CRITICAL PRAISE

"This relevant resource for travelers combines two intersecting components of travel today; health and safety. The up to date information makes for a great travel companion to help you sort out problems on the road and protect your security. Whether traveling for business or pleasure, on a Scouting adventure or an expedition, stow this book in your carry-on luggage!"

Dr. Robert Gates
Former US Secretary of Defense
Former Director, Central Intelligence Agency
President, Boy Scouts of America

-

"*Lizard Bites & Street Riots* is a much needed addition to the list of essential reading for every traveler."

Terry Garcia
Chief Science and Exploration Officer
National Geographic Society

-

"From Ebola to blizzards; from dog bites to food safety, and social unrest, this easy-to-read book provides comprehensive information for every health or safety situation a traveler might confront regardless of whether one's destination is Tibet, Paris or a ski vacation in Colorado. As an Eagle Scout, outdoorsman, and business person, I travel frequently - over 160 days this year including Saudi Arabia, Panama, Costa Rica, France, and Sweden - and I would not leave home without this book!"

Glenn A. Adams
Energy entrepreneur
President, National Eagle Scout Association

-

"We support millions of travelers around the globe each year and often deal with devastating outcomes as a result of people not spending time on health, safety, and security preparations. In hindsight, the person or the family left behind always wishes they had. This book allows a busy traveler to jump right to topics of concern and get to the 'so what' quickly. This knowledge will help the traveler or loved ones avoid many problems and hopefully return only with happy memories."

Bruce McIndoe
Chairman and CEO
iJET International

CRITICAL PRAISE

LIZARD BITES & STREET RIOTS

WIND RUSH
PUBLISHERS

Dallas, Texas

To Helen:

Thanks for your support!
Hope this keeps you safe
on the road.

Mike

Be prepared!

Mike Maceijek

LIZARD BITES
& STREET RIOTS:
Travel Emergencies and
Your Health, Safety & Security

Stay Safe

Warren Yens

Healthy travels.

Joyce Johnson

Published by WindRush Publishers, Dallas, Texas.
WindRush Publishers and colophon are trademarks of
WindRush Ventures, LLC.

First Edition 2014

10 9 8 7 6 5 4 3 2 1

WindRush publications are available at special discounted rates for volume and
bulk purchases, corporate and institutional premiums, promotions, fund-raising,
and educational use. For further information, contact:

WindRush Publishers
P.O. Box 670324
Dallas, Texas 75367
www.WindRushPub.com

Printed and bound in the United States of America.

ISBN-13: 978-098590974-1

Cover design, book design, and layout by Charito Jones, Dallas, Texas.
Creative Direction by John K. Shipes, Dallas, Texas.
Check out John's photographic work at: www.ShipesShooter.com
Production assistance by David C. Scott

Stay Informed and Travel-Inspired at www.LizardBites.com

This book is dedicated to the memory of
L. Scott Harrison,
a decorated security specialist
and brother-in-arms for many adventures and travels.

TABLE OF CONTENTS

M

N

O

P

R

S

T

U

V

W

NOTES TO THE READER

Medical Disclaimer

This book is provided by WindRush Publishers for educational and informational purposes only and is not intended and should not be construed as medical or legal advice. This publication is not meant to be a substitute for professional clinical judgment or in any way to supplant or interfere with the relationship between a patient and his/her medical provider. The authors, publisher, and any party involved in the preparation of this book are not responsible for the results obtained from use of this publication.

Use of QR Codes

Due to the constantly changing environment regarding current medical and safety recommendations, we include a topic-specific QR code reference at the end of each section that connects with a specific page within our website (www.LizardBites.com). Each topical page has additional instant access web links and useful travel resources. To be taken to a resource link page, simply scan the QR code with your smartphone.

Scan for more resources.

FOREWORD

The dry, dusty heat and high altitude of Afghanistan, plus a long evening with two Russian archaeologists and their vodka, was taking its toll. My first thought was "last night was probably a mistake." Nauseous and light-headed, I was sweating rather heavily. One of my Afghan colleagues helpfully offered me one of his nitroglycerin pills (a bad idea for lots of reasons). As luck would have it, a medic with an ISAF patrol happened to be passing and quickly determined that I was suffering from dehydration. Water with rehydration salts and a day in bed were all I needed and the next day I was back at work. Had the medic not come along, my condition likely would have worsened because I had no resource to help me figure out what was wrong.

On another occasion while on a National Geographic assignment in Egypt, I was sitting outdoors on the bank of the Nile enjoying a meal with friends at a popular restaurant. As our meal was being served, the wake from a passing ship hit the sea wall and a small amount of water splashed onto our table. I was certain that essence of Nile had soaked our food but my companions laughed off my concerns and proceeded to enjoy the meal. I placed a second order of food with our waiter and avoided the first. The next day my companions failed to show for an early morning meeting due to gastrointestinal problems. Fortunately, previous bad experiences with water supplies helped me avoid Cleopatra's revenge this time.

Ok, so you are probably not planning a trip to Afghanistan to spend a day in the field and then spend a vodka-soaked evening with a couple of Russian archaeologists. And maybe your dinner reservations don't involve a table on the banks of the Nile. But you don't need to travel far or to exotic locales to find trouble. It is remarkably easy to have a close encounter with a health issue as one travels. Fortunately, if you read this book you will be ready to avoid most problems. A few simple precautions, as Dr. Manyak points out, are all that's required to be prepared. If you do run into problems, whether medical or involving security, this book provides practical information for assistance.

As Chief Science and Exploration Officer for the National Geographic Society,

I have experienced or had occasion to witness all manner of travel mishaps. How I wish a book such as this had been available when I first started my work. *Lizard Bites and Street Riots* is a thoroughly researched and practical guide written by three of the world's top experts that should be on every traveler's book shelf or better yet, in your hand luggage. Not only does it provide a comprehensive look at the many different health issues a frequent, or even occasional, traveler may encounter and how to avoid or treat them but it also provides sound, practical advice for dealing with a host of non-health issues that could pose a threat to a traveler's well-being. Whether you face civil unrest (do your research in advance and heed the advice of locals), terrorism (keep a low profile and avoid places frequented by foreigners, my personal mantra), air safety questions (no copilot or liberal use of duct tape, in my experience, shouts to you to find another flight), seasickness (the bane of my existence), an allergic reaction or a broken limb, it is covered in the pages that follow.

Very importantly, whether you are an occasional or frequent traveler pay special attention to the chapter on Medical and Evacuation Insurance. Anyone can fall victim to an accident or sudden illness whether in Ireland or Afghanistan. Know the extent of your coverage. Does your policy provide coverage outside the United States? Is medical evacuation covered? If not find out what is available because without insurance, hospitalization in a foreign country and medical evacuation can have ruinous financial consequences.

Lizard Bites and Street Riots is a much needed addition to the list of essential reading for every traveler.

> *Terry Garcia*
> Chief Science and Exploration Officer
> National Geographic Society
> Washington, DC

INTRODUCTION

We were in heavy chop in the Mindoro Strait at 3 am in the South China Sea, off the coast of the Philippines, when the first victim was spotted. Barely visible in the dark, clinging to a small board, we maneuvered to fish the woman out of roiling seas. Her tale was chilling…..their overloaded vessel had sunk eight hours earlier with over a hundred passengers and we were 5 miles from shore with the current headed out to sea. No sharks had arrived yet. As a newly-minted medical school graduate and the only doctor on board, medical responsibilities were mine, but despite extensive ambulance experience and Eagle Scout training, I was immediately struck by the lack of resources in this remote area. Our rescue of 87 people, including many children, really sparked my lifelong interest in remote medical care.

Since that maritime disaster, expedition medicine has been a major interest alongside my academic medical career, allowing me to contribute to many exciting adventures. Whether avoiding a coup while traveling to the most remote jungles in Africa, descending the deep ocean where the *Titanic* rests, riding camels in Mongolian deserts, rescuing a trapped ship in Antarctica, exploring the Amazon rain forest, or traversing the deepest canyon in the world, each destination has had its unique problems for preparation and safety, yet many share common elements. It has been said that a medical degree is a passport to travel and that certainly holds true for me.

The growing public interest in adventure travel, easier access to remote areas, and improvements in travel and communication results in over 50 million annual travelers to the developing world. They encounter medical problems on the road, some of them predictable and potentially avoidable while others may be dynamic and unpredictable, like the Ebola outbreak or a tsunami. But they also face security issues, particularly in today's world of unrest in many areas. Health and security are intertwined and travelers must consider both. Medical issues are security issues and vice versa. Although there are resources for each topic, very few today address both together. This book is intended to fill that gap with essential, basic information on a wide range of topics from avalanches and typhoons to abdominal pain, taxi security, and legal advice. Links to more detailed resources of topics and a frequently updated website (www.LizardBites.com) with emerging information are an added benefit for our readers.

The title *Lizard Bites and Street Riots* arises from an incident that catalyzed its creation. The medical office at National Geographic consulted me about a photographer who had a Komodo dragon spit in his eye while getting close up photos. While that is unusual to say the least, you cannot make up some of the circumstances they are presented. Well, what DO you do? What do you do in other situations where medical assistance may not be at hand? Or if faced with sudden civil unrest in your destination? Or caught in a legal predicament? You may have to make decisions with no one to hold your hand.

My co-authors are world experts with vast experience. Dr. Joyce Johnson is the former Surgeon General of the US Coast Guard and designed their algorithms for medical problems at sea in addition to her international medical humanitarian work. Warren Young is a former Australian special forces officer with an MBA and Director of Security for the International Monetary Fund. I urge the reader to examine their biographs which reveal their breadth of experience.

No text is complete without acknowledgement of assistance and support. We are certainly grateful for such efforts provided by several friends and colleagues, all of whom have been supportive of our vision. IJET, an industry leader in operational risk management, provided expertise and corroboration of up to date health and security information. Several subject matter experts, many of them fellow Explorers Club members, provided information or critiqued content: Dr. Craig Cook, Medical Director of *Sport Diver Magazine*; Kristin Larson, environmental attorney at Palladin Law Group, LLP; Dr. Chris Macedonia, former Defense Advanced Research Projects Agency project manager; Bruce McIndoe, CEO of IJET; Dr. Martin Nweeia of the Harvard School of Dental Medicine; Dan Richards, CEO of Global Rescue; Dr. Richard Williams, NASA Chief Health and Medical Officer. Thank you all for your many years of friendship, professional camaraderie, and shared interest in remote medical issues.

One must always recognize the support provided by our families and loved ones, it is given unconditionally and much appreciated. They keep the home fires burning while we are on the road and keep the coffee pot stoked while we write. It is the little things and the unspoken support that comforts us all while on travel or engulfed in projects like this. They are as much a part of this book as we are.

Michael J Manyak, MD, FACS
Washington, DC

ABOUT THIS BOOK

We have organized this book in alphabetical order for easy, quick reference on any number of subjects. However, before leaving on your journey, there are a number of entries you will want to read before departure. It is advisable to read several resources to be informed. For US citizens, the websites for the US Department of State and the Centers for Disease Control and Prevention (CDC) are very useful. Many other countries have similar information for their citizenry on consular or governmental websites. In addition, the World Health Organization (WHO) website contains useful information for travelers related to health. Websites about weather (weather.com) help you prepare for the climate at your destination.

Depending on the type and destination of your travel, the climate, and your planned activities, reading lists might include, but not be limited to, the following suggestions before departure.

General Information for All Travel

Entries Based on Destination Environment

In addition to General Information, the following are suggested for travel to specific areas or climates:

Medical Emergencies

ABDOMINAL PAIN
Appendicitis to Ulcers

Your travel companion has had dull lower abdominal pain for a few hours that waxes and wanes but is increasing in intensity and associated with nausea. There have been no previous episodes and no regular medication use. Is this an emergency?

Abdominal pain causes a great deal of concern for both patient and companions. There are many causes of abdominal pain, ranging from minor and short-lived to serious and life-threatening. It may be difficult to differentiate between causes of abdominal pain but the key is to determine if medical attention is needed and how rapidly that should occur. *Anyone with severe abdominal pain should be taken to an emergency room if possible as soon as possible.*

KEY POINTS

» Pain is evaluated according to location and character.

» Location is best described by dividing the abdomen into four areas created by drawing imaginary perpendicular lines through the umbilicus. These four sections are identified as the right and left upper quadrants and right and left lower quadrants. It is also possible to have central upper and lower abdominal pain and it should be described as such.

» The character of the pain is described as sharp, dull or aching, intermittent, or cramping. Pain can rise to a peak and decrease in waves (colic).

» It is important to note pain location, whether it radiates to another area, and whether it began in one location and moved to another.

» Did the pain began suddenly or gradually and how long has it persisted?

» Have there been previous instances of similar pain?

» Is the patient still or constantly moving? Does any particular position relieve or increase the pain?

» Observe or ask about other symptoms such as nausea and vomiting, diarrhea, shortness of breath, dizziness, fever, and urinary symptoms.

» Other important information includes the medical history, medication use, previous surgical history, and menstrual history.

Generalized severe abdominal pain can be caused by gastroenteritis, blockage of the intestine or its blood supply, intestinal perforation, an abdominal aneurysm, appendicitis with the appendix in an abnormal location, or incarcerated abdominal hernia. The common serious and potentially life-threatening causes of abdominal pain by location are listed. Note that gastroenteritis, heart burn, and urinary tract infection are not necessarily life-threatening but cause significant distress and that true emergencies must be ruled out.

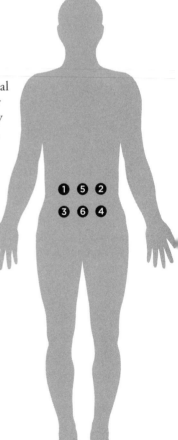

Numbers correspond to the patient abdominal location, not as you look at the patient.

Scan for more resources.

❶ RIGHT UPPER QUADRANT
- Gall stones (dull or sharp, constant)
- Hepatitis (dull, constant)
- Liver injury (after trauma, dull)
- Pneumonia (with cough, fever)

❷ LEFT UPPER QUADRANT
- Pancreatitis (sharp, constant)
- Gastroenteritis (cramps, nausea, vomiting)
- Spleen injury (after trauma, dull)
- Pneumonia

❸ RIGHT LOWER QUADRANT
- Appendicitis (dull becoming sharp)
- Kidney stone (colic, may radiate from flank)
- Ovarian infection or cyst (dull, constant)
- Hernia (dull, sharp if incarcerated)
- Bowel obstruction (waves of cramps)
- Tubal pregnancy (dull to sharp)

❹ LEFT LOWER QUADRANT
- Diverticulitis (dull to sharp)
- Kidney stone (colic, may radiate from flank)
- Ovarian infection or cyst
- Hernia
- Bowel obstruction
- Tubal pregnancy

❺ CENTRAL UPPER
- Heart attack (dull or sharp)
- Ulcer (sharp, constant)
- Gastroenteritis
- Pancreatitis (sharp, constant)
- Heartburn (sharp, burning)

❻ CENTRAL LOWER
- Aortic Aneurysm (sharp, constant)
- Bladder infection (dull, constant)
- Ovarian infection, cyst, or tubal pregnancy
- Bowel obstruction
- Irritable bowel syndrome or colitis

AFTER YOUR TRIP
Latent Infections to Legal Matters

You have returned from your adventure trip to a tropical climate during which you visited a rain forest. You have intermittent diarrhea but people on the trip said that is common and not to worry. Since your return you have had a nagging cough that you attribute to seasonal allergies but you do have a low grade fever. You did see local health services for which you paid cash.

No two trips are the same because travel agenda, seasons, conditions, length of stay, and people involved may vary. The risk of bringing home an illness and responsibilities associated with your particular travel will differ with each trip.

Pre-travel planning may help prevent illness but does not guarantee that health-related consequences of the trip will not occur. Some illnesses are acquired before travel and brought with the traveler while others occur during or appear after travel, whether or not related to the travel itself.

KEY POINTS

» Travel to more remote areas or more strenuous trips obviously have higher risk for medical adverse events. People traveling to a remote place may be exposed to unusual diseases or those not present in their native environment.

» A medical officer may be responsible for a group on remote travel or an expedition including follow up, but individuals need to be aware of potential aftereffects of travel.

» Over 50 million travelers annually visit underdeveloped countries and anywhere from about 25 percent to 65 percent will report medical problems with 8 percent (4 million) becoming ill enough to seek medical care abroad.

» 90 percent of infections acquired during travel will present within 6 months. However, some such as TB, leprosy, filariasis, Chagas disease, and some other parasites, may not present for months or years after exposure.

BASIC GUIDELINES

- Fever is a common complaint after travel. Fevers can have many causes ranging from common respiratory viruses to exotic diseases found in the location of travel. Malaria is a common cause of fever in travelers returning from an endemic area. The cause of the fever may never be identified. However, any persistent fever and anyone with a fever occurring within 3 weeks of travel to the Middle East or SE Asia, sources of emerging virulent avian and swine flu as well as coronavirus infections should be evaluated promptly. The same is true for any travelers returning from Africa, especially in light of the Ebola outbreak (see Ebola and Emerging and Resurgent Viral Diseases).

- Diarrhea is another common medical complaint following travel (or during travel). Diarrhea can be caused by many organisms and is classified as acute, lasting only a few days, or chronic. Chronic diarrhea must be evaluated, preferably by a physician familiar with infectious diseases (see Traveler's Diarrhea).

- Any swelling of the legs, particularly if only one is swollen, requires immediate evaluation to rule out blood clots which are potentially life threatening (see Deep Vein Thrombosis).

- Psychological issues can occur after travel, particularly if the trip was physically or mentally stressful. Post-traumatic stress disorder (PTSD) can occur in travelers who have endured threats or danger, witnessed a violent act, or had physical trauma. Those surviving a traumatic event can suffer from survivor syndrome, experiencing feelings of guilt and abandonment after an apparent random event (see Mental Health).

- Records of your trip and reports about any medical or legal events are very important. It is necessary to document circumstances surrounding such events to fulfill insurance requirements or to resolve disputes, provide evidence for legal issues, and record medical events (see Legal Matters).

Scan for more resources.

AIRLINE HIJACKING: WHAT TO DO IN THE EVENT OF
A Flight Nightmare

You and your family are taking a flight within a foreign country, when suddenly a young man stands up and tells the passengers that the plane is being hijacked and flown to another country.

Statistics indicate that airline hijackings have declined in recent years, but they still occur.

KEY POINTS

To reduce the trauma and stress of hijacking, all travelers should be familiar with the following considerations.

» In selecting your seat assignment, consider requesting a window or center seat, since passengers in such seats are less accessible to interactions with hijackers. In addition, if a rescue is attempted, those sitting in window or center seats are less vulnerable to gunfire in the aisles.

» Get rid of anything that you cannot explain or that might offend the hijackers. If you are wearing or carrying anything that could provoke or irritate the hijackers, discreetly remove it and try to get rid of it.

» Try to remain calm and obey the hijackers.

» Have your passport protected with a cover case to make the nationality harder to see and less prominent.

» If you are asked questions by the hijackers, respond simply.

» Avoid saying or doing anything that might cause them to take an interest in you.

» Do not resist the hijackers unless it is an absolute last resort. Those who react aggressively place themselves at greater risk than those who behave passively.

» During the hijacking, try to appear uninterested in what is going on around you. Sleep, read a book, or do some activity that will not attract attention to yourself. Hijackers are less likely to bother people who are not a threat to them.

» If you speak or understand the hijacker's language, do not make this fact known. Although it is sometimes assumed that speaking the language could enhance your rapport with the hijacker, experience indicates that you are better off speaking your native tongue and acquiring information by listening to the hijacker's conversation. This could provide you with information as to what the hijacker intends to do next.

» Do not appear sullen or uncommunicative. Doing so depersonalizes you in the eyes of the hijacker and could increase your risks.

» Try to maintain your composure. Fear of death or injury is natural. Recognizing this may help you manage the crisis more effectively. Pause, take a breath, and attempt to organize your thoughts.

» Should there be a rescue attempt, slide down in your seat as far as you can or get on the floor. Cover your head and arms with a pillow to avoid being injured.

Scan for more resources.

AIRLINE SAFETY
Weather & Maintenance

You are on an transoceanic flight and are awakened by significant turbulence and an announcement by the captain to remain seated. You notice the flight attendants are scurrying for a seat. You were aware of a possible weather front over the ocean but figured the plane could fly above the turbulence. Should I be worried?

Aircraft accidents on commercial airlines are very rare, but when they happen, they are usually catastrophic and make for impressive headlines. Most governments have some form of Civil Aviation Authority that is responsible for enforcing minimum standards for air safety within their airspace although the application of standards may vary.

However, there are many parts of the world where airline profitability is the only concern and where airlines cut corners in operations and maintenance to improve profits. Most of these airlines are relatively easy to spot but not always apparent.

Despite some less-than-desirable airline operators, improvements in maintenance programming and aircraft technology in recent years in many parts of the world have made air travel one of the safest forms of mass transport. Even where airline operators and aircraft may be less stringent about safety, travel by air is statistically still much safer than ground transportation. The odds of being killed as a result of an airline accident these days are a remarkable 1 in 19.8 million if you are on one of the top 39 airlines with the best accident rate—and a still impressive 1 in 2 million even if you are flying one of the airlines with the very worst accident rates. Put another way, commercial airlines have a fatal accident rate of one for every five million flying hours, bearing in mind that substantial improvements have occurred since the data was prepared. —This means that an airline passenger theoretically could fly 24 hours a day for 570 years before his/her number is likely to come up. The recent Malaysian Airline crashes are rare exceptions.

Harro Ranter, the president of the Aviation Safety Network, an independent aviation industry research organization located in the Netherlands, stated in 2013 that "Since 1997 the average number of airliner accidents has shown a steady and persistent decline, probably thanks to the continuing safety-driven efforts by international aviation organizations such as ICAO, IATA, Flight Safety Foundation, and the aviation industry."

However, if you want to do some safety record checking of your own for a particular flight that you intend to take, the internet makes finding such information much easier. Some useful website links are provided at the end of this chapter. So much information is available these days that the challenge becomes making sense of it all.

For example, the United States leads the world by a substantial margin when it comes to the number of aircraft accidents involving one or more fatalities. However, the USA, accounts for 54 percent of all the air traffic worldwide. Africa, on the other hand, accounts for approximately 20 percent of all fatal aircraft accidents worldwide, but only accounts for approximately 3 percent of the world's aircraft traffic. How is a traveler to make use of such esoteric information? Shoddy aircraft maintenance is often considered a major cause of aircraft accidents, but thanks to improvements in technology and generally stricter oversight by aviation regulatory, the chances of a disaster are on the decline. The statistics indicate that an airline accident is more likely to be caused by pilot/human error than any maintenance-related factors. However, improved aircraft technology, pilot training, and regulatory governance have significantly reduced the likelihood of pilot/human error as well.

KEY POINTS

In Making a Fly/ Don't Fly Decision:

» Despite all the good news about the improving general standards of airline safety, there may come a time when a traveler sees something that causes concern. In such cases, travelers are well advised to trust their instincts and, depending on the imperative to travel, may want to consider alternative arrangements.

Examples of things that might be a cause for concern, though not usually found on large commercial airlines, include:

>> There is no co-pilot on the plane.

>> The aircraft is clearly overloaded, such as too many passengers for the number of seats or excess baggage and/or freight visible in the cabin.

>> There is no seat with attached safety belt available.

>> In winter, snow and ice removal procedures for aircraft are not observed prior to flight.

BASIC SAFETY GUIDELINES

Good safety practices at the travel planning stage include:

• Plan itineraries with sufficient flexibility in scheduling to allow for delays and the possible need to defer or re-schedule flights.

• Plan flights to arrive and depart during hours that are considered safe.

• Take account of seasonal and local weather conditions in travel planning. Excessively bad weather or a forecast of such weather should be considered a good reason for delaying your travel.

ON THE DAY OF TRAVEL:

>> Dress appropriately for the environment in which the flight occurs.

>> Provide the flight crew or ground staff with an accurate weight for yourself and all baggage if you are asked to do so.

>> Do not smoke in or around the aircraft and never during flight.

>> Remove hats/headgear before approaching or leaving the aircraft.

>> Do not leave loose articles on the aircraft parking area.

>> Request an aisle seat nearest the emergency exits. If there is unassigned seating, try to be one of the first to board the aircraft and select a seat adjacent to an emergency exit. The over-wing exits allow less drop distance to the ground than those away from the wings;

» Stow baggage in the approved baggage storage area, which will ideally be secured by a door or net. Do not stow unsecured baggage in the aisle or adjacent to any emergency exit and ask for the removal of any unsecured baggage or baggage in the path of exits.

» Check that your seat has a safety belt installed and functioning. If it doesn't, move to another seat.

» Remain in your seat and always keep your safety belt fastened when in the aircraft; in case of severe turbulence, remain seated until the pilot signals that it is safe to unfasten the seatbelt and to leave the seat after the plane has landed.

» Be attentive to flight briefings and safety instructions. Study the flight safety card where provided.

» Be aware of the location of exit doors, hatches, and the way to operate them.

» Note the location of fire extinguishers, flashlights, life-rafts, first aid kits, crash axes, smoke hoods, and survival packs.

» If your flight is over water, ensure that a life-vest is available and wear it when instructed by the flight crew.

» Wear ear plugs during flights on noisy aircraft; adjust ear pressure as needed while climbing or descending to avoid discomfort.

PREGNANCY AND AIR TRAVEL

If it is necessary to travel by air while pregnant, some airlines may require assurance that pregnant travelers are "fit to fly," so a prior medical clearance certificate should be obtained and carried to ensure that there are no problems with travel plans.

KEY POINTS WHEN MAKING A DECISION TO FLY, PREGNANT TRAVELERS SHOULD CONSIDER THE FOLLOWING:

» Whether they need assistance for carrying luggage, climbing stairs, taking local transport, or other actions.

» Determine availability of adequate medical facilities and assistance throughout the journey.

» Seek the advice of your doctor.—Travel plans should be discussed at an early stage so that the necessary advice can be given and other options can be considered.

USEFUL WEB SITES

http://www.airlineratings.com/

http://www.icao.int/

http://www.iata.org/

http://flightsafety.org/

http://aviation-safety.net/

http://planecrashinfo.com/

Scan for more resources.

ALLERGIC REACTIONS
From Hives to Hypotension

You are on an international trip and are asked to try the local cuisine. You have had some mild allergic reactions in the past to shellfish and avoid eating them. You have been assured that this dish does not contain seafood. However, shortly after you begin the meal, you notice a flushing sensation and start to feel constriction in your throat and itching.

Allergic reactions range from very mild to potentially life-threatening respiratory and circulatory collapse. It is important that you know the signs of an allergic reaction so that you can react appropriately as soon as possible.

KEY POINTS

There are wide variety of allergic reactions possible. For example:

» Allergic rhinitis involves sneezing, nasal congestion, and a watery nasal discharge. These symptoms may be accompanied by mild itching, red eyes from congestion, and wheezing. A wide variety of pollen, dust, animal dander, and fungi can be responsible for this condition—the typical seasonal allergy. Other causes of allergy include foods, drugs, insect stings, and other types of environmental proteins.

» More pronounced allergic reactions can announce themselves with hives, itching, and swelling of lips, around the eyes, or in the throat.

» The most severe form of allergic reaction is anaphylaxis, A LIFE-THREATENING EMERGENCY. Anaphylactic symptoms can occur from seconds to several hours after exposure but usually occur very quickly. The first signs of an anaphylactic reaction may include a warm or flushed feeling, tingling in the mouth, or a red and itchy rash or hives. Additional symptoms may include light-headedness, shortness of breath, severe sneezing, anxiety, stomach cramps, and vomiting and diarrhea. Airway constriction, drop in blood pressure, rapid pulse, dizziness or loss of consciousness signal anaphylactic shock. In extreme cases, decreased blood pressure and respiratory failure can lead to shock and death. If you suspect anaphylaxis, GET IMMEDIATE EMERGENCY MEDICAL ASSISTANCE IF POSSIBLE.

BASIC TREATMENT GUIDELINES

Treatment depends on the severity of the symptoms and history of previous allergic reactions. Here are some guidelines your should know:

- Mild allergic reactions are best handled by oral antihistamines and bronchodilator inhalational sprays.

- People with itching, hives, and swelling around lips, eyes, and throat should be given diphenhydramine (Benadryl) and be observed for worsening symptoms.

- At the first sign of severe allergic reaction, inject epinephrine (prepared dose known as Epi-pen, Auvi-Q, or Adrenaclick) into the thigh. Most patients with known severe allergies carry epinephrine for injection. Epinephrine for injection may be in an emergency supply kit.

- Repeat injection of epinephrine at 5 to 15 minute intervals if the patient has persistent symptoms or a recurrence of symptoms. Most patients require only one or two doses.

- There are no contraindications for epinephrine use for anaphylaxis treatment including cardiovascular disease or high blood pressure.

- See Bee and Wasp Stings for management of allergic reactions from insect stings.

- Seek medical assistance for any moderate to severe reaction. Evacuate for any difficulty breathing or signs of shock (rapid faint pulse, dizziness, altered mental status).

Scan for more resources.

ANIMAL (WILD) ATTACKS
Rare But Increasing

You are traveling in the countryside and a herd of elk by the roadside have attracted some travelers to get out of the car and approach the animals. You would like to do this as well but note the people are quite close to the elk. Is this safe?

Wild animal attacks are rare but are increasing in areas where man encroaches on wildlife habitats. Fatal animal attacks in the United States occur less than 200 times per year with the majority caused by domestic farm animals and then dogs. Injuries from wild animals include puncture wounds, extensive complex lacerations, crush injuries, and blunt trauma(see Trauma to the Abdomen, Trauma to the Chest, Lacerations). No reliable statistics exist for global annual animal attacks but reports increase in areas with higher animal exposure, such as sub-Saharan Africa. Travelers should familiarize themselves with local wildlife behavior and causes of provocation. Do not approach wild animals. Remember, everything bites!

KEY POINTS

» Predators are more prone to attack humans. Large exotic animals and predators are not discussed here and travelers need to rely on local resources for safety advice. However, perceived threats may cause rather docile animals to attack.

» Small mammals usually avoid humans but beware of unusual and aggressive behavior because of the risk of rabies. Dogs, skunks, fox, and raccoons are the most likely rabies carriers but other animals can harbor this deadly disease.

» Bats have minimally detectable bites but are another source of rabies. Fecal matter from bats can also transmit disease. Any exposure to bats should raise suspicion of exposure to rabies but also other viral diseases.

» Swine can be aggressive and produce significant wounds. Feral and wild pig species are more aggressive, may attack in packs, and should be avoided.

» Canine attacks have increased in proximity to natural habitats though there is a disproportionate fear of wolf attacks which are rare. Large canine predators such as hyenas can be quite aggressive. In urban areas, packs of "domesticated" dogs can also be dangerous.

» Primate bites can be very serious and even small monkeys can be aggressive if threatened or habituated to humans and food handouts. Baboons and chimpanzees are aggressive and dangerous because of their size, strength and bite capabilities.

» Deer, elk, and moose are aggressive during mating season and if calves are threatened. Bison, when provoked, can cause significant injury from blunt trauma and goring.

» Camels are notoriously unpredictable and temperamental, but that is associated with improper past treatment. Serious bites and fractures can result from a camel attack.

» Most bear attacks can be prevented. Techniques to avoid contact differ with the species. Running from bears in a sudden encounter may elicit a predatory response from brown bear species but black bears will usually flee from aggressive human response.

BASIC GUIDELINES

- If attacked by an animal, the following issues should be considered.

- Rescuers need to make sure the scene is safe. Large predators may remain in the vicinity after an attack.

- Serious injuries should be evaluated like any other trauma with airway preservation, control of blood loss, and spinal immobilization (see Trauma to the Abdomen, Trauma to the Chest, Lacerations, Animal and Human Bite).

- Wound care should be initiated if evacuation is delayed (see Lacerations).

- All bites should be considered infected (see Animal and Human Bite). Treatment and appropriate antibiotics should be started as soon as possible.

- Post-exposure prophylaxis for rabies should be considered for animal bites depending on the type of animal, behavior, and country of exposure (see Rabies).
- Post-traumatic stress disorder (PTSD) is a potential consequence of animal attack.

Scan for more
resources.

ANIMAL & HUMAN BITE
From Canines to Komodos

You are in Cambodia with a tour group and are off to see some temples in a rural area. Your tour bus stops in a small village for a restroom break and, as you walk around the corner, a rather scrawny village dog heads toward you. No one is in sight. It looks harmless enough and you are wondering whether to be friendly and pet the dog.

It is important to remember that everything can bite, so do not corner or try to pet that dog or any other cute furry animal. The most common animal bite is from a dog. Dog bites usually involve the hand or arm with infection resulting, fortunately, in only about 5 percent of bites. However, feline, human, primate, and non-venomous reptile bites are often followed by infection from a combination of bacterial organisms necessitating wound treatment and use of broad spectrum antibiotics. In fact, it appears that causing infection may be part of the hunting strategy in some species like the Komodo dragon, a very large monitor lizard found in Indonesia. If the prey of a Komodo dragon ambush attack escapes, the lizard can follow the prey for days, waiting for it to die of the effects of its venom and infection from bites. (Also see Snake Bite).

Larger bites can cause lacerations and significant bleeding. Wounds to the hands and feet as well as puncture wounds, typical from a bite, are at greater risk to develop infection. Bites can result in avulsion, laceration, crushing of tissues, and tendon damage so proper medical evaluation and treatment is required.

Human bites can inflict significant damage. Approximately 10 -15 percent of human bite wounds become infected because of multiple anaerobic (do not require oxygen) bacteria that flourish in damaged tissue. Most of these injuries occur on the hands which have a higher infection rate than do similar wounds in other anatomic locations. These infections are often far advanced by the time they receive appropriate care because victims often wait until infection is well established before seeking medical treatment. Wounds are frequently more extensive than estimated on initial examination by the inexperienced observer and are frequently managed inadequately.

BASIC PREVENTION AND TREATMENT GUIDELINES

Dogs and other animals in rural villages pose a threat to the traveler. Avoid animals, particularly dogs, in unfamiliar surroundings. If you are traveling to an area where rabies is endemic, or you may have contact with urban or wild animals, consider getting rabies vaccine before you travel. The standard treatment for all bite wounds mirrors that for other lacerations with control of bleeding by pressure as the first step (see Lacerations and Puncture Wounds). Familiarize yourself with the following:

- Human bites may seem minor but 10 to 15 percent can become infected with a variety of organisms. Victims usually wait until infection is well established before seeking care. Many bites occur on the hand which has a higher rate of infections than other anatomic locations. Human bites can transmit serious infections such as hepatitis.

- Remove all jewelry from an injured hand and wrist because swelling may occur to prevent removal later and compromise circulation.

- Clean the wounds with soap and water and irrigate them profusely with clean water.

- Do not close wounds unless severe hemorrhage occurs. Closure of bite wounds can lead to a serious infection. Wound edges from a large laceration can be held together by tape or wraps until medical assistance can be obtained.

- If in a remote area and evacuation is delayed, it is prudent to begin antibiotics if available. Additional antibiotics may be administered by medical personnel later.

- Victims at high risk for infection such as diabetics, the elderly, and immunocompromised patients should receive broad spectrum antibiotics.

- If motion of a digit or extremity is compromised, tendon damage must be considered and splinting may be necessary for transportation.

- A tetanus shot is required if the victim has no record of tetanus prophylaxis or if the last booster shot was given more than ten years ago. Rabies prophylaxis must be considered for bites from any unvaccinated or unobserved animal including domestic pets in rural areas (see Rabies).

Scan for more resources.

AVALANCHE SURVIVAL
A Real Snow Emergency

You are staying at a ski lodge and friends suggest a snowmobile ride in an area away from ski slopes with sparse timber for good runs. It has been snowing heavily on top of a good snow base and is beautiful. It seems too good to pass up.

Winter vacationers and outdoor adventurers are usually cautious about hypothermia and frostbite but unless skiing in an area where warnings are announced, they rarely concern themselves with worries of an avalanche. An avalanche is perceived as a rare occurrence with death from this natural disaster even more rare but there were 752 avalanches involving 1504 people in Switzerland alone over a recent eleven-year period. The International Commission for Mountain Emergency Medicine reports that the median annual mortality rate from avalanches in Europe and North America was 141 between 1994 and 2003.

Rapid rescue is the key to survival. The Swiss Avalanche Research Center data revealed a greater than 90 percent chance of survival if buried less than 15 minutes but less than 30 percent chance of survival with burial for 45 minutes. Research by the Austrian Mountain Rescue Service has shown that about 18 percent of people rescued after total burial survive to hospital discharge. Reinforcing the need for rapid rescue are studies that have shown probability of survival was highest with visual localization and lowest for those located by avalanche transceiver and no survival difference for those found by avalanche probes compared to rescue dogs. However, use of an avalanche transceiver did reduce time of burial and mortality compared to those without the device. Death from avalanche occurs overwhelmingly by asphyxiation with less than 10 percent attributed to trauma and virtually none by hypothermia.

KEY POINTS

The obvious first step to avoid becoming an avalanche statistic is to know the site and make prudent decisions about your activity.

» Assess the terrain. High risk of avalanche occurs with slope gradient of 30-45 degrees, convex slope contour, north-facing slopes in winter and south-facing slopes in spring, and smooth slopes without much ground cover.

» Look for evidence of recent avalanches or old slide paths; these are definite signs of danger.

» Snow conditions are very important with dry, loose snow, especially composed of small crystals, more likely to cause an avalanche.

» Smooth surfaces with a crust and areas with loose, non-compacted underlying snow are dangerous.

» Rate of snow fall one inch or greater per hour increases avalanche danger rapidly.

» Snow instability is increased by rapid temperature change and wind 15 mph or more.

Portable avalanche airbags and avalanche transceivers are available for those in potential avalanche situations. The airbag pack weighs about 3 kg (6.6 lb) and deploys easily but is expensive, about the cost of good skis. When deployed, the airbag protects against trauma, acts as a flotation device to keep the victim on the surface, and provides sharp contrast with the snow to aid localization. People equipped with an avalanche airbag had lower mortality (3% vs 19%) than those without it.

Transceivers transmit by manufacturer agreement at the same emergency frequency. They weigh roughly 3 oz, run on 1 AA battery, have a range of 125 feet, and cost a few hundred US dollars. Avalanche transceivers lower the average duration of burial (25 min vs 125 min) and therefore mortality (55% vs 70.6%).

KEY POINTS

If you are in a potential avalanche situation, spend the least time possible on the open slopes.

» Either stay high and try to travel on ridge tops or else in a valley away from the slope bottom.

» Take advantage of dense timber or rocky outcrops.

» If you are on an open dangerous slope, go straight up or down, do not traverse.

» Snowmobilers should stay away from lower parts of slopes and long, open slope areas and certainly resist the temptation to ride up steep hills.

» Reduce risk by having only one person at a time on a dangerous slope.

BASIC GUIDELINES

If caught in an avalanche, you must think quickly and stay as calm as possible.

• Abandon all equipment, including snowmobiles, and seek shelter behind rocks, trees, or vehicles.

• Brace for impact, crouch low, turn away from the onrushing snow, cover your mouth and nose.

• As the avalanche slows, pull your arms and hands toward your face to create space.

• Thrust and kick toward the surface and try to work toward the edge of the snow slide.

• If trapped in a vehicle, turn off the engine to avoid carbon monoxide poisoning and do not abandon it unless certain of your safety.

• If you are the survivor, stay with those still trapped, time is essential and you are the most likely source to rescue others.

• However, if help is only a few minutes away, mark the route for the returning search party.

• There is real danger to rescuers and survivors alike from another avalanche.

Scan for more resources.

BED BUGS
Hotel Misery

After camping for two weeks, we finally decided to spend two nights in a hotel. The hot shower was great! However, the second morning I woke up itching my legs, and noticed large red welts all over them—I must have at least 10 or 15 welts. What happened?

The likely cause of the welts is bed bug bites. The common bed bug, *Cimex lectularius*, looks a lot like an apple seed in size, shape, and color.

Bed bugs' only source of food is blood from warm-blooded animals. They generally feed on people but will also bite pets such as dogs and cats.

KEY POINTS

» Bed bugs have five nymph stages as they become an adult—and each of these requires a blood meal to go on to the next.

» A feeding takes about five to ten minutes, and the "victim" is usually asleep and unaware.

» At the beginning of the bite, the bug injects an anesthetic and an anticoagulant so the bite isn't felt.

» Some people have no reaction to the bite. For others, over several days to a week or more, the site of the bite can become a red itching bump. The bite can be distinguished from a flea bite because it doesn't have the characteristic red center of a flea bite. Though uncomfortable, bed bugs are not known to spread disease.

» Bed bugs evolved from bugs that lived in caves and fed on bats. This history explains these bugs behavior today. They hide in narrow spaces such as folds in mattresses, under peeling wallpaper, and in cracks in walls. They emerge from hiding to feed, and then retreat back to the isolated area.

» Though they prefer to stay within about 8 feet of their feeding area, they can travel over 100 feet in a night. When food is available, they will feed several times a week. However, they can go for several months without food, especially when the temperature is cooler.

» An adult bed bug can live ten months.

» Bed bugs are prolific, and in usual household conditions, about 80-90 percent of offspring survive. The number of bed bugs can double every 16 days.

» Because bed bugs live in hidden areas, they can be difficult to find and control. They are easily transported on clothing, suitcases, used mattresses. They are a growing problem in hotels, especially in some large cities.

» Signs of beg bugs are itchy bites on the skin. Other signs include seeing the small (1/16 inch to 1/4 inch) bug in mattress creases or other areas. Crushed bedbugs may leave small bloodstains. Reddish-brown spots, especially noticeable on pillows, may be the blood-tinged excrement from the bugs.

Remember, bed bugs aren't a sign of poor hygiene or filth. Any hotel, in any economic tier, can have bed bugs. Though common early in the twentieth century, bed bugs became rare by the 1950's. Unfortunately they are re-emerging.

When checking into a hotel, check the bed linens for signs of bedbugs—especially small brown or red spots. If you see them, change rooms or change hotels. However, if you find you have slept in a room with bedbugs and awaken with bites, the most important thing is to make sure you don't take the bed bugs home with you. Again, prevention is helpful. Don't leave suitcases on the bed. Use storage racks. Also, keep things packed in suitcases as much as possible.

BASIC GUIDELINES FOR ERADICATING BED BUGS

If you continue to get additional bites once home, you have probably brought the bed bugs with you. Because bed bugs hide, reproduce so efficiently, and live such a long time without food, they can be very difficult to eradicate.

- The best approach to control bed bug infestation is a combination of pesticides and environmental control.

- If you live in a multiple family dwelling (high-rise, row house, townhouse), it is helpful to take a community approach and for everyone to attack the problem together.

- Call a licensed exterminator for accurate assessment of the problem, and safe chemical treatment.

- Additionally, it is important to treat any items that may be infested. Heat and freezing cold kills the bugs and the eggs. Wash affected clothes and linens in the hottest water, and dry thoroughly at high heat. Iron with a hot iron if possible.

- If you take clothing or bed linens to the dry cleaners, wrap in sealed plastic bags and let the laundry know about the problem so they can help control it and keep it from spreading.

- Mattresses and box springs can be replaced….. but wait until all signs of bed bugs are gone. If you plan to try to salvage the mattress, wrap it in an airtight plastic cover for a year.

- In your home, destroy any bed bug hiding areas.

- Replace torn and peeling wallpaper.

- Caulk areas where bedbugs can hide.

- Remove any clutter around the bed—place books, papers, and other things that may be infested and that you can dispose of in a plastic bag, label the bag "bed bugs" and discard. If the items can't be discarded, heat or freeze—place in a sealed plastic bag and freeze in a home freezer for two weeks.

Even with a professional exterminator, handling a bed bug problem can take several chemical applications and continued vigilance and cleaning. Bed bugs are a difficult problem to treat.

Scan for more resources.

BEE & WASP STINGS
Winged Assault

You are traveling with your family and having lunch at a roadside festival. Your wife is bitten on the lip by a bee. What should you do?

Stings from insects belonging to the insect order Hymenoptera are among the most important causes of systemic allergic reactions. The most likely culprits come from three families within this order: the honeybees and bumblebees; the hornets, wasps, and yellow jackets; and fire ants.

KEY POINTS
Most insects sting to defend themselves and their nests. The venom from these three families of insects are different with little cross reactivity between families. Therefore, it is very unlikely that a wasp sting will cause an allergic reaction in a person with allergies to bee stings. However, within families there can be significant cross reactivity so that a wasp sting may cause an allergic reaction in someone allergic to yellow jackets.

» Only females can sting because the stinger is a modified egg-laying organ.

» All stings contain venom with vasoactive substances that cause pain, itching, and swelling at the site of the sting.

» Protein enzymes in the venom are the cause of systemic symptoms in those who are allergic. In these sensitized patients, the chain reaction of the immune system can cause a wide spectrum of reactions ranging from local reactions to itching and cardiovascular collapse known as anaphylaxis resulting in death (see Allergic Reactions).

» Anaphylaxis from bee and wasp stings cause at least 40 deaths per year in the United States.

» Less than 10 percent of patients with a large local reaction have systemic reactions to subsequent stings. However a previous systemic reaction correlates with a high risk of a subsequent systemic reaction.

» Severe systemic allergic reactions occur in less than 1 percent of children and about 3 percent of adults.

» Honeybees are less aggressive but their sting is more likely to lead to a systemic reaction. Africanized honeybees are more aggressive but their venom is no more toxic than other honeybees though with multiple stings from an aggressive swarm, life-threatening reactions may result.

» Bee stings are a source of rare neurological disorders and kidney failure from delayed reactions.

BASIC TREATMENT GUIDELINES

Local Reactions:

- Most stings cause acute pain and transient localized swelling.
- Treat with ice, pain meds, oral antihistamines, and topical steroid creams to reduce itching, swelling, and pain.
- Scrape the skin with your fingernail or credit card to remove retained stingers from honeybees. Bumblebees do not leave stingers behind. The stinger will likely be emptied of venom after 30 seconds with no consequence if not removed.
- Large local reactions of the tongue or mouth may compromise the airway and oral steroids, if available, may be useful. SEEK IMMEDIATE EMERGENCY MEDICAL CARE IF THE AIRWAY IS COMPROMISED. SWELLING CAN INCREASE QUICKLY.
- The severe allergic reaction known as ANAPHYLAXIS IS A LIFE-THREATENING EMERGENCY. Anaphylactic symptoms can occur from seconds to several hours after exposure but usually occur very quickly. The first signs of an anaphylactic reaction may include a warm or flushed feeling, tingling in the mouth, a red and itchy rash, or hives. Additional symptoms may include light-headedness, shortness of breath, severe sneezing, anxiety, stomach cramps, and vomiting and diarrhea. Airway constriction, drop in blood pressure, rapid pulse, dizziness or loss of consciousness signal anaphylactic shock.

- Infections of sting sites are very rare so antibiotics are rarely necessary.
- Fire ant stings typically form pustules 1 to 2 days after stinging. Keep them intact and clean.

Systemic Reactions:

- Severe systemic reactions usually occur rapidly after a sting but may be delayed or followed by a recurrence typically within 8 hours. Less than 20 percent of people with allergic reactions have a recurrence.

- At the first sign of a severe allergic reaction, inject epinephrine (prepared dose known as Epi-pen, Auvi-Q, or Adrenaclick) into the thigh. Most patients with known severe allergies carry epinephrine for injection. Epinephrine for injection may be in an emergency supply kit. GET IMMEDIATE MEDICAL CARE. ANAPHYLAXIS IS LIFE THREATENING.

- Delayed injection of epinephrine often results in more severe reactions.

- Repeat injection of epinephrine at 5 to 15 minute intervals if the patient has persistent symptoms or a recurrence of symptoms. Seek immediate medical treatment if at all possible. (Most patients require only one or two doses).

- In a life-threatening situation in a remote area, there are no contraindications for epinephrine use for anaphylaxis treatment including cardiovascular disease or high blood pressure.

If you experience systemic reactions to stings, there are a number of precautions you should consider. Wear long sleeves and pants, avoid activities where exposure may occur. Carry an epinephrine auto-injector and get a prescription for more in case of a recurrent episode.

If you have had an allergic reaction to a sting, make an appointment with an allergist/immunologist to be tested for specific venom sensitivity and consider longer term immunotherapy if identified.

Scan for more resources.

BLIZZARDS
Wisdom During Whiteouts

You are driving through the mountains in winter with a companion and decide to take a scenic but primitive back road shortcut to save time. The weather report says there may be snow but you think you have time to make it back to the main road. It is slow going because of poor road conditions and then it starts to snow, rapidly deteriorating into blizzard conditions. Your car slides off the side of the road. No other travelers have been seen since you left the highway.

It is imperative to understand the skills necessary to survive in a blizzard, or other extreme winter storm, if you live or have to travel in areas where such weather conditions can occur. You should maintain an appropriate emergency kit in your car and in your home.

KEY COMPONENTS IN CAR WINTER EMERGENCY KIT

- » Winter blanket and extra warm clothing
- » Bright colored waterproof panel or tarpaulin
- » Flashlight (with extra batteries or hand-cranked energy source)
- » Radio (either battery or hand-cranked)
- » First aid kit
- » Swiss army knife or similar style pocket knife
- » Small quantity of nonperishable food (high-energy food, such as dried fruit or candy, and food requiring no cooking or refrigeration is best.)
- » Container for melting snow
- » Waterproof matches
- » Paper towel
- » Shovel
- » Compass and road maps

KEY COMPONENTS IN HOME WINTER EMERGENCY KIT

- » A flashlight and extra batteries

- » A battery-powered portable radio to receive emergency information and extra batteries

- » Extra food and water. High energy food, such as dried fruit or candy, and food requiring no cooking or refrigeration is best.

- » Extra medicine and essential items for family members

- » Pet food and pet medications if applicable

- » First aid kit

- » Heating fuel and emergency heating source. Be sure the source can be properly ventilated.

- » A fire extinguisher, smoke detector, and carbon monoxide detector. Make sure the batteries are refreshed.

If you were caught stuck in your home or vehicle during a blizzard, would you know what to do? Here are some tips that may save your life.

BASIC GUIDELINES

- If you are in a vehicle in an isolated area, stay with the vehicle. A vehicle will provide you with good protection from the harmful effects of cold and wind. A vehicle is also much easier to find than a person.

- Do whatever you can to make the vehicle as visible as possible using anything that attracts attention to the car. That was the reason your emergency kit contained a brightly colored tarp or blanket. If the snow has stopped, open the hood so that it is obvious you need assistance.

- Try and keep your blood flowing and your body warm by exercising to the extent you can inside the car. Stomping your feet and clapping your hands vigorously will help. Work actively to maintain a positive mental attitude.

- If possible, clear your car's exhaust pipe from the snow and start the engine intermittently for short periods of time to provide some heat. When you do this, remember to open the window a small amount to allow for some air circulation and to avoid the possibility of carbon monoxide build up, which can happen very quickly if the exhaust pipe is clogged with snow or buried in the snow.

- If you are outside, find shelter quickly. Wind can cause your core body temperature to drop dangerously low and the risk of frostbite and hypothermia increase with every minute you are exposed to the cold weather. Wind multiplies the debilitating effect of cold weather on your body. Deep snow can provide very good protection from the wind and cold. Digging a snow cave can provide you with life-saving protection from the elements. (see Frostbite and Hypothermia)

- Do whatever you can to get dry if you are wet. Don't allow snow to stay settled on clothing, remove it as quickly as possible before it has a chance to melt and soak into the clothing.

- Stay hydrated, but do not be tempted to eat snow. It will lower your core temperature. To melt snow, find a way to gather it into any sort of container and place it under your clothing, but not right against your skin.

- If you are at home, it is wise to have an alternative power source available, such as a generator, if you live in areas that are prone to winter storms or blizzards,. Keep a supply of fuel readily available during the winter weather period.

- Ensure the home is capable of ventilating periodically, especially if you are using non-electric forms of heating. Remove snow from outside the windows and open the window a small amount if necessary. If your electricity has gone out, be very cautious about using other forms of heating such as open fires or kerosene heaters, as these can be extremely dangerous without proper ventilation.

- Find one room in the house that is capable of being sealed up and warmed, but also periodically ventilated. Close other rooms that are not in use. Keep windows uncovered when the sun is shining and covered when it is not.

- Fill a bathtub with water in case the water supply is jeopardized.
- Remember that pets and other animals need to be protected from the cold and wind as well.

Scan for more
resources.

BURNS
From the Sun to the Stove

You are walking barefoot on a public sandy beach on your way back to your vacation resort cottage and in the darkness step on a campfire site with live embers. The burned area of your foot continues to hurt despite soaking it in cold water. It affects your toes and you cannot walk on it.

Burns can be caused by chemicals, electricity, or radiation but, aside from sunburn, most burns received while traveling are caused by high heat sources that produce flame burns, contact thermal injury, or scalds.

KEY POINTS

»   Thermal injury causes tissue coagulation and destruction of blood vessels resulting in inflammation.

»   If the injury occupies less than 10 percent of the total body surface area, the reaction remains local but, as the surface area affected increases, the body undergoes significant fluid loss, decreased cardiovascular function, and kidney failure.

»   Calculate burn size in adults by the Rule of 9s: From neck to pelvis is 18 percent for front and back, each leg is 18 percent, each arm and the head are 9 percent, and the genital area is 1 percent. Burns affecting greater than 30 percent of the surface area are often fatal.

»   Thermal burns are classified as being superficial (first degree) if only the outermost skin layer is involved (e.g., sunburn), partial thickness with penetration into the deeper tissues (blisters common), and full thickness if all layers of skin and underlying dermal tissue are involved. Most burns are a mixture of types. Both superficial and partial thickness burns are exquisitely painful while deeper burns are paradoxically less sensitive because the nerves have been severely damaged or destroyed.

» Sunburn is the most common burn and is an acute skin inflammatory reaction that follows excessive exposure to ultraviolet (UV) radiation. UV exposure can come from a variety of sources, including sun, tanning beds, and certain lamps. UV light is divided into UVA and UVB by wavelength. UVB causes the classical signs of sunburn such as reddening and warmth. UVA does not cause those responses but also damages cellular DNA leading to an increased cancer risk over time. UV exposure increases for those at high altitudes or in environments where sunlight is reflected such as on snowfields or open water. Certain medications (such as some classes of antibiotics and diuretics) can cause increased sensitivity to UV light in some people.

» Contact burns result from exposure to hot metals, plastic, glass, or other heated items. These tend to be limited in area but deep. Hot coals from a campfire are a common source of contact burns.

» Scalds usually result from hot liquid or steam and almost always cause deep partial or full thickness burns in a matter of seconds if over 140°F (hot coffee is around 180°F). Cooking oils and grease usually exceed 300°F. Clothing tends to keep liquids in contact with the skin longer, extending the burn process.

» Electrical burns occur from conversion of electricity into high intensity heat in the tissue through which it passes. Damage depends on the electrical resistance in the tissue and the amperage. Electrical burns are often accompanied by other injuries such as fractures and cardiac damage. Nerve tissue is particularly susceptible to electrical injury. Severe electrical burns often cause excretion of proteins from destroyed muscle cells that can lead to kidney failure if untreated. It is imperative to avoid touching the victim if still in contact with the electrical source of the injury. Use a wooden stick or log to push the person away from the source of electricity. Also, if the person is in cardiac arrest, begin and continue CPR until medical help is available. A lightning strike is another example of an electrical burn (see Lightning Strikes).

» Chemical burns are unlikely to be encountered during travel unless there is exposure to strong acids or alkalis. Chemical burns continue to cause damage until neutralized and early recognition of this problem is important to limit damage. The extent of a chemical burn is often deceptive and may appear superficial.

BASIC PREVENTION AND TREATMENT GUIDELINES

- Many sunscreens do not block UVA radiation so people using sunscreens may be exposed to high UVA levels without realizing it. A broad-spectrum sunscreen provides protection through the entire spectrum of both UVA and UVB.

- Sunscreens should be applied 15 to 30 minutes before exposure thickly enough to provide full protection, followed by one reapplication 15 to 30 minutes after the sun exposure begins, and then about every two hours. More frequent reapplication is necessary only if activities such as swimming or sweating affect sunscreen coverage.

- Check with your doctor about medications that may cause increased sensitivity to the sun. For example, about 3 percent of people who take tetracyclines have increased sensitivity that can cause a serious sunburn quickly. That may cause a problem if you are taking tetracycline for malaria prophylaxis in a tropical climate.

- Treatment of sunburn involves re-hydration with fluids and treatment of symptoms. Studies are inconclusive but mild improvement may result from use of steroids, anti-inflammatory meds like ibuprofen, antioxidants, or antihistamines.

- Treatments seldom decrease recovery time. Burn recovery of any type requires time for the cells to regenerate.

- Damage to cells is not reversible by treatment.

- Aloe-containing lotions may provide pain relief.

- Black tea contains tannic acid and theobromine which may reduce sunburn pain. Soak cloths in cooled black tea and apply to the sunburned area, do not remove it. This is a useful remedy if in a remote area without access to pharmaceutical products.

- Management of other burns depends on the type, extent, body location, associated injuries, and ease of evacuation. Most medical kits do not have specific burn dressings. The key objectives of burn management are keeping the wound clean and controlling pain, and managing fluids and electrolytes..

- Remove the victim from the burn source without endangering yourself.

- Clothing should be removed because it can continue to smolder or retain heat in the case of a scald or cooking oil burn. Synthetics can leave a hot residue that continues to burn.

- Remove all jewelry from burned areas because swelling will compromise circulation.

- People rescued from a closed space must be considered to be at risk for smoke inhalation.

- Burns to the face may result in swelling that can obstruct the airway. Regularly check the airway.

- Immediately evacuate any victim with partial or full thickness burns over greater than 10 percent surface area, facial burns, circumferential burns of an extremity or the chest, and deep burns to the armpits, hands, feet, and genitals.

- If the victim cannot be rapidly evacuated, wash burns with soap and water and dry the area. Apply antibiotic ointment lightly, if available, and wrap with clean gauze. Do not apply a tight bandage.

- Chemical burns should be flushed with copious amounts of water as soon as possible.

- Give pain and anti-inflammatory medication like ibuprofen.

- Keep the victim flat and warm, loss of skin leads to hypothermia and shock.

- Elevate burned extremities to decrease swelling.

- If evacuation is delayed for an extended time, have the victim move the burned areas to decrease the chance of immobility after recovery. Change the dressings twice daily. Begin antibiotics if signs of infection occur.

- Electrical burns are difficult to evaluate because much of the damage is internal. Evacuate people with significant electrical burns, including those struck by lightning (see Lightning Strikes). Electrical burns can cause heart and other internal organ damage and can require life-saving hospital treatment.

Scan for more resources.

CHEST PAIN
Is This the Big One?

You are a busy 52-year-old executive but are proud of the fact that you make time for exercise every day. Shortly after arriving in Jakarta from San Francisco, you notice a sharp stabbing pain in your left chest that radiates to your back. The pain is so intense you break out in a cold sweat and feel like you cannot catch your breath. This is the last thing you remember before waking up in the hospital.

If you are reading this and are having chest pains, have any major health concerns or cardiac risk factors, and the pain is not from an obvious cause, put down this book and seek immediate medical attention. This section of the book is best read when you are not suffering chest pain but want to know what risks are associated with this condition so you can be better prepared.

Chest pain is a major cause of emergency room visits for adults. The majority of individuals experiencing chest pain do not have life-threatening problems, but early treatment is often very important for those who do. It is critical to understand that awareness of risk factors, triggers, and key warning signs will improve your odds of preventing or surviving life-threatening chest pain.

Most emergency physicians view chest pain through the lens of the big three killers—heart attack, pulmonary embolism (blood clot in the lung), and dissection of the aorta (see Deep Vein Thrombosis) These three potentially fatal problems must be ruled out before determining that the chest pain is something less serious. Healthcare professionals will want to know key information including history of the onset, duration, and the character of the pain, risk factors and health history, and any precipitating factors.

KEY RISK FACTORS

» Smoking

» Obesity

» Family history of cardiac problems

» High cholesterol

» High blood pressure (hypertension)

» Diabetes

» Pregnancy, malignancy, and prolonged immobilization add additional risks to pulmonary embolus.

BASIC TREATMENT GUIDELINES

• Certain risk factors cannot be corrected. You can't change your family history nor a history of cancer.

• You can choose not to smoke.

• You can get treatment for high blood pressure or high cholesterol.

• You can exercise and follow a sensible diet.

• During prolonged air travel, you can get up and walk about the cabin and keep well hydrated. Wearing compression stockings helps to prevent formation of blood clots in your legs that can cause a pulmonary embolism.

Several other potentially life-threatening causes of chest pain have a more gradual course that include shortness of breath. These include pneumonia, pleurisy (inflammation of the lining of the chest cavity around the lungs), pericarditis (inflammation around the sac enclosing the heart), and pneumothorax (collapsed lung). Pericarditis is also characterized by pain in the left chest on inspiration or lying down.

If the pain is very superficial, not deep in the chest, and not accompanied by shortness of breath, this is usually a good sign of a less serious problem. Common causes of this type of pain include inflammation or injury to the ribs or muscles of the chest, and shingles, a viral infection causing intense pain along rib outlines.

The upper GI tract is often a source of chest pain, particularly esophagus or stomach problems like reflux disease or gastritis. Sometimes the esophagus can spasm mimicking a heart attack. Gallstones can also present with pain in the chest.

Chest pain that persists longer than 5 minutes without a clear reason, pain accompanied by shortness of breath, or significant chest pain accompanied by the major risk factors should be evaluated by a doctor.

The best treatment for chest pain is prevention. Staying compliant with medicines prescribed by your doctor for conditions such as hypertension, diabetes, or indigestion reduces your risks of complications from these disorders. Be sure you travel with adequate supplies of medications. Include enough to see you through unexpected delays or trip extensions.

Scan for more
resources.

CIVIL UNREST:
WHAT TO DO
Protests & Riots

While returning on foot to your hotel, after a day of tourist activities in Thailand, you find yourself in a street where police have set up a roadblock. Suddenly, with no warning you are surrounded by thousands of placard waving, screaming protesters who start to throw rocks at the police. The police immediately respond with tear gas, and then you hear some shots fired. In their effort to contain the rioters, the police quickly barricaded the streets behind you, and you cannot see any easy way out.

Each year many thousands of people are killed or injured in riots or other forms of civil unrest. Civil unrest can occur in just about any country and takes many forms, from small disorganized and impromptu protests to massive, well-organized riots. Even though it is rare for visitors or expatriates to be directly targeted during periods of civil uprising, it is not out of the question. Sometimes just being in the wrong place at the wrong time is all it takes.

Most incidents of civil unrest are related to labor disputes or social and political issues and therefore are most often predictable and/or known about by locals. Before you travel abroad, research conditions in the place you'll be visiting by reading news stories about the area and checking for travel advisories issued by the U.S. Department of State or equivalent agencies. If there is a strong possibility of civil unrest, consider postponing or rerouting your trip. Obviously, the best way to avoid becoming a victim of civil unrest is to stay away from areas where civil unrest may be occurring. However, if you are unfortunate enough to be caught in the midst of a riot, knowing what to do can mean the difference between getting away safely and becoming one of those thousands of victims such events claim each year.

KEY POINTS

» Contact your embassy, your hotel, or your traveling companions and notify them of your whereabouts. Remember cell phone communications are often impaired during times of civil unrest, but text messages often can get through. Try texting if you cannot make a call.

» Residents of the area are usually aware ahead of time that something big is going to happen. If there is a possibility of impending violence, leave the area immediately. Most victims claim afterward that they should have heeded the warning signs they were given, but failed to do so.

» Avoid large groups of people. It takes a lot of people to make a mob, which is why riots are far more common in densely populated areas. The more people that come together in one place the more chance the gathering has of becoming violent. Even peaceful protests can quickly turn violent.

» Maintain a low profile by avoiding discussions with locals about the contentious issues behind the civil uprising.

» During violent or potentially violent unrest, think carefully before seeking shelter in places that might be targeted by the mob. Such places often include police stations, government buildings, and embassies. In many places nationally affiliated hotels and fast food restaurants are among the first to be attacked.

» If violence erupts or is imminent, leave the area as quickly as possible. If you cannot leave the area, seek shelter in large, public buildings such as libraries or museums. Wait until the crowds have gone before going back outside.

» If curfews are imposed, strictly observe regulations, and monitor the media for immediate updates to the situation.

» Avoid using any form of public transportation and stay away from bus and train stations. Such places can become dangerously crowded quickly when civil unrest starts. Use hotel taxis or private car services if possible.

» If civil unrest is possible, always have adequate amounts of cash on hand and/or travelers checks in case banks close. In extreme cases, cash is useful to buy your way out of a tricky predicament.

» Severe civil unrest can significantly disrupt businesses, industries, and services. If you must travel during unrest, ensure that hotels and businesses will be open, services will be available, and transportation will be running. Confirm all meetings and reservations ahead of time.

» Carry a supply of any medications you are taking in case you can not get back to your hotel.

» Carry a copy of your passport with you at all times.

Scan for more resources.

COMMUNICATION
Can You Hear Me Now?

You are on an adventure vacation in the Andes Mountains at 9000 feet elevation when a companion falls, sustaining non-life threatening injuries that require medical evacuation. Your camp is in a narrow valley in an area flat enough to accommodate helicopter evacuation. How do you call in the cavalry?

A communication plan is important for even a simple local hike. Poor communications during travel have plagued us all at times despite advanced technology and you cannot rely on smart phones alone. Situations that arise may well deteriorate with poor communication. Effective communication is essential on an adventure to connect with trip members, your operations base, or to the outside world.

More complicated travel needs a detailed communication plan which, depending on how remote the event, may include standard and alternate radio frequencies and laminated cards with instructions for use of satellite communications equipment. For international travel, it is advisable to notify the embassy of your plans and how to reach you in an emergency.

KEY POINTS

- » Start with alerting someone that you will be in a remote location and arrange for emergency contact.

- » Terrain has the greatest influence on the quality of telecommunications. Common personal communication equipment is designed for urban environments and clear line of sight. Remote places have sparse cellular coverage and steep terrain can block overhead satellite networks. In a deep valley or cave, communication is very limited beyond what is in sight.

- » No single communications device is perfect for all conditions but a mobile phone configured for the local mobile network is the most common and versatile communications tool. Mobile phones not only provide communication but also act as a homing beacon. Mobile phones can potentially provide search and rescue teams with a valuable means to find you. However, mobile phones are limited by terrain and atmospheric conditions. New technologies combining both cell and satellite capabilities are emerging.

» Applications useful for travelers include SMS texting which is available over a broader range than voice or data and may be available when a voice call is not.

» A location stamp app allows you to update or log your location.

» Apps that provide location and compass headings are very helpful to orient satellite equipment.

» A weather app can warn about deteriorating conditions that affect your safety and communications.

» Satellite phones are expensive to operate and don't always work better than a cell phone. Reliable satellite phone service depends on your location. Check with people with experience in the area because some satellite phone providers cover only certain regions. Some services are optimized for maritime use and others for terrestrial use. It is very important to select the right plan depending on your needs for voice, data, and video transmission.

» VHF communications with two-way radios are very handy in the field and use proven technology that is inexpensive to operate. These units limit communications to individuals monitoring the chosen frequency within range which is line of sight unless repeaters are used. Sophisticated radio systems can cost more than satellite phones but provide long duration, high-quality internal communications. If the radios are a survival tool, ensure they are designated "Mil Spec" which stands for "meets military specifications" for shock, drop, and weather durability. Privacy is an issue unless using an encrypted communicator.

BASIC SAFETY AND EMERGENCY GUIDELINES

- An unbreakable mirror is a handy tool for daily hygiene as well as for signaling aircraft if you are lost.

- Powerful LED torches are versatile and can be used as signaling devices.

- Radio distress beacons can and do save lives. EPIRBs are emergency position-indicating radio beacons used at sea.

- ELTs are emergency locator transmitters used in aviation.

- PLBs are personal locator beacons used for terrestrial location remote from 911 access.

Not all expeditions need these devices and a backup mobile or satellite phone is advisable because search and rescue teams often desire more than just your location. One major advantage of distress beacons over cellular devices is the automated activation feature. Some are activated by salt water or impact. Such beacons on aircraft and vessels may be required by law.

Scan for more resources.

CONTACT DERMATITIS: POISON IVY, POISON OAK, POISON SUMAC
Toxic Tendrils & Trees

I am on a hiking trip in northern Minnesota and have been trekking through the woods for several days. This morning when I woke up I noticed two patches of itching, oozing bumps on my ankles. Is this dangerous? What should I do? Will it spread to other body parts or to others?

This sounds like a classic poison ivy allergic contact dermatitis. Poison ivy is a vine growing wild in much of the United States and also found in temperate climates in China, Japan, and Taiwan. It is recognizable by its shiny three-leaf cluster that may grow close to the ground or may climb high into trees. The rash many people get after contact with the plant is also called "poison ivy," after the plant's name. The rash is caused by urushiol, a resin in the leaves, stems, and roots. Urushiol is also found in poison oak and poison sumac, which look different than poison ivy but cause a similar rash.

KEY POINTS

» The skin lesion or rash looks like clusters of small oozing vesicles or blisters and is very itchy. The rash occurs on areas of the body that come in contact with urushiol which is in the leaves and stem of the plant.

» Though the rash can be on any part of the body, it is most common on sensitive areas of the skin that commonly contact the plant such as the ankles, trunk, neck, face, back of the legs, and inner arms.

» The rash lasts a couple of weeks, and can be very uncomfortable because of the itching.

» The poison ivy rash is a contact dermatitis, or a skin problem that comes from contact with the urushiol in the plant. It is a delayed hypersensitivity type of contact dermatitis. The first exposure often "sensitizes" one to the plant, but rarely causes a rash. At the next exposure, when the toxic resin from the plant touches the skin, the body "remembers" the resin, and the allergic response results in the rash. It often takes a day or two from the time of exposure until the rash appears.

» The rash can occur from touching the plant itself or from touching something that touched the plant, such as clothing or a pet dog.

» Though the plant transmits the allergen, the "oozing" from the skin rash does not contain urushiol, and thus cannot transmit a poison ivy rash from one person to another.

» Urushiol stays active for many years—so even touching a dead root in the ground or a dead vine on a tree can cause the rash.

TREATMENT GUIDELINES

• Mild cases of poison ivy don't require any treatment, though they can be very uncomfortable.

• Warm compresses and frequent bathing can help to relieve the itch.

• Some people find over-the-counter anti-histamines helpful.

• Others find some relief from over-the-counter steroid creams.

• If the poison ivy is severe, see your health care provider who may prescribe oral steroids for a couple of weeks, and/or a topical ointment.

• If the rash gets infected, oral antibiotics may be indicated.

• If you happen to touch a poison ivy plant, as soon as possible, ideally within an hour or two, gently wash the area with soap and water. Wash enough to remove any resin, but be careful not to abrade the skin since injured skin is even more susceptible to it.

• Bathe children and pets who may have contacted the plant.

• Since the poison ivy rash can be transmitted by urushiol on clothing, be sure to wash all clothing that may have touched the plant. Remember the urushiol on the clothing can still spread the rash. Be careful when washing the clothes, and wash with soap, even if it is in the local stream.

- Never burn poison ivy plants. The smoke from burning poison ivy can also spread the allergic reaction deep into the lungs. This can be very dangerous and difficult to treat.

With poison ivy, prevention is the best treatment. Avoiding contact with the plant resin urushiol is the best prevention. The poison ivy plant can be found almost everywhere—it is a common weed in many areas. When young, it is small and often goes unnoticed. As it matures, it can climb trees and be 20 or more feet high, with a vine stem of an inch or more in diameter. Be extra careful in wooded areas and avoid any contact with the poison ivy plant.

Remember even dead leaves, stems and roots contain the urushiol, the active allergen, and can cause a rash. The chemical causing a rash is potent for many years.

Scan for more resources.

DEEP VEIN THROMBOSIS & PULMONARY EMBOLISM
Dangerous Blood Clots

You have just returned from a business trip to Spain and slept most of the time on the seven-hour flight. Aside from being tired, you notice a nagging discomfort like a muscle strain in your calf and attribute it to a cramp from being on the long flight. You are not worried about it and will wait to see if this persists over the next couple of days.

Thrombophlebitis is an inflammation of a vein associated with a development of a blood clot (thrombosis). If the clot develops in the deep veins of the pelvis or leg, there is a risk that a piece of the clot may break off forming a plug (embolism) to block circulation in the lung. A large pulmonary embolism (PE) is a relatively common cause of sudden death so early recognition and treatment are essential. This is a medical emergency.

KEY POINTS

» People who are at risk for formation of deep vein thrombosis (DVT) include smokers, inactive people, women using oral contraceptives, pregnant women, cancer patients, and those with known blood clotting disorders. Certain ethnic populations may have undiagnosed clotting disorders. For example, about 5 percent of people with European ancestry have an abnormal clotting factor which predisposes to blood clot formation.

» Others at significant risk are those who have sustained lower extremity or pelvic trauma or have had recent abdominal or pelvic surgery. Prolonged inactivity in a single position, such as cavers experience, also creates a greater risk.

51

» There has been a great deal of interest in the link between DVT and flying. Prolonged inactivity and dehydration may contribute to development of DVT on a long flight. All travelers, regardless of their risk level, should avoid dehydration and frequently exercise leg muscles.

» Symptoms of DVT classically include swelling of one lower extremity and pain which resembles a muscle strain or cramp. Alert should be raised if the pain does not follow exercise, does not abate with rest, and is in one leg (usually the calf), particularly if there has been a period of prolonged inactivity or if you have the risk factors listed earlier. People tend to dismiss these symptoms which increases risk of clot extension and PE.

» Symptoms of life-threatening PE are sudden sharp chest pain which may be worse with deep breathing, cough, shortness of breath, and increased breathing rate and heart rate.

» DVT and PE can occur without warning signs or symptoms.

BASIC PREVENTION AND TREATMENT GUIDELINES

- Travelers with one or more risk factors for DVT should consider graduated compression stockings or possibly prescription anticoagulants for flights longer than 6 hours.

- Get up and walk periodically on long flights and stop for breaks on long car rides.

- Drink fluids on trips preferably water, avoid excessive alcohol intake.

- Aspirin does not prevent DVT.

- Aspirin may be given if DVT is suspected and should be given if PE is suspected while awaiting medical evacuation and assessment.

Scan for more resources.

DENTAL EMERGENCIES
Cavities, Lost Fillings, & Trauma

You are at dinner in a small resort town and bite into the local fruit with a seed, you feel part of your tooth come loose in your mouth. The area is now sensitive to cold fluids. There is no local dentist. What should you do?

One of the health areas paid the least attention before travel is dental health. Whether it is loss of a filling or oral trauma, we are often ill-prepared to deal with a dental emergency. Dentists may be found in urban areas but are a rare luxury in remote locations and extraction of an abscessed or damaged tooth may be the only care possible.

KEY POINTS

» A dental emergency causes anxiety and can be extremely painful.

» The most common problems encountered on travel are cracked and broken teeth, oral infections and dental abscesses, and lacerations and trauma to the oral region.

» The most common cause of non-traumatic oral pain is an acute abscess. The best prevention is to have a thorough dental exam before leaving to resolve existing or unsuspected problems.

» Oral trauma needs to be recognized with appropriate medical and dental care for initial treatment. Evacuation is likely after stabilization unless in a country with high-quality health care. Oral injuries can compromise the airway. Always make certain the airway is clear.

» Visible tooth fractures without exposure of a nerve or blood supply will be sensitive to cold and air but should not be sensitive to light tapping. These fractures can be covered with a temporary material.

» Fractures below the gum line and into the bone will often be detected by a blood clot beneath the gum tissue. Such areas will also be sensitive to touch. It is important to document the circumstances of the incident causing the trauma (see After You Return).

BASIC PREVENTION AND TREATMENT GUIDELINES

- Make sure to have a visit to the dentist no more than six months before your trip to identify and treat any problems.

- If going to a remote area for any length of time, assemble a minimum kit with a topical anesthetic, temporary dental filling, oil of clove, cotton balls, dental wax, and an antibiotic. This will not take up much space.

- If a filling is lost during travel, the area should be cleaned, dried, and isolated using cotton rolls. For the short term, sugarless gum or dental wax can be placed in the defect if there is no temporary filling. If available, a temporary paste of zinc oxide eugenol (oil of clove) or other material should be applied to the area and allowed to set and dry. The surface needs to be smooth and the temporary material cannot interfere with the bite or impinge on an area of gum tissue.

- If an abscess is suspected, start a ten-day course of penicillin, 500 mg, four times per day. For those with penicillin allergies, clindamycin is the drug of choice. For pain relief, oral pain medication and anti-inflammatory medicine like ibuprofen will help but may not eliminate the pain.

- A dental abscess may require evacuation if the infection appears to involve surrounding tissue, if antibiotics are not available, or if pain cannot be controlled.

Scan for more resources.

DIABETES & TRAVEL
The Silent Killer If Not Controlled

You have invited your father on a family trip to Spain. His health is generally good but he is moderately overweight and takes medication for diabetes and high blood pressure. He has had a cardiac stent in the past. Is it safe for him to accompany you?

Diabetes mellitus (DM) is serious chronic condition that affects over 350 million people globally with an expected 50 percent increase over the next decade. DM is characterized by high levels of glucose caused by defective insulin production or action. Adult-onset DM (Type 2), the most common, usually has a direct relationship to obesity and inactivity. DM is directly associated with development of high blood pressure, cardiac disease, and stroke. Because DM affects small blood vessels, complications from this disease commonly affect many organs including the eyes, kidneys, legs and feet, and skin. It is imperative for travelers with this condition to prepare and be alert for problems related to DM. With proper attention, diabetics can travel as freely as others in most instances.

KEY POINTS

» Travelers with DM need to have the condition well controlled. Diabetics are strongly recommended to consult with their physician before travel.

» Expedition and trip leaders should be aware that diabetics may hide their condition to avoid being excluded from the mission or trip. Failure to disclose DM may have very serious consequences for the patient as well as the other members of the trip if someone has to be evacuated.

» Travel often comes with increased stress, changes in meal schedules and types of food available, changes from daily exercise routines, and lack of quick access to medications. All of these can have an effect on DM management.

» Diabetics may have a suppressed immune system. Routine vaccinations must be up to date (see Immunizations).

» Travelers with DM should consider receiving pneumococcal vaccine, additional Hepatitis B vaccine, inactivated flu vaccine, and *Herpes zoster* (shingles) vaccine.

» Yellow fever vaccine must be discussed with a physician and a waiver will not guarantee prevention of quarantine, refusal of entry, or mandatory vaccine upon arrival.

» Make sure you have good evacuation insurance.

BASIC GUIDELINES

• Pack twice as much insulin or medicine needed for the trip to ensure that you have adequate supplies in case of trip delays or extensions.

• Hand carry all medical supplies because luggage can be lost. Bring a letter from your doctor stating that you have DM and need to hand carry medication and supplies including needles and syringes.

• Diabetics who use insulin pumps or monitors need to check with the manufacturer to determine if equipment is affected by scanners and configured for use on planes.

• Carry snacks on the plane. It is prudent to alert flight attendants to your condition if it is not stable.

• Wear a medical bracelet or necklace and carry a medical card stating that you have DM.

• Pay attention to storage temperatures for insulin at your destination.

• Check feet frequently for possible infections. Quickly seek medical attention if there are signs of infection in the feet or anywhere.

• Seek medical evaluation for excessive thirst, more frequent urination, sudden visual changes, tingling in feet or hands, or excessive fatigue.

Scan for more resources.

DIARRHEA (TRAVELER'S)
Common Scourge On The Road

You just returned from a vacation to Mexico where you indulged in local cuisine and did not always drink bottled water. On the last day you noted some rumblings in your stomach and had increased gas but dismissed it as expected when you eat unfamiliar food. Now you have some nausea and loose stools. Everybody gets this, right? Won't this just go away?

Intestinal infection causing diarrhea is one of the most common illnesses among travelers. About 80 to 90 percent of traveler's diarrhea (TD) is caused by bacteria with the most common culprit being E. coli species. Viruses and unicellular protozoan organisms (amoeba species, Giardia, Cryptosporidia) are also sources of TD.

KEY POINTS

> » Collectively, these organisms are responsible for "food poisoning" and "stomach flu" and though more common in developing countries, TD can be contracted anywhere. Improper food handling and poor hygiene in restaurants are major contributors to TD risk. Areas of poor access to safe drinking water and sanitation likewise significantly increase the risk.

> » Symptoms of bacterial and viral TD usually begin within 6-48 hours of infection and can include intestinal cramps, urgent loose stools, severe abdominal pain, fever, and vomiting. Bloody diarrhea can be noted on occasion with severe infections.

> » Uncomplicated bacterial or viral TD can last 2-5 days without treatment. Noroviral infections are short-lived but violent diarrheal infections.

» Protozoal TD usually has a longer incubation period of 1-2 weeks. Symptoms of protozoal TD are more subtle at the outset with a gradual onset of low-grade symptoms and 2-5 loose stools per day. Symptoms can be intermittent with a few days of somewhat normal stools followed by return of loose stools and symptoms may persist for months without treatment. Pay attention to persistent diarrhea after travel, it should trigger evaluation for protozoa or other parasites.

» The traveler with diarrhea is generally miserable and should seek medical care early after onset of symptoms to prevent dehydration as well as to rule out more serious diseases that have diarrhea as a symptom. These include typhoid fever and, less commonly, cholera which usually occurs in localized epidemics. Symptoms are generally very intense with these more serious infections. Transmission of these diseases follows the same route of exposure to contaminated food and water.

BASIC PREVENTION AND TREATMENT GUIDELINES

- Travelers who are careful about food and water sources may reduce their risk of TD yet still may not be able to completely protect themselves from TD.

- Wash your hands after each use of the bathroom, and use hand sanitizer before eating. Make certain everyone in your travel party does the same.

- All meat, fish, shellfish, and vegetables should be fully cooked and served hot.

- Buffets and salads should be avoided.

- Fresh fruit that is eaten unpeeled should be avoided and fruits with peels should be peeled by the person who eats them.

- Drink bottled water, soft drinks, and other beverages opened in front of you.

- Do not use ice, this is made with local water that may be contaminated. Restaurants often say the ice is "safe" – don't trust it.

- Avoid food and beverages from street vendors. Sub-standard hygiene is common.

- Vaccine for typhoid fever provides some but not complete protection.

- Vaccines for cholera are ineffective.

- Due to rising bacterial resistance to antibiotics, prophylaxis for TD with antibiotics is no longer recommended.

- Solutions containing bismuth (Peptol-Bismol) have been shown to provide some protection against TD if taken four times a day.

- Treatment for TD depends on the causative organism. All treatment involves fluid replacement.

- The large majority of TD is caused by bacteria so antibiotics, anti-diarrheal medication, and fluids are the usual prescription. There is growing bacterial resistance to commonly used antibiotics and you should seek medical attention for treatment guidance.

- Viral causes of TD cannot be treated and supportive care with fluids, anti-diarrheal medication, and anti-emetics are advised for these self-limiting afflictions.

- Protozoan causes of TD require different types of antimicrobials than bacterial causes. You should suspect a protozoan cause if diarrhea continues without significant improvement after 24-hour use of an appropriate broad-spectrum antibiotic. Be aware that alcohol must be avoided while on this medication.

- Don't 'self-treat' with over-the-counter antibiotics available in many countries. They are rarely effective and lead to antibiotic resistant and extremely difficult to treat infections.

**Scan for more
resources.**

DRINKING WATER SAFETY
Foiling Montezuma's Revenge

A lawyer, retained by a client in Morocco for a complicated international mineral rights case, is on travel to Casablanca and Rabat. From there he will go to the Sahara Desert where the mineral rights are in dispute. This experienced traveler previously had diarrhea from poorly treated water and wants to take appropriate precautions to avoid this problem.

In the United States and Canada, clean water is taken for granted. Clean potable water is plentiful and freely available virtually everywhere where there is human habitation.

KEY POINTS

» American households use about 400 liters per day while the average European household uses half that amount.

» The average human is composed of 60 percent water. Replacing lost water each day depends on the type of activity, body size (men need more water than women), and environmental factors such as ambient temperature. Most people need to replace 2-3 liters of water every day with water found in food and potable liquids. An easy way to calculate daily fluid requirements is that a person should try to drink 8 servings of 8 ounces of liquids each day. This is particularly important in arid climates or at high altitude.

» As a general rule, traveling to highly developed countries generally frees one from worry about contaminated drinking water. The taste of the water varies based on the mineral content and the use of disinfecting agents such as chlorine or ozone.

» Using bottled water is preferred by many travelers because both the safety of the water and the taste generally tend to be more agreeable. A note of caution on the "safety" of some bottled water: in poor and overcrowded countries, unscrupulous water companies may package contaminated water in unsealed plastic bottles. Do not drink from a water bottle that has not been opened in your presence.

» When traveling in a region with potential for contamination, you should avoid water without the protective seal of a reliable brand of bottled water. Beware of ice which is usually made from unprotected water sources. Tap water is to be avoided as well, even on a tooth brush.

» The hazards from untreated water include microorganisms including bacteria, viruses, and protozoan parasites as well as chemical contaminants. The most common bacterial contaminant in water worldwide is E. coli. Contamination to drinking water can come from both human and animal fecal waste.

BASIC GUIDELINES

- Several commercial methods of disinfection are available for personal use.

- Chlorine dioxide or iodide tablets pack easily into a travel bag and are a good backup in case no source of clean bottled water is available.

- Water filtration systems are another useful item. There are a variety of filter types including ceramic, carbon, siphon or pump. Carbon filtration adds the benefit of removing some chemical contaminants in addition to most microorganisms.

- Filters don't remove viruses. Small and portable personal UV light sterilization tools will kill viruses in addition to bacteria and protozoan contaminants.

- If filtration systems, UV light sources, and chemical sterilizers are not available, you must boil all water before using it. One common reason for the popularity of tea in many countries is its relative safety as a potable beverage. It can also settle a mildly upset stomach, particularly mint or mint-flavored tea.

- DO NOT FORGET to pack supplies to treat travel-related diarrheal illnesses.

Scan for more resources.

DROWNING
Submersion Survival

You are on vacation in the islands and while out for a stroll on the beach see a commotion surrounding a young man just pulled from the water who appears unconscious.

Drowning causes death by impairing respiration during submersion or immersion in liquid. Over 500,000 deaths occur each year worldwide from drowning which is the leading cause of death among boys age 5 to 14. Incidence of drowning in developing countries is at least ten times higher than in the United States. Risk factors for drowning are male gender, age less than 14, alcohol use, risky behavior, lack of supervision, low income, poor education, and rural residency.

KEY POINTS

» Submersion of the airway below the liquid surface or water splashing over the face (immersion) causing respiratory impairment starts the drowning process.

» Rescue of the person at any time to interrupt this process is termed a nonfatal drowning.

» A submersion or immersion incident without respiratory impairment is considered a water rescue and not a drowning.

» When the airway can no longer be kept clear, water is aspirated into the airway leading to hypoxia, loss of consciousness, cessation of respiration, and cardiac arrest. This sequence takes seconds to a few minutes. In unusual situations of very cold water and hypothermia, this process can last for an hour.

» If the person is rescued alive, the amount and type of water aspirated (fresh versus salt water) determines the degree of damage to the lungs and subsequent respiratory function. Fluid in the lungs greatly interferes with the exchange of oxygen and carbon dioxide.

» If cardiopulmonary resuscitation (CPR) is needed, neurological damage is the same as with other situations requiring CPR. The only exception is in drowning with hypothermia where brain oxygen requirements are less. Cerebral oxygen requirements are reduced about 5 percent for each degree of reduced temperature from 37° to 20° C.

BASIC RESCUE GUIDELINES

- Many drowning persons can help themselves or are rescued by bystanders. Where there are lifeguards, about 6 percent of victims need medical care and 0.5 percent need CPR.

- Untrained rescuers must avoid drowning and should provide assistance from outside of the water if possible. Reach for the victim with a pole, towel, or branch or throw a buoyant object to them.

- Call for emergency medical services immediately. Begin rescue and CPR immediately if needed. Do not wait for emergency medical services to arrive.

- Conscious victims should be brought to land to start life support as soon as possible.

- Resuscitation of unconscious victims is more successful in the water but must be done by highly trained rescuers. Otherwise the more rapidly you bring the victim to land, the better the chances of survival.

- Drowning victims with only respiratory arrest usually respond after a few rescue breaths. If the patient is non-responsive, begin CPR for presumed cardiac arrest.

- Cervical spine injuries are rare but must be suspected in cases where diving, waterskiing, surfing, or watercraft are involved. Five to 10 percent of all spinal cord injuries occur during water sports, the majority from diving. Immobilization of the spine in the water is optimal before moving the victim or attempting resuscitation. Keep the airway open.

- Place the victim flat with head and abdomen at the same level.

- If unconscious but breathing, position the victim on his/her side.

- CPR for drowning requires 5 rescue breaths before chest compression because ventilation can be harder because of water in the lungs.

- Vomiting of stomach contents is a significant problem and may lead to more aspiration and impair airway exchange. Do not use abdominal thrusts to expel water. Keep the victim on their side and clean any vomit from the airway with your finger.

Scan for more resources.

EARACHE
A Real Pain

You recently landed in Denver, Colorado, to head toward a ski resort nearby. You notice the gradual onset of a sharp earache that begins to become severe enough that skiing seems out of the question.

Earache (otalgia) is a common problem. It encompasses a broad variety of conditions with one obvious thing in common: ear pain. Earache can be more than a nuisance. Depending on the source of the pain, earache can be a self-limited problem or a harbinger of a life-threatening emergency.

KEY POINTS

» Earaches can originate from problems within the ear like infection or trauma from rapid or extreme changes in pressure. Rapid ascent or descent, particularly if the traveler has some obstruction of the natural internal drainage from the ear (through the eustachian tube) can cause a pressure mismatch across the eardrum which is painful. This happens most commonly when the traveler has a respiratory infection or allergies.

» Earaches can also arise from problems external to the ear itself as in dental problems or even cardiac pain that radiates into the ear.

» Fortunately, most cases of earache though painful are not life threatening, are often self-limited, and respond to simple and commonly available treatments.

BASIC TREATMENT GUIDELINES

• The first step in dealing with an earache is to determine the cause.

• One common cause of earache in travelers and explorers is barotrauma (trauma from rapid or extreme changes in pressure). When you cannot clear your ears during rapid ascent or descent in air or water you can develop an earache and in extreme cases you can have rupture of the eardrum. Chewing gum during takeoffs and landings can help improve the natural process by which the ears balance inner ear pressures.

- If you have sinus and inner ear congestion, it is always prudent to avoid air travel or SCUBA diving until this congestion is resolved or treated.

- Earache from infections are often accompanied by other symptoms such as fever, discharge, loss of appetite, and vertigo (dizziness). Earaches associated with the common cold can be treated with analgesics such as acetaminophen or ibuprofen along with warm compresses and decongestants.

- If the ear has an actual discharge along with fever it is best to seek medical attention soon. This may require antibiotic therapy but only after a health care provider has been able to directly view the ear canal and ear drum.

- Ear pain can sometimes arise from a foreign body lodged in the ear, such as an earplug that is forgotten (yes) or pushed in to the canal too far. Children can put items in their ears. Rarely, insects can lodge there at night while sleeping in tropical climates and need to be extracted.

- Earaches that arise from dental pain must be treated by addressing the underlying dental problem. An infected or cracked tooth should be treated without delay. Analgesic medication can help make the pain tolerable but delay in dental treatment should be avoided as the pain can become incapacitating.

- If you are prone to ear problems, then you are likely already on medications to mitigate these problems. Make sure these medications are packed with your medical kit on travel particularly to a remote area. Anyone prone to ear canal cerumen (wax) blockages should have their ears cleaned before their trip, and also pack an approved ear suction irrigation bulb along with a small vial of mineral oil.

There are a few causes of ear pain that are rare but if untreated could have serious consequences. Tumors in or near the ear can cause earache.

Certainly unexplained ear pain accompanied by vertigo (dizziness) unresponsive to conventional conservative approaches should be evaluated by a healthcare provider. Pain in the ear that is accompanied by neck pain and limb numbness during exertion may be a variation of angina, chest pain related to cardiac problems, particularly for older individuals at risk for coronary artery disease.

Scan for more
resources.

EARTHQUAKE
Drop, Cover, & Hold

You are in the Philippines at an international conference and while at breakfast, you feel a peculiar shaking and notice the hanging plants and chandeliers rocking significantly. You realize that you are in an earthquake.

Earthquake-prone areas are generally well known but the exact timing of an earthquake cannot be predicted. People living in such areas can take a number of safety measures to minimize the impact of earthquakes. Most of the casualties and damage are not caused by the earthquake but by the fires that often follow. Therefore, particular attention should be paid to reducing the risk of fire (from open flames, stoves, electrical wires, and appliances). Subsequent earthquakes often occur, and these aftershocks can still cause considerable damage and topple buildings made unstable by the first quake.

KEY POINTS
Before an Earthquake:

» If you are living in or visiting an earthquake zone for any length of time, ask if your residence is constructed to meet local building codes for earthquake locations, if they exist.

» Check that your accommodation is on solid ground, not land fill.

» Check every part of the house for fire prevention.

» Put bottles of flammable materials in a safe place to ensure they will not fall.

» Do not store on shelves items that are likely to fall and cause injury.

» Make a habit of checking the safety of cooking stoves.

» Get a fire extinguisher with appropriate capacity and keep it up to date. Fire extinguishers need to be renewed.

» Choose stoves designed not to turn over, and do not keep any flammable articles beside the stove.

» Identify an emergency exit and ensure it is free of any obstacles. If possible, avoid staircases. If this is not possible, stairs should be kept clear of any kind of obstacles.

» Ensure that all doors to the emergency exit always have a key near and accessible.

» Conserve drinking water in tanks, cisterns, or other storage containers. But be sure the water is kept fresh. Once a year at least, replace all water supplies.

» Allot tasks to each person in case of earthquake, such as firefighting, emergency evacuation, and rescue.

» At work, take the same precautions as those taken at your residence and adapt them to the characteristics of your work place.

» Emergency equipment must be clearly marked and ready for use at any time.

» Designate an assembly point, outside and a safe distance from the building, where people can assemble after the earthquake for a roll-call to determine if any individuals are trapped in the building. This procedure is the same as it would be for a fire drill.

» Keep your automobile fueled. If electric power is cut off, filling stations may not be able to operate pumps for several days.

During an Earthquake:

» During an earthquake, wherever you are, do not panic, be calm. The motion of the earthquake is frightening but, unless it shakes something down on top of you, it is harmless. It is very rare for a building to collapse immediately. Keep calm and ride it out.

» Stay inside: "Drop, Cover, Hold" Find a place to get down low, preferably under a strong table or other heavy furniture that will create air pockets in case of a collapse. If you run outside, you may be hit by falling debris.

» Do not use an elevator, and only use a stairwell after the building ceases to move.

» Stay away from windows and chimneys.

» If you are at a public place (movie theater, department store, bus terminal), do not panic. It is dangerous to rush to the exit. Try to protect yourself under doorways or against inner walls. Walk out (do not run) when shaking has stopped.

» If you are outdoors, move away from buildings, high walls, and utility wires.

» If you are beside a large building, seek shelter under archways or doorways that offer protection from falling debris. Do not run through or near buildings.

» If you are in a moving vehicle in the countryside, stop the vehicle in the closest safe place, away from slopes where landslides may occur, underpasses, or overpasses and, if possible, away from trees. Remain inside your vehicle until the shaking stops.

» In a city or town, stop your vehicle as quickly as safety permits (far from tall buildings, if possible) and stay in the vehicle until the tremors subside.

After an Earthquake:

» After the earthquake, you should first take care of any fires if possible.

» Do not use candles, matches, or other open flames, either during or after the tremor. Gas lines may have been disrupted.

» Do not turn utilities on. Earth movement may have cracked water, gas, and electrical conduits.

» If you smell gas, open windows and shut off the main valve, then leave the building and report gas leakage to authorities. Do not re-enter the house until a utility official says it is safe.

» If water mains are damaged, shut off the supply at the main valve.

» If electrical wiring is damaged, close the switch at the main meter box.

» Turn on your radio or television (if conditions permit). Information and instructions will be broadcast by radio.

» Stay off the telephone except to report an emergency.

» Calmly get out of the building (do not run) and go to open spaces. Look out for falling debris. If you are in town, keep away from buildings (for a distance of at least half the height of the tallest one).

» Stay out of severely damaged buildings; after-shocks can shake them down.

» Stay outdoors and go to open spaces.

» If in a vehicle, drive slowly and listen carefully to traffic information on the radio and follow the instructions.

» In a severe earthquake, roads will be broken up, traffic signals will not work, and there will be confusion. It may be safer to evacuate on foot than by car.

» False rumors are apt to circulate after tremors and even more so after a severe earthquake. Await instructions from the authorities, which will probably come by radio or through the hotel management system, before evacuating.

» Take with you minimal personal belongings that you would need in case of emergency.

» Avoid walking along a wall, under any overhangs, or beside water courses. Be careful of broken loose electrical wires.

Scan for more
resources.

EBOLA & EMERGING & RESURGENT VIRAL DISEASES
MERS, Dengue & Other Bad Actors

Your business takes you regularly to the Middle East but you have been hearing news reports of a disturbing respiratory disease originating in that area. You keep hearing about bird flu coming from China... again. You worry that more rapid spread of bad diseases puts you in the crosshairs in travel hubs like Dubai or Shanghai. There are always people coughing on planes and in airports. Ebola is on the march again in west Africa. Do I really need to worry about these viruses?

Viruses are small, complex, very efficient infectious agents which are the most abundant biological organisms on earth. Viruses infect animals, plants, bacteria, and fungi. They are much smaller than a cell and have no cellular characteristics except genes. Surrounding the genetic material is a membrane envelope containing various proteins that function to attach to and invade cells. Once in the cell, the virus corrupts the host cell metabolism to reproduce and escape to infect other cells. Viruses mutate frequently and can acquire traits to allow more rapid spread or resistance to medication.

Ebola is a deadly viral disease which kills 30 to 90 percent of humans who become infected. There are five strains of Ebola virus with varying degrees of fatality rates for humans. One strain, Ebola Reston, found in monkeys in the Philippines does not appear to cause disease in humans. Three different Ebola virus species have caused large outbreaks in sub-Saharan Africa.

Influenza (flu) and other viruses that can kill humans remain of great concern to experts because of their potential to mutate to easily infect victims like the common cold or measles.

Other emerging and resurgent viral diseases also pose risks in areas where they occur.

KEY POINTS

EBOLA

» The largest Ebola outbreak in history began in 2014 and is caused by Ebola Zaire. It remains uncontrolled in West Africa as this went to press with over 10,000 cases and a greater than 50 percent death rate.

» Ebola virus is transmitted through close personal contact and exposure to excretions and bodily fluids from infected patients, particularly blood products and tissue.

» The Ebola outbreak has been maintained because of cultural funeral practices, community distrust of international medical services, and the eating of bush meat.

» Healthcare workers and others with close direct contact with people infected with Ebola are particularly prone to infection.

» The first symptoms of Ebola are a sudden onset of fever, sore throat, muscle aches, fatigue, and headache followed in more advanced cases by vomiting, diarrhea, rash, and both internal and external bleeding.

» Once a person is infected with Ebola, the incubation period (time it takes for symptoms to appear) can vary between 2 and 21 days. The 2014 epidemic has averaged about 10 days to time of symptom appearance.

» At this time, only people with symptoms are contagious. Ebola does not appear to be airborne currently. Screening procedures at major airports are likely to greatly reduce the chance that a person infected with symptomatic Ebola would be on a plane.

INFLUENZA (FLU)

» Influenza is a viral infection of birds and mammals. Influenza-like illnesses such as the common cold and the 24-hour stomach flu are generically called "flu" but are caused by other viruses.

» Flu viruses are named by their H protein (17 subtypes known) and N protein (9 subtypes known).

» The rapid mutation of viruses that cause common flu is the reason you have to get a shot every flu season (see Immunizations).

» New strains emerge when a flu virus acquires the ability to spread to humans or when a human virus picks up new genes from an animal or bird flu. The real problem occurs if the virus develops the ability to transfer easily between humans like SARS did and has a significant fatality rate associated with it.

» Three flu pandemics within the twentieth century have killed tens of millions worldwide. Fortunately, we have been relatively lucky with recent flu outbreaks.

» Avian flu H5N1 emerged in the 1990s with over 600 cases and 60 percent fatality rate. However, despite periodic outbursts, it has not yet been able to transmit between humans.

» A flu that combined swine, avian, and human genes emerged in 2009 and spread between people but fortunately this H1N1 swine flu has a low mortality rate.

» A recent emergence from eastern China of H7N9 avian flu has killed about 20 percent of those infected but unlike H5N1, birds are not very sick so there is no warning in the community. Ominously, it possesses traits that suggest an easier spread to man and may be resistant to medication.

» Two other avian flu strains, H7N1 in South African ostriches and H7N3 in Mexican poultry have not jumped to humans yet but are under close scrutiny.

OTHER DANGEROUS VIRAL DISEASES

Other emerging or resurgent viral diseases arising from animals besides flu can mutate to cause serious consequences in humans. A coronavirus infection (not a flu) called **Severe Acute Respiratory Syndrome (SARS)** arose from bats in 2002, rapidly spread to 37 countries, and killed 10 percent of those infected before being contained.

No vaccine or specific antiviral treatments are available for the following diseases at time of this publication.

» Five strains of coronavirus including the one responsible for SARS are known to infect man. A sixth strain has now emerged from the Middle East, primarily in Saudi Arabia, but 3 cases appeared in London after travel to that area. This deadly **Middle East Respiratory Syndrome coronavirus (MERS-CoV)** has killed nearly 40 percent of those infected though direct human transmission has been a rare occurrence at the date of this publication. Camels have been implicated but not proven as the animal host.

» **Dengue** is an Aedes mosquito-borne viral disease that affects about 400 million people yearly in tropical and subtropical climates. It is endemic (always present) in these areas but epidemics occur periodically. An upsurge of dengue has occurred in the Caribbean and Latin America and it is now reported in Florida and Texas in the United States. There is no vaccination or cure. Though debilitating, there is a low fatality rate (less than 5 percent) if treated (see Fever).

» **Chikungunya** is another Aedes mosquito-borne viral disease, with symptoms similar to dengue, in Asia, Africa, and the Pacific regions. It recently spread to the Caribbean and Latin America and is now reported in the subtropical United States. The fatality rate from Chikungunya is less than 1 percent (see Fever).

» **West Nile Virus (WNV)** is another viral illness transmitted by mosquitoes after biting infected birds. WNV transmission occurs in Europe, the Middle East, Africa, India, Australia, North America, and parts of Asia. About 70 to 80 percent of people infected with WNV do not develop any symptoms while 20 percent have fever and other symptoms such as headache, body aches, joint pains, vomiting, diarrhea, or rash. Most people with these symptoms recover completely, though fatigue and weakness can last for weeks or months. A small percentage of people with symptoms will develop serious neurologic problems such as encephalitis or meningitis (inflammation of the brain or surrounding tissues).

Other deadly viruses but with low risk for most travelers include:

» **Marburg** viruses causes hemorrhagic fever with similar symptoms to Ebola, have bat reservoirs, and cause sporadic outbreaks in isolated areas of sub-Saharan Africa. Marburg virus is transmitted through close personal contact and exposure to excretions and bodily fluids from infected patients, particularly blood products and tissue. Like Ebola, the first symptoms are sudden onset of fever, sore throat, muscle aches, fatigue, and headache followed in more advanced cases by vomiting, diarrhea, rash, and both internal and external bleeding. Outbreaks are rare but fatality rates have been around 90 percent.

» **Lassa Hemorrhagic Fever**, also similar in presentation to Ebola, is found in West African grains stores and can transmit from human to human. The rat is the reservoir and excretes the virus which can also be transmitted from infected people or through particles in the air. The fatality rate is relatively low but can reach 50 percent during epidemics.

» **Nipah** virus in Bangladesh which originated in Malaysia, has bat reservoirs, and is associated with unpasteurized date palm juice. The fatality rate approximates 30 percent.

» **Crimean-Congo Hemorrhagic Fever (CCHF)** is caused by a virus transmitted through tick bites or through contact with contaminated tissue and blood from infected animals. CCHF can spread among people from an infected person through close personal contact. CCHF is found in Eastern Europe, particularly in the former Soviet Union, throughout the Mediterranean, in northwestern China, central Asia, southern Europe, Africa, the Middle East, and the Indian subcontinent. Fatality rates vary from 10 to 50 percent.

BASIC GUIDELINES

• Stay away from live birds and undercooked poultry if you are traveling to an area of reported dangerous viral diseases. Avoid live markets with birds.

• Wash hands regularly or use hand sanitizer. Masks will not help. Masks are useful if you are the one coughing or sneezing to prevent particulates in the air but will not filter viruses.

- Do not eat bush meat, particularly from primates.

- Take precautions to avoid mosquito bites: use mosquito bed nets, use DEET-containing insect repellent, empty free standing water in your environment, wear long sleeves and pants if possible.

- If you develop a fever within thirty days of traveling to an area known for flu or other viral diseases, report to health authorities quickly.

Scan for more
resources.

EYE DISORDERS
An Eye For An Eye

You have been out deep sea fishing with an ocean breeze blowing for most of the day and your contact lenses are now bothering you and starting to cause your eyes to hurt. Removing your lenses has not helped much. What should you do?

We rarely think about optical care until problems occur. Perhaps those who wear contact lenses are more aware of their eyes, but most people do not consider their eyes when going on a trip. Yet the eyes are extremely sensitive and can be a source of significant irritation or misery often complicated by limited access to resources for help while traveling.

KEY POINTS

» Many acute eye disorders present initially with a red eye, a symptom of inflammation. Common causes of this condition include viral or bacterial conjunctivitis that affects the membranes lining the eye socket.

» An infection is usually accompanied by a discharge.

» Other causes of inflammation include allergy, presence of a foreign body (such as a splinter, dirt, or cinder), corneal abrasion, contact lens complications, irritation from chemicals or smoke, snow blindness, and trauma.

» If one eye is affected, the cause is commonly a corneal abrasion, presence of a foreign body, an infection, or trauma. If both eyes are affected, causes include infections, allergic reactions, irritation from chemicals or smoke, and snow blindness, Both infections and contact lens problems can affect one or both eyes.

» Always travel with sunglasses, the color does not matter, but those that block the full range of ultraviolet light (UVA and UVB) are optimal.

» People who have had corneal corrective surgery by the LASIK or

PRK procedures are not at any increased risk in various austere environments. However, those with the earlier corrective types of surgery such as radial keratotomy may have visual defects because of a shift in the cornea due to changes in pressure. Travelers who have had these types of surgery should seek the advice of an ophthalmologist before going to locales where pressure changes are expected such as at high altitude.

BASIC GUIDELINES

- Any sudden loss of vision, including loss of part of the visual field, requires immediate evacuation.

- Vision loss, especially loss of part of the visual field in one eye, can be a sign of a detached retina which must be repaired within 24 hours for best visual recovery.

- Vision loss can also signal a stroke.

- Corneal abrasion is a common cause of eye pain and results from physical damage to the outer layer of the eye from a scratch or foreign object, including contact lenses. Although difficult to see with the naked eye, corneal defects can be confirmed using a fluorescein dye and ultraviolet (UV) light, something easily performed by medical personnel with this equipment.

- Do not wear contact lenses longer than recommended.

- The common problems associated with contact lenses include infections and abrasions. At the first sign of an eye problem, remove the contact lens.

- Very serious infections can occur with the use of non-sterile water or solutions so avoid them and cleanse hands with antiseptic wipes or gel preparations before handling lenses or touching your eye. However, clean water is best as some residue from hand cleansers can cause further eye discomfort.

- A foreign object in the eye is another cause of irritation and pain. The eyelid must be pulled up and away from the eye and a light and possibly magnification can be used to identify the culprit. Most foreign bodies can be removed by flushing with sterile saline or water, but if not easily removed, the foreign body is likely embedded and removal should only be attempted by a professional with sterile conditions. This may require evacuation.

- Solar keratitis is a problem that occurs in any environment where eyes are exposed to high levels of UV light. Corneal damage can arise from either direct or reflected light and is enhanced by dry air or wind. High dry altitudes, deserts, snow, and oceans are environments where eye protection is important. Blurred vision and extreme pain several hours after exposure are the hallmarks of solar keratitis. With treatment, vision should return and pain should subside. Sunglasses prevent this problem and the lens color does not matter. Even plastic absorbs UV well. In particularly higher risk areas, such as snowfields or high altitude, wrap-around sunglasses are advised. Most importantly, it is imperative to wear sunglasses even on cloudy days because the UV light penetrates clouds.

- Trauma to the eye while traveling presents a significant challenge with diagnosis often difficult and treatment limited. Traumatic injuries include closed eyeball trauma, retinal detachment, rupture of structures including the eyeball, fractures of the skull with eye involvement, lacerations, and penetrating injuries. The significance of an eye injury may not be readily apparent so it is important to evacuate anyone who has double vision, protracted or progressive visual impairment, loss of central vision, an open wound, or irregular pupils. Furthermore, these eye symptoms can all be signs of serious brain and skull injuries that require immediate medical intervention (see Traumatic Brain Injury).

- The most important personal supplies for eye safety for a long or remote trip include ophthalmic antibiotic (ofloxacin drops, bacitracin/polymixin ointment), a topical ophthalmic anesthetic (tetracaine), eye drops for allergy (neosynephrine), a broad spectrum oral antibiotic, and artificial tears. If you wear contact lenses, bring extra lenses, supplies, and glasses. Most importantly, bring sunglasses.

BASIC TREATMENT GUIDELINES

- Treatment of conjunctivitis depends on the cause. The best treatment is antibiotics and allergy eye drops. Do not patch the eye if infection is suspected. For chemical causes, the best therapy is copious flushing (called irrigation) followed by antibiotics.

- Corneal abrasions are treated with ophthalmic antibiotics and an eye patch but only if the abrasion occurred in a non-contaminated environment, unlikely in remote areas. Abrasions usually heal within a few days and evacuation is not usually needed. The victim should try not to move the eyes – no reading or other similar activities.

- Contact lens irritations or pain are treated by removing the lens and treating as a corneal abrasion.

- Foreign bodies in the eye should be identified if possible and the eye irrigated to dislodge the object. If not successful, use ophthalmic antibiotics, patch the eye, and seek professional help. Evacuation may be required.

- Treat solar keratitis with topical anesthetic drops, artificial tears, and antibiotics.

- Traumatic eye injuries are all difficult to deal with. The best course is to stabilize the victim, provide pain medication, cover the surface gently, administer oral antibiotics, and evacuate immediately. Be aware that other head injuries may be present and monitor the victim (see Traumatic Brain Injury).

- Evacuate anyone with sudden complete or partial loss of visual field.

Scan for more resources.

FEVERS
Common Symptom of Many Disorders

One of the highlights of your vacation in Costa Rica was the day-long jungle and canopy trail hike. Now a week later you have developed a fever, chills, and headache. You are not sure about a rash that seems to be developing. Is this dangerous or is it a common cold?

Fever is an elevation in body temperature. Although fever is associated with many systemic diseases, fever in travelers is almost always from a bacterial, viral or parasitic infection. Fever also usually occurs with other general symptoms like chills, headache, muscle pains and weakness, and fatigue, and as well as common specific respiratory or gastrointestinal symptoms such as nausea and vomiting. Although other symptoms often pinpoint the causes of fever, some of the more serious disorders should be considered, especially if you are in an area known for such problems. Some serious causes of fever are listed below.

KEY POINTS

»   Over 100 subtropical and tropical countries frequented by 125 million travelers each year are endemic for malaria.

»   The four species of malaria are transmitted by Anopheles mosquitoes and cause fever cycles that vary with the species. However, depending on the species, clinical signs of malaria can present from about 10 days to several months after being bitten. This disease is characterized by a fever that recurs in patterns which vary depending on the species. Malaria is a medical emergency because rapid organ damage and possibly death can occur. One hallmark of malaria is that it does not produce a rash, unlike many other viral and bacterial diseases. Because of the delay in onset, it is important to seek a doctor and report your travel history if fevers begin after your trip.

»   **Dengue Fever** is a common tropical viral illness transmitted by Aedes mosquitoes. The incidence of dengue is rising throughout the world and has now been reported in Texas and Florida in the United States. The incubation period is 3 to 8 days and is characterized by a rapid onset of fever, chills, headache, back pain, and often a rash is present at the onset. Severe bone and joint pain then develops. A small number of victims may develop a hemorrhagic fever with a high mortality rate. Avoid aspirin products if dengue is suspected. Mosquito protection is the best prevention. There is no treatment except supportive care (see Ebola and Emerging and Recurrent Viral Diseases).

» **Chikungunya** is another tropical viral illness transmitted by mosquitoes with a rising incidence throughout the world. It is primarily found in Africa and Asia but has now been reported in the Americas. Chikungunya causes symptoms similar to dengue fever. The disease generally resolves within two weeks without medication, but patients are often unable to walk during the acute phase, which is characterized by debilitating joint pain. Mosquito protection is the best prevention. There is no treatment except supportive care (see Ebola and Emerging and Recurrent Viral Diseases).

» **Meningitis**, an inflammation of the covering of the brain and spinal cord, may be caused by viruses, bacteria, fungi, and parasites. The most common causes are viral and bacterial. Symptoms develop 3 to 7 days after exposure. Meningitis presents with sudden onset of severe headache, fever, stiff neck, and often nausea, vomiting, and light sensitivity. Bacterial meningitis may present with a purplish rash. Viral meningitis resolves in 7 to 10 days without treatment. Bacterial meningitis has more severe symptoms, has a 10 to 15 percent mortality rate, may have significant side effects, and requires immediate treatment. Vaccination is recommended for travel in areas of known bacterial meningitis (see Headaches).

» Low-grade to high-grade fever can also be caused by encephalitis from insects (Japanese encephalitis, tickborne encephalitis, West Nile virus), influenza, leptospirosis, hepatitis, parasites, and tuberculosis. A diverse range of symptoms accompany the fever depending on the infectious agent.

Fever is very common but medical care should be sought quickly if accompanied by skin rash, difficulty in breathing, shortness of breath, persistent cough, decreased consciousness, bruising or unusual bleeding without apparent injury, persistent diarrhea or vomiting, jaundice, and paralysis.

Any chronic or recurring fevers should be investigated upon your return from travel. Fevers related to travel may be delayed before presentation. Provide your travel itinerary to your physician. Note the pattern of your fever and its intensity. Two of the more common serious diseases to consider with chronic or recurring fevers acquired on travel are malaria and tuberculosis (TB).

> ***Malaria should always be considered for those who have traveled to areas endemic for this disease even if they have taken anti-malaria prophylaxis medication.***

About 30 percent of the world population is exposed with TB. Travelers to high-risk countries, particularly sub-Saharan Africa and Southeast Asia, are more susceptible to acquiring TB. Two-drug treatment for a positive TB test takes 9 months, but the real problem occurs with multidrug-resistant TB (MDR-TB). MDR-TB incidence is increasing and accounts for 1 to 7 percent of US cases and requires quarantine. Current global estimates attribute 490,000 cases and 110,000 deaths annually to MDR-TB. More ominous is the emergence of an extensively drug-resistant TB (XDR-TB) resistant to nearly all medications and causing a high fatality rate. Originally associated primarily with HIV patients, XDR-TB has now established a presence in the general population. While still limited to about 4 percent of MDR-TB cases in the US, the World Health Organization estimates about 40,000 cases of XDR-TB will emerge annually.

Scan for more resources.

FISH HOOKS &
FOREIGN BODIES
Slivers & Shrapnel

Your fishing companion screams in pain, and you see that he has a fish hook imbedded in his finger. He begs you to remove it. What do you do?

Injury from a foreign body is a relatively common problem—whether it is a simple wood sliver from grabbing a board, a small piece of glass imbedded in the bottom of a foot from walking on the beach, or a finger impaled with a fish hook. Superficial foreign bodies can be removed using simple tools and basic first aid. However, foreign bodies that are deeply imbedded, in a very sensitive area like the eye, or those that would cause further damage by manipulation should be left in place until medical assistance is available.

BASIC GUIDELINES

- Sometimes it is best to leave the foreign body in place, stabilize it, and transport the victim to medical care.

- Small and superficial foreign bodies can often be removed and treated with simple first aid.

- If possible, clean the area before removing the foreign body. Skin areas can be washed with soap and clean water.

- After removing the foreign body, cleanse again. Wash with soap and water and irrigate with water under pressure. Do not use rubbing alcohol, merthiolate, iodine, or other over-the-counter antiseptics. These may prevent wound healing and some are painful (see Lacerations). Cover with a loose bandage.

- Small pieces of glass, metal, wood and other thin sharp objects that have only superficially penetrated the skin can often be removed with a sterile sewing needle. Cleanse the skin. Sterilize the needle by heating it under a match flame. When cool, gently pick at the foreign body, and try to lift it to remove it. Then cleanse and lightly bandage.

- A fish hook, even a small one, requires very specific steps for its removal. If only the point has entered the skin, the hook may be pulled out directly. However, if the barb has engaged the skin or underlying tissue, extreme care must be taken. If the fish hook is superficial and not in sensitive tissues, continue to push the hook through until it comes out the other side. Cut off the barb and then pull out the remainder of the hook without the barb in the same direction of entry. In many cases, it is best to stabilize the fish hook, and immediately take the victim to a healthcare provider for removal.

- Foreign bodies in the eye are quite painful. The eyelid must be retracted from the eye. Use a light and possibly magnification to identify the object. Most foreign bodies can be removed by irrigation but if not easily removed, the foreign body is likely imbedded and removal should only be attempted by a professional with sterile conditions. This may require evacuation (see Eye Injuries).

- Children sometimes put small objects in their nose, ears, and other orifices. These can be difficult to remove. Be careful not to push the objects further into the orifice. Because the nose is connected to the airway, a small object lodged in the nose pushed in further can block the airway. A foreign body firmly lodged in the nose or other orifices is often best left in place while seeking medical care where appropriate instruments are available for removal.

- Foreign bodies that cause a puncture wound or remain imbedded have a risk for developing tetanus if vaccinations are not up to date. A victim who has not had a tetanus vaccination within 10 years must receive tetanus toxoid. A particularly dirty wound may require additional tetanus prophylaxis.

Scan for more resources.

FLOODS
When the Plumber Can't Help You

Recent heavy rains had flooded low lying areas but roads appeared clear so you decide to continue to your destination. You come across a flooded area but it only looks about a foot deep. Halfway across a wave smacked into the side of your sports utility vehicle and the engine died. Water suddenly has risen halfway up the door and the vehicle is moving sideways. What should you do?

While both floods and flash floods are capable of causing great damage to people and property and can happen anywhere, flash floods are far more likely to cause significant injuries and death. Flash floods, as the name implies, happen far faster than most people realize, which explains why they claim a higher toll of injuries and death.

KEY POINTS

» The most important step to avoiding floods of any type is to stay informed and heed warnings issued by local authorities. Keep listening for flood updates on radio or television.

» Weather terminology (watches and warnings) used in the United States by the Federal Emergency Management Agency (FEMA) and the National Weather Service is increasingly becoming common terminology in other countries as well and should be understood.

» Understand the difference between a flood "watch" and a flood "warning." A "watch" means a flood or flash flood is possible in your area, and you should be alert to the possibility. A "warning" means a flood or flash flood is already occurring and will probably impact your location imminently.

» When a flood watch is issued, check all your preparations and, if you have a vehicle, be sure it is filled with gas and be prepared to move at very short notice.

» If a flood warning is issued, listen carefully to local radio stations and television stations for advice, and if advised to evacuate do so immediately.

» Beware especially aware of flash flooding. Do not wait for instructions to move if authorities think flash flooding is possible.

BASIC GUIDELINES

• Keep critical documents and valuables in a waterproof transportable container, in an easily accessible location, and if possible one that is high enough above ground to be protected from the floodwaters.

• Make up an emergency supplies kit in a bag that is capable of being padlocked in case you are required to take temporary shelter in a communal location. The kit should include the following items, which should be inside waterproof bags:

- If appropriate, written instructions to turn off electricity, gas and water if advised by the authorities to do so.

- Warm and protective clothing and sleeping apparel (sleeping bags, blankets) wrapped in waterproof bags, appropriate for the climate.

- Bottled water—enough for 3 or 4 days at a gallon per person per day.

- First aid kit and appropriate medications—plus any special items necessary for family members, particularly young children.

- Canned foods and a can opener.

- Battery-powered radio, flashlight, and extra batteries.

- Identification, such as a passport, driver's license, or other papers.

• Take the time to do a reconnaissance, either physically, or by using a map—to predetermine your evacuation routes and destinations. Choose more than one of each, and make sure someone outside the affected area has a list and contact details for each destination.

- If you must evacuate your home—and if you have time, do the following:

  - Secure your home.

  - If you have time, bring in outdoor furniture.

  - Move essential items up off the floor, or to a higher floor.

  - Unplug electrical appliances.

  - Turn off utilities (gas and electric) at the main switches or valves if instructed to do so.

  - Do not touch electrical equipment if you are wet or standing in water.

  - If you must walk through water, only go through standing water. Six inches of moving water can make you fall. Use a stick to check the firmness of the ground in front of you.

  - Never drive through flooded areas—this is extremely dangerous.

- If caught in a flood while on foot, do not be tempted to walk through moving water. If it is essential to do so, use a stick or some similar long object to test the ground ahead of you. Flooding may have caused familiar places to change. Floodwaters often erode roads and walkways. Flood debris may also conceal dangerous objects. If you are swept away by moving water, point your feet downstream and maneuver your body over obstacles as best you can.

- Never drive through flooded areas—this is extremely dangerous. If you are caught in fast-moving floodwaters while in a vehicle, get out of the vehicle as quickly as possible. One foot of water is enough to float most cars, and two feet of rushing water can carry away cars, SUVs, and pick-ups. If your car does begin floating, do not be tempted to ride it out inside the vehicle. Your chances of survival are higher outside the car than inside.

- If water is rushing so quickly that your car becomes submerged, open the window as fast as you can – before you submerged or as soon as possible after. Keep your seat belt on until the water reaches your neck. Do not try to open the door until the water stops flooding the car because pressure from the water outside will be too great. The pressure becomes equal once the interior is flooded. If you cannot open the door, attempt to break a side window, never the windshield. Once you open the door or window so you can escape, grip the steering wheel and release the seat belt. This will allow you to free yourself from the car. Once free of the car, let your body take you to the surface, it will rise with the breaths you have taken.

• If stranded on a rooftop or in a tree, stay where you are until help arrives. Avoid the temptation to get into the water unless it is absolutely critical to do so. It is very likely to be more dangerous in the water than to stay put and wait. Flood waters are often contaminated with sewage or harmful chemicals and conceal dangerous objects.

Scan for more resources.

FOOD SAFETY
Keep Healthy on the Road

Almost everyone I know gets traveler's diarrhea or Montezuma's revenge when they go to remote places. However, a couple of my friends never seem to get sick. I am going on a trip to Thailand that will include urban and rural areas. What food precautions should I take?

Eating is one of the pleasures of travel, and with a few precautions, some common sense, and occasionally some restraint, most travel diarrhea can be prevented. Prevention is definitely the best approach.

BASIC GUIDELINES

- Consistently following safe food precautions is essential—it only takes one lapse in procedures to cause a long bout of diarrhea.

- Eat hot foods hot, and cold foods cold.

- Check the bathrooms in a restaurant for a clue to food cleanliness. Remember, food is only as clean as the people who prepare it. Dirty hands among the food preparation staff is a common cause of contamination. The people who prepare food are only as clean as the bathrooms they use. If the bathrooms do not have handwashing facilities, hands probably haven't been washed.

- If you eat food that requires a lot of handling during preparation, such as potato salad and fresh fruit salad, try to make certain the hands touching it were clean.

- Dry and packaged foods are generally safe—bread, dry cereals, crackers, and similar foods.

- Never eat fruits and vegetables that could have been grown on contaminated ground or washed with contaminated water. Raw sewage is often used for fertilizer. Lettuce, strawberries, and unpeeled fruits and vegetables should be avoided.

- If you peel fruits and vegetables, wash them first with clean water, or a clorox-water solution. Peel them with clean hands. Eat fruit right after peeling.

- Avoid perishable food that has not had proper refrigeration. This includes most street food.

- All animal products should be fully cooked—meat, poultry, and seafood.

- Eggs should be well cooked.

- Milk should be sterilized or pasteurized and refrigerated.

- Never use ice in a drink. Freezing does not kill most organisms that cause diarrhea. Do not drink lemonade and other drinks made with unboiled water.

- Hot tea and coffee are safe to drink if brought to a boil while being brewed.

- If you get traveler's diarrhea, drink a lot of fluid to help flush out your system. This will temporarily increase the amount of diarrhea but mechanically helps remove the disease-causing organisms from your system faster. Furthermore, diarrhea dehydrates you, so you must replace fluids (see Traveler's Diarrhea).

- Medications for diarrhea may temporarily stop the diarrhea, but the micro-organisms causing it remain. These medications only provide symptomatic relief and do not address the underlying infectious problem. Diarrhea medications should be used in conjunction with medications to eradicate the organism causing it.

- Standard antibiotics only work against certain bacteria and have no impact on viral or protozoan causes of diarrhea.

- Anyone with vomiting or diarrhea must stay hydrated. Diluted sports drinks that provide some electrolytes are a good source of fluids. Sports drinks have a lot of salt and sugar, so caution is indicated for anyone on a low sodium or low sugar diet.

- If you are on a short trip to an area with questionable sanitation, pay more attention to the cleanliness aspects of what you eat than to the nutrition. A short-term imbalanced diet will not have a long-term impact. Take a pass on that local salad.

Scan for more
resources.

FUNGAL SKIN INFECTIONS
Fungus Among Us

You are in the remote provincial Philippines as part of a disaster response team after the typhoon. Over the past few days the soles of your feet and palms of your hands have started turning bright red, they burn a little, and now the skin is peeling off. It's scary. You had something similar once before but it just affected the bottom of your feet. The doctor prescribed an anti-fungal cream and the blistering stopped. Should I try anti-fungal cream again? Where can I get it?

It sounds like you have an acute case of a skin fungal infection. "Athlete's foot," "jock itch" and "crotch itch" are common fungal infections.

KEY POINTS

>> Fungi can cause skin problems especially in warm, moist areas of the body. In warm climates they can progress faster than when at home.

>> Fungal infections can sometimes be prevented by keeping skin clean and dry. Also, helpful are changing socks frequently and wearing flip flops in shower and pool areas.

BASIC GUIDELINES

• Fortunately, with fungal cream applied two or three times a day, the infection should go away almost as fast as it came.

• Always carry fungal cream with you when you travel.

• If you didn't bring a fungal cream, check at a local pharmacy. Topical medications, including topical anti-fungal creams, should be readily available. Oral fungal medications may be available but are usually reserved for more widespread fungal infections or to treat areas of the body where it is difficult to apply fungal ointment.

- Women taking antibiotics are more prone to develop vaginal fungal infections, especially in tropical climates. If you have a history of fungal infections following antibiotic use, bring medication with you on travel.

Scan for more resources.

HEADACHES
When a Headache is More Than a Headache

After a long day of photographing wild game on a preserve in South Africa, you and your partner return to your cabin in the early evening. She tells you that she is having a migraine headache and needs to rest. She takes medicine prescribed by her doctor before the trip, drinks some water, and retires to the bedroom to take a nap. An hour later, she comes out of the room significantly improved and ready to accompany you to dinner.

A headache is a word to describe a myriad of problems with one thing in common, pain in the head, scalp, or neck. Most headaches are an unwelcome nuisance. A rare few can be harbingers of a life-threatening emergency. Knowing how to prevent headaches, how to treat them before they ruin your day, and knowing when a headache is more than a headache is important for every traveler to know.

KEY POINTS

» Three quarters of the population will have at least one headache in any given year. Women are more likely to suffer headaches than men and three times as likely to suffer from migraine headaches.

» There are two main categories of headache, primary and secondary. Primary headaches are mostly of the migraine type or the tension type although many primary headache sufferers have a combination of migraine and tension components. Primary headaches are the most common headaches. They can be debilitating but with proper knowledge and preparation they can be very manageable and often preventable. Primary headaches are not usually a warning sign of a more dangerous condition.

» Secondary headaches, as the name implies, are the result of some other process. While these processes can be benign such as the side effect of a new medication or a sinus infection, they can be the result of a more ominous event such as a stroke, an aneurysm, or an expanding tumor.

Some secondary headaches are called a "thunderclap headache." With this condition the sufferer feels an abrupt and forceful onset of a severe headache that is often accompanied by some other sensory phenomena like a flash of light, temporary blindness, hearing loss, or mental confusion. A thunderclap headache should prompt immediate access to emergency medical care. Any sudden, severe headache, or a persistent chronic headache requires further investigation.

» Another important but uncommon cause of headache is meningitis, an inflammation of the covering of the brain and spinal cord. Meningitis may be caused by viruses and bacteria, and occasionally by fungi and parasites. Symptoms develop 3 to 7 days after exposure. Meningitis presents with sudden onset of severe headache, fever, stiff neck, and often nausea, vomiting, and light sensitivity. Bacterial meningitis may present with a purplish rash. Viral meningitis resolves in 7 to 10 days without treatment. Bacterial meningitis has more severe symptoms, has a 10 to 15 percent mortality rate, may have significant side effects, and requires immediate treatment. Vaccination is recommended for travel in areas of known bacterial meningitis.

» Many primary headache sufferers have had enough experience with these to have sought medical advice and to have come up with ways to cope with their headache. Often the right combinations of medicines and avoidance of headache triggers fits an individual's unique profile. However, it is sometimes difficult to distinguish between a primary headache, and one caused by more serious underlying conditions.

» Travelers who have frequent headaches but have not had a discussion with their doctor about prevention and treatment of their primary headaches should do so. This can take time and often requires a bit of trial and error. There are, however, some generic steps that most headache sufferers can take to reduce the quantity and intensity of their headaches on travel.

BASIC GUIDELINES

• Sleep deprivation or an irregular sleep schedule can contribute to headaches. Trying to get at least 7 hours of sleep a night and maintaining a regular sleep-wake schedule is important. Sleep can also be a good therapy for an emerging headache. Being prepared with an eye mask and a good travel pillow and earplugs can allow a traveler sleep better, even on an airplane.

- Staying well hydrated helps to prevent primary headaches. Clean cool water is best. Caffeinated beverages can also hydrate and for some headache sufferers the caffeine can help sooth headaches caused by vascular spasm. Though caffeine does increase urine output because it is a diuretic, the idea that caffeinated beverages dehydrate you is a myth. Used in moderation, caffeinated beverages are safe and do hydrate.

- Headaches can be related to carrying heavy items for prolonged times. Travelers often carry several bags and sling bags and packs to rush from place to place. Holding unbalanced loads can exert enough tension to create muscle spasms in the shoulders, neck, and scalp and trigger a headache. Being mindful of how you carry loads can reduce your chances of getting a headache.

- Good sunglasses can help prevent headaches. They have clear optics in both the central and peripheral regions. Cheap sunglasses can look cool but they are no bargain if they cause you to miss a safari or a once in a lifetime travel experience because strong light caused your irises to go into spasm and your head is throbbing. Update your prescription if you wear prescription glasses or contacts.

- Keep analgesic medicine handy. Acetomeniphen, ibuprofen, naproxen, or aspirin are common useful medications. Whatever works best for your headaches should be handy. They do no good if they are back at the hotel.

- Know your triggers. Pollen, alcohol, dust, animal dander, and fluorescent light can precipitate a headache in different people. If you have a trigger, then you know what you need to try to avoid it.

- If you or any of your travel partners are having a headache that is accompanied by problems such as alterations in vision, slurred speech, lateralizing or focal weakness, double vision, sudden weakness or paralysis, or other unusual symptoms, you should seek immediate medical attention.

Scan for more resources.

HEAT EXHAUSTION & HEAT STROKE
Boiling Over

You are running in a 10 kilometer race for charity and rounding a corner come upon a runner who is stumbling and appears confused. There is no water station near. What should you do?

Human metabolism requires a very narrow temperature range for basic daily function. Our body at rest generates enough heat to raise our core temperature 2.5°F per hour and strenuous activity can increase that 15 times. We release heat through our skin to the cooler atmosphere but this process slows as the external temperature increases towards the 95°F of skin temperature. As temperature increases and heat loss through skin decreases, sweat glands spread a layer of water on the skin surface (perspiration) that evaporates, cools the skin, and releases heat. Higher temperatures speed up evaporation but this highly effective cooling system requires a constant source of water. However, this system is limited because the higher the humidity, the less sweating can release its moisture into the more highly saturated air.

It is critical to recognize the signs and symptoms of heat exhaustion and heat stroke. Different environments can be treacherous for heat regulation, such as high altitude where significantly less humidity than ground levels increases evaporation and higher oxygen demands cause the body to work harder, producing more internal heat. Furthermore, your body loses at least 2 liters of water per day and you can lose 5 liters on a hot day even at rest. Exertion increases water loss. Core body temperature rises if water is not replaced or cannot evaporate, leading to heat illness.

KEY POINTS

» Signs of impending trouble are gradual in onset and the common symptoms are not unique to heat-related illness. These symptoms also occur for other reasons so it is important to have a high index of suspicion for heat illness.

» Heat exhaustion is characterized by a rapid weak pulse, dizziness, nausea, headache, diarrhea, and mild temperature elevation. Some confusion or irrational behavior may be present. Sweating may be either present or absent and the skin may feel cool to touch. Heat exhaustion must be treated immediately. Heat exhaustion can rapidly progress to heat stroke.

» Heat stroke is more severe and life threatening. Heat stroke presents with extreme confusion, diarrhea, vomiting, dark urine, shortness of breath, bleeding, low blood pressure or shock, seizures, or unconsciousness. The failure of multiple organs is the ultimate cause of mortality and heat stroke recovery may leave the victim with permanent mental or physical problems. Immediate medical care is critical to prevent death.

» Currently heat stroke remains more preventable than treatable. Chances of getting heatstroke are increased if you had it once before but awareness and preventive measures can help avoid a repeat.

BASIC TREATMENT GUIDELINES

• The most important principle of treatment is rapid lowering of the core temperature. Oral thermometers do not reliably reflect core temperature, therefore a rectal thermometer is needed to monitor progress. Do the following:

• Get the victim to lie down in a shaded area.

• Remove or at least loosen clothing.

• If oral fluids can be taken, encourage intake of water or electrolyte solution. Try to get a liter or two into the victim over the first few hours.

• Wet the victim down and fan vigorously if possible. Use ice packs for the armpits, groin, or around the neck.

• Rectal temperatures should be taken frequently in the initial phase of treatment to avoid overcooling. Monitor the temperature every half hour or so for the next few hours after cooling as there can be a rebound temperature rise requiring more cooling procedures.

- Restrict all activities that day and monitor closely for recurrence the next day.

- Evacuate suspected heat stroke victims rapidly.

- Do not give oral liquids unless the victim is awake and can swallow upon command. An uncooperative or confused person may choke.

- Do not use aspirin, acetaminophen (Tylenol), antihistamines, antipsychotic drugs, or amphetamines. These all have detrimental affects on a patient in this condition.

- Do not use alcohol to sponge the victim.

Scan for more
resources.

HIGH ALTITUDE MEDICAL PROBLEMS
Acute Mountain Sickness

*Your college friends and their spouses are planning
to hike part of the Inca Trail to Machu Picchu in Peru
for the 25th reunion of graduation. All are in reasonably good
shape but urban coastal dwellers. The altitude ranges
from about 10,000 feet to 14,000 feet depending on the route.
How do you prepare for this event?*

Travel to sites with high elevation requires proper preparation to avoid medical complications caused by high altitude. The oxygen content in air at 10,000 feet is 69 percent of that at sea level. The effects of hypoxia (oxygen deprivation) for travelers at these heights are compounded by cold temperatures, low humidity, decreased air pressure, and increased ultraviolet radiation exposure. These factors not only affect mountain trekkers but travelers who go to cities at high altitudes like Denver, Colorado; Taos, New Mexico; La Paz, Bolivia; Quito, Ecuador; and Addis Ababa, Ethiopia and other high altitude locations.

KEY POINTS

» Humans require time to adapt. Problems with altitude occur for those who do not have the time or inclination to acclimate to the decreased oxygen levels.

» However, the body is incapable of permanent acclimatization above 17,500 feet.

» Significant variability in acclimatization exists among individuals, likely related to genetic differences.

» No simple screening tests predict the risk of developing altitude illness for a particular individual.

» Risk is not affected by training or physical fitness and children are as susceptible as adults.

» The incidence of altitude illness increases in those with a previous history of altitude illness, obesity, and slightly increases in females but does not increase for those who smoke or use oral contraceptives and is somewhat decreased in those over age 50.

» Maximum overnight altitude and days of acclimatization also predict high altitude medical problems. Travelers with cardiac and respiratory conditions or diabetes should consult a medical provider familiar with high altitude issues before doing any high-altitude travel.

» Travelers who fly into high-altitude destinations directly from lower altitudes should spend three to five days before ascending beyond 8000 feet and spend an extra day for every 3300 feet of higher ascent. It is recommended to ascend no more than 1500 feet per day.

BASIC TREATMENT GUIDELINES

• Altitude illness has three syndromes: acute mountain sickness (AMS), high-altitude cerebral edema (HACE), and high-altitude pulmonary edema (HAPE). HACE is a severe progression from AMS while HAPE can occur by itself or in conjunction with AMS or HACE.

• Gradual ascent is the safest method of prevention for all forms of altitude illness. Limit exertion and avoid alcohol and sedative medications for the first few nights at high altitude. It is very important to remain hydrated.

• The most commonly used medication for prevention of AMS is acetazolamide (Diamox) which is about 75 percent effective to prevent AMS in travelers who cannot gradually ascend. A physician familiar with this medication should prescribe, determine the dose, and discuss side effects and allergies.

• Acetozolamide should be taken from 24 hours before ascent to at least 2 days after reaching altitude. Although less effective, acetazolamide can be used to lessen symptoms once AMS has begun.

• Many travelers to high altitude experience temporary headache, fatigue, difficulty breathing with exertion, and sleep disorders. AMS symptoms are similar but more pronounced and include headache, fatigue, loss of appetite, nausea, and vomiting which typically begin within 12 hours of arrival at high altitude and usually subside after 1 to 3 days of acclimatization.

- AMS is commonly confused with other conditions like viral flu, hangover, dehydration, or medication effects.

- Travelers with AMS will NOT improve with hydration or while at rest and should not continue to ascend until symptoms have resolved.

- Treatment of mild AMS includes rest and to stop ascent, symptomatic treatment with analgesics, and descent without improvement.

- More severe AMS requires the initiation of acetazolamide, use of oxygen, possible use of dexamethasone 4mg every 6 hours, and immediate descent. A hyperbaric pressure bag is also useful if available and very desirable if descent is delayed. Such a device can provide the same effect as a 5000 foot descent.

- HAPE is a severe consequence of altitude illness from fluid accumulation in the lungs.

- HAPE is the most common cause of death related to high altitude, usually occurs within the first 4 days of ascent, and is easily reversed if recognized and treated.

- Symptoms of HAPE include difficulty breathing with exertion and at rest, persistent dry cough, and weakness.

- The most effective treatment of HAPE is immediate descent. While that is being arranged, keep the patient warm and provide oxygen if available.

- Dexamethasone should be used for severe or worsening cases. Nifedipine, if available, is also useful but must be administered under medical guidance. Use of a hyperbaric pressure bag is advised if available.

- HACE is a rare but severe result of altitude illness that causes swelling of the brain.

- Symptoms of HACE include extreme fatigue, drowsiness, confusion, and loss of coordination.

- HACE is often confused with AMS in its early stages and usually takes 1 to 3 days to develop from AMS but can develop more quickly in those with HAPE.

- If HACE develops, the individual must immediately descend to a lower altitude or risk death.

- Treatment for HACE is immediate descent or evacuation, oxygen, dexamethasone, and hyperbaric therapy if descent is delayed.

- If in doubt or medication is not available to start treatment, the definitive treatment for altitude related illnesses is to descend to a lower altitude.

Scan for more
resources.

HOSTAGE SURVIVAL GUIDELINES
Improving Your Chances

> *"This is the worst thing I've ever gone through in my life. I've never gone through anything worse. You sit, day in and day out, and I look at my friends here and at the end of the day here, we think to ourselves, 'We're alive another day. We will be alive tomorrow? Do we have a future? Can we see our families?"...Keith Stansell, survivor of five-and-a-half years of captivity at the hands of Colombia's FARC.*

Statistics prove that your chances of survival during a kidnapping event are very high if you follow some simple guidelines. Every hostage or kidnap situation is different, however, and there are no strict rules of behavior; but there are a number of options which could enhance your ability to deal with the crisis, and survive.

KEY POINTS

The following techniques have been successfully employed by persons taken hostage:

» Avoid the temptation to do anything heroic. Aggravating the hostage takers may lead to you being injured, especially if the kidnappers are armed.

» Follow the instructions of your hostage takers without appearing to be either too docile or too aggressive. Your kidnappers will almost certainly be in a highly agitated and emotional state themselves—and may respond unpredictably if provoked. Remember, your job is to survive.

» Maintain a low profile; avoid eye contact and the appearance of being observant. Do not let a hostage taker feel that you recognize them if they are trying to conceal their identity. You should make mental notes about their mannerisms, clothes and apparent rank structure. This may help the police after your release.

» Do not try to escape unless you are certain of being successful.

» Maintain faith that authorities will be working to secure your release.

» Emotionally prepare yourself for a long ordeal, but also understand that longer hostage situations usually result in the safe release of captives.

» Remain mentally and physically functional by establishing a daily program of mental and physical activity and figure out a way of keeping track of the days and dates.

» Keep reminding yourself that you are much more valuable to your captors alive and in good condition.

» Do not make any threatening remarks or give hostage takers any cause to be concerned about action you may take against them at a later date.

» Ask politely but firmly for anything you want—especially drink, food, or medications, but ask in a dignified manner.

» Try to consume food and drink when it is offered to you—even if it looks unappetizing. It is more important to drink than to eat. Thank your captors for any concessions made on your behalf.

» It is important that your abductors view you as a person worthy of compassion and mercy. Never beg, plead, or cry. If possible, stay well-groomed and clean to gain your captors' respect as well as their sympathy.

» Try to establish some rapport with your captors, but be aware of, and avoid the potential effects of Stockholm syndrome—a situation whereby hostages start to empathize with their captors.

» Avoid getting engaged in discussions about controversial or confrontational subjects. A good topic to discuss, if possible, is family and children. Unlike the advice offered with respect to a hijacking situation, if you speak the language of your captors, use it—it will enhance communications and rapport.

» Do not admit to any accusations.

» If there is a rescue attempt using force, drop quickly to the floor or get in a position that offers some cover. Keep your hands high and behind your head so rescuers immediately know you are not a threat. Identify yourself at the first available opportunity.

Scan for more resources.

HOTEL SAFETY & SECURITY
Personal Protection & Fire Safety

A traveller checked into a well-known hotel for a two-week holiday. At 11:30 pm a phone call from someone who claims to be a front desk employee, explains that a computer malfunction had deleted all of today's credit card details, and the problem must be corrected before automatic backups at 2 am. The guest was asked to come to the lobby if possible, or just give his credit card details over the phone. The caller sounded professional, polite, and credible. The guest was even offered a discount from his hotel bill to compensate for the inconvenience. The guest decided not to go downstairs and gave the caller his credit card details. The next day, the guest had to cancel the credit card when it became obvious it had been used for items he did not purchase.

Whether travelling on business or pleasure, at some time all of us will stay in a hotel. There are too many variables to consider for any one list of suggestions to be applicable in every case, but the following checklist provides a handy guide that any traveller can use.

KEY POINTS

» Ensure that all your financial business transactions are taken care of face-to-face, and never give your credit card details to an unknown caller.

» Ask for a room near the elevator (this location is likely to have more passing pedestrian traffic and not be as attractive a target for a criminal intent on breaking into a room).

» Ensure that your room door is always locked and close your curtains.

» Use all lock mechanisms while in the room including the door chain.

» Purchase and use your own rubber door-stop while in your room—these are very effective.

» Don't leave "Please Clean" or "Make up my Room" signs outside your door. This announces the room is probably unoccupied.

» Don't open your door to strangers. Use the door viewer then speak with the door partially opened with the chain on.

» Avoid rooms located on the ground floor. Ideally take a room situated between level 2-6 (harder for a criminal to gain access via a window or balcony yet the room will probably still be within the operational capability of fire rescue equipment if necessary).

» Read the hotel safety and security instructions provided in your room and know where the emergency exits are.

» Place cash, passport, and other valuables in the room safe or contact the reception for safe-deposit facilities every time you leave your room—there are a number of tools thieves use to get a hotel door open including electronic breaching devices, but getting into a room safe is significantly more difficult.

» Inform the manager or someone at the reception desk if you see anyone acting suspiciously or you hear unusual noises.

» Don't leave handbags, laptop computers, wallets, bags, documents, or other valuable items unattended in hotel conference rooms, restaurants, or other public areas.

» If using hotel facilities such as a swimming pool or sauna, leave your room key and other valuables with reception or a trusted friend/colleague. Do not leave them unattended in clothing or bags nearby.

BASIC FIRE SAFETY GUIDELINES

• Familiarize yourself with the fire escape routes upon arrival and know how to get to them in the dark.

• Don't use the elevator if there is a fire.

• Don't smoke in bed.

- If you discover a fire or smell smoke, raise the alarm.
- If you smell smoke, stay low as smoke rises and the air is cleaner closer to the ground.
- Do not stop to collect valuables or other personal belongings if there is a need to evacuate.
- Check doors for heat before opening—if the door feels hot, do not open it.
- Open the door slowly and partially if it feels cool to touch. Check for smoke and flames before moving out into the hallway or into a stairwell.
- Do not try to walk through thick smoke.
- Shut the door when you leave (this will reduce the spread of smoke and flame).

If you cannot evacuate:

- Turn off the air-conditioning to prevent smoke from being drawn into the room.
- Telephone the reception and/or hotel operator and advise them of your location.
- Place wet towels, sheets, blankets, or clothing under the door to prevent smoke entering through the gap.
- Close louvers and air vents using wet towels if necessary to prevent smoke from entering the room.
- Remove curtains from windows.
- Fill the bathtub with water and have a waste can nearby. Use the waste can to carry water to the towels you used under the door and remoisten them if/when necessary.
- Stay close to the floor and tie a wet handkerchief or cloth over your nose and mouth to help with breathing.
- Throw water onto hot surfaces (walls, doors) using the waste can.

- Do not break windows unless it is absolutely necessary and you are certain of escape. You may need the windows intact later to assist in keeping smoke out.

Be Prepared. Fire or robbery will probably never happen but responsible and diligent behavior and actions beforehand will make you more confident to deal effectively with any incident and reduce the chance of panic and poor decision making that could place you, family, friends, or colleagues at greater risk.

Scan for more
resources.

HUMAN IMMUNODEFICIENCY VIRUS (HIV) & ACQUIRED IMMUNODEFICIENCY SYNDROME (AIDS)
The Continuing Scourge

You are helping a good friend on a medical mission in Botswana and pick up a bag of medical supplies when your finger is pierced by a discarded needle. You know Africa has a high incidence of HIV infection. What do you do?

HIV is a retrovirus that attacks human immune cells and weakens immune response as the infection progresses. AIDS is an advanced stage of HIV infection that can take 10 to 15 years to develop. AIDS may present with specific rare cancers, unusual infections, and other severe medical conditions usually associated with immunosuppressed individuals.

KEY POINTS

- » Approximately 75 million people have contracted HIV and 36 million AIDS-related deaths have occurred since it was first described in the early 1980s. Despite major advances, HIV/AIDS remains a serious public health problem. The 2012 estimated total number of individuals living with HIV/AIDS is 35 million with about 1.6 million deaths from AIDS-related illnesses representing a slight decrease compared to the year before.

- » HIV is transmitted through close contact with infected body fluids such as blood, semen, vaginal secretions, or breast milk.

» Common routes of transmission include unprotected sexual contact, sharing needles and syringes for drug use or other skin-piercing activities such as tattoos, receiving a transfusion infected with HIV, accidental needle sticks, and mother-to-child transmission during pregnancy, childbirth, or breastfeeding.

» HIV is not spread through normal contact such as kissing, hugging, shaking hands, or sharing food or drink.

» Sub-Saharan Africa continues to report the highest prevalence of HIV and AIDS.

Countries with the highest prevalence of HIV/AIDS (percent of people with HIV/AIDS in individuals ages 15-49):

Swaziland...	28	Lesotho...	24.7
Botswana...	24.4	South Africa...	18.4
Zimbabwe...	15.6	Namibia...	15.2
Zambia...	13.7	Mozambique...	12.9
Malawi...	11.4		

Regions with a lower prevalence of HIV/AIDS:

Caribbean...	1.0	East Europe...	0.7
Central Asia...	0.7	N America...	0.5
Latin America...	0.4	S and SE Asia...	0.3
W Europe...	0.2	ME, N Africa...	0.1
E Asia...	0.1		

WHO statistics, 2014

BASIC PREVENTION GUIDELINES

All methods of prevention involve blocking exposure to infectious body fluids.

- Practice protected sex. Correct and consistent use of condoms has been shown to reduce the risk of HIV and other sexually-transmitted diseases by 85 percent. Condom use significantly reduces – but does not eliminate – the risk of HIV transmission.

- Avoidance of blood product transfusions in regions with high prevalence unless there is a life-threatening hemorrhage.

- Avoidance of reusable or shared needles for injections, fluid replacement, and tattoos. Note that it is often difficult to know whether needles are being reused. Except in life-saving situations, if in doubt about the sterility and safety of needles, it is usually better to avoid needle use.

- For people who may have significant risk of occupational exposure to HIV or who engage in risky sexual behavior, pre-exposure prophylaxis with medication is an option. Anyone in these categories should seek medical advice about the need and type of prevention to use.

- For people unexpectedly exposed to HIV, first irrigate and clean the wound. Determine the need for tetanus and Hepatitis B prophylaxis. The risk of acquiring HIV from a needle stick used for an HIV contaminated person is roughly 0.3 percent. People exposed should be counseled about risks of HIV transmission based upon their specific exposure.

- The need for post-exposure prophylaxis is based on assessment of risk using the Centers for Disease Control and Prevention (CDC) scale.

- Determine exposure code: Exposure to intact skin only, no risk of HIV transmission. If the exposure is to broken skin or mucus membranes determine if contact with blood, body fluid, or an instrument contaminated with one of these substances, is small (Code 1) or large (Code 2). If exposure was a puncture, solid needle or superficial scratch it is Code 2. If exposure was from a large-bore hollow needle, a device with visible blood, or a needle used in a source patient's artery or vein it is Code 3.

- Determine code for HIV status of exposure: HIV negative, no HIV prophylaxis needed. If HIV positive, and source has no symptoms, Code 1. If HIV positive with symptoms, Code 2. HIV status may be unknown.

- Add the two codes for exposure and HIV status to obtain CDC scale. Total score of 0 or 1, no prophylaxis is necessary. Score of 2, decide with your doctor about benefit versus risk of prophylaxis. Score of 2 or 3 from exposure code with unknown HIV status or score of 3, the basic regimen is recommended. Score of 4 or higher, expanded prophylaxis regimen is recommended.

- Basic regimen (at time of publication): 4 weeks of zidovudine (600 mg/d in 2-3 divided doses) and lamivudine (150 mg twice daily)

- Expanded regimen (at time of publication): Basic regimen plus either indinavir (800 mg q8h) or nelfinavir (750 mg 3 times/d).

- Interferon ribavirin prophylaxis decreases risk by 40%.

Scan for more resources.

HYPOTHERMIA & FROSTBITE
Pay Attention to Your Feet

You are on a ski vacation and want to maximize your time on the slopes despite the high wind chill factor. Your new ski boots are too tight so you wear lighter socks. Your feet are tingling but you really do not notice much in the excitement of the day.

Prevention and treatment of cold-related injuries is important both for travelers anticipating and for those caught unexpectedly in cold weather.

KEY POINTS

» Injuries range from chilblains and trenchfoot to frostbite.

» Breathing problems can be caused by cold air due to increased secretions and decreased pulmonary function.

» The high surface area structures farthest from the heart—ears, nose, fingers, and toes—are most susceptible to cold injury because the body constricts vessels to non-essential organs to conserve heat.

» Foot protection and comfort is essential because feet are particularly susceptible due to mechanical trauma and moisture condensation. Moisture in footwear is the most important variable that affects thermal insulation and comfort. Moisture in combination with motion may reduce insulation and thus protection against cold by 45 percent.

» Hypothermia is the first step for cold injury and starts the cascade of physiological responses leading to tissue injury. Maintenance of heat production requires proper attention to food, exercise, insulation with non-constrictive clothing, and protection from moisture.

» Tissue is susceptible to non-freezing cold injuries. Symptoms of chilblains and a similar condition known as pernio are itchy, painful, swollen skin after a few hours of exposure to intense cold. Early administration of pain medication and the avoidance of secondary exposure are important. Both conditions resolve after drying and rewarming with no prolonged damage.

» Trenchfoot is a much more serious condition that may occur following several days of cold, wet feet. The white, cold feet become red, hot, and painful after warming. The symptoms intensify over the next few weeks with the possibility of permanent hypersensitivity and disability.

» Frostbite occurs at both work and in leisure activities and is more common in men. Frostbite occurs when tissue freezes, forming internal ice crystals. Skin freezes at 25°F but occurs more rapidly and at higher temperatures with wind and moisture. Cells can survive freezing and thawing but small blood vessel damage causes clots to obstruct circulation leading to tissue death. Factors that increase frostbite risk and complications include diabetes, cardiac problems, peripheral vascular spasm (Raynaud's phenomenon), and heavy alcohol consumption.

BASIC MANAGEMENT GUIDELINES

• Know and look for the signs of hypothermia: prolonged shivering, confusion, loss of muscular control manifested by staggering, clumsy movements, inability to perform simple physical tasks. Hypothermia is a medical emergency requiring immediate intervention.

• If frostbite develops, the best treatment is rapid and continued submersion of the affected body part in warm water (104°-107°F) for at least 30 minutes. Do not submerge the entire body because cardiac arrhythmias may result. Heating water to a specific temperature may be difficult because sufficient fuel and water may be lacking and a thermometer is needed for tight temperature control.

• Too much heat or the dry heat from a fire can dessicate tissue and extend the damage.

• Do not thaw the body part if there is a chance of a refreeze. That could result in greater damage.

- Do not massage the body part to minimize further trauma to the damaged tissue.

- The body part will turn red as it thaws denoting return of blood flow but nerve reactivation will cause pain and strong medication may be needed.

- Blister formation after thawing suggests more severe injury, especially if filled with blood.

- The body part should be wrapped with sterile bandages with pads between digits and elevated.

- Rapid evacuation should be initiated. If you are in a location with access to the Internet or a satellite phone, digital images can allow immediate access to hospital-based specialists who can assess cold injuries and advise on early care at your location.

- Resolution of frostbite may take weeks to demarcate the area of damage. The condition where tissue recovers within a few days without permanent damage is sometimes called frostnip. With actual frostbite, the salvaged tissue may be cold sensitive for years.

Scan for more resources.

IMMUNIZATIONS & PROPHYLAXIS
An Ounce of Prevention

You have decided to take that East African safari you have put off for a long time. Your close friends think it is safe because the tour company is reputable but you have heard stories of travelers getting tropical diseases on travel. What do you do about preventing malaria? What about yellow fever? You had polio vaccine as a child but do not know when you last had a tetanus shot. Your have confidence in your local doctor but he is not experienced with travel medicine. What do you do?

It is not possible to eliminate the possibility of illness completely while traveling but you can certainly reduce the risk by immunization against vaccine-preventable diseases and by pharmacologic prophylaxis for others. Go to the Centers for Disease Control website (http://wwwnc.cdc.gov/travel/destinations/list) and determine which immunizations are recommended for the destination you have chosen.

KEY POINTS

» Vaccines stimulate antibody production against a particular antigen from a disease. Antibodies prevent or reduce the severity of illness when exposed again to the antigen. Vaccines can be made from whole or parts of live, inactivated, or dead organisms or the toxins produced by them. Some vaccines require more than one dose and the type of vaccine will determine the schedule for administration.

» Adverse reactions can occur with any vaccine but are uncommon and the majority produce mild local or general symptoms. Severe reactions are rare.

» Routine immunizations are administered in childhood or regularly throughout adulthood. Routine immunizations should be up to date to protect you and people you may come in contact with. Travelers with children should confirm immunizations with their pediatrician. The following immunizations are recommended:

- Diphtheria, Pertussis, Tetanus. These diseases are worldwide and require booster shots.

- Hepatitis A. Recommended for all travelers.

- Hepatitis B. Recommended for all travelers.

- Measles, Mumps, Rubella (MMR)

- Herpes zoster vaccine (shingles) for older adults

- Polio. Travelers to India, Afghanistan, Pakistan, Nigeria should receive a one-time booster dose.

- Streptococcus pneumoniae. For diabetics, immune compromised people, the elderly, or those with severe liver or lung disease and those whose spleens have been removed.

- Varicella (chickenpox).

BASIC VACCINATION GUIDELINES

Required vaccinations are necessary for entry into certain countries. Recommended vaccinations depend on the destination and varying degrees of risk.

- Yellow fever. Required for entry to several African countries. Required in Brazil if coming from several other Latin American countries.

- Meningitis. Required for entrance into Saudi Arabia during the Hajj and Umrah pilgrimages. Recommended for sub-Saharan Africa.

- Rabies. Recommended if in rural village areas for extended time or expect contact with potentially infected animals.

- Typhoid. Soft recommendation. Modestly useful, may interfere with certain medications.

BASIC PROPHYLAXIS GUIDELINES

The use of medication for prevention of disease is called prophylaxis. Certain diseases require prophylaxis if traveling in an area where the disease exists and exposure can occur. Again check with the centers for Disease Control website for the latest information.

- Be aware of MALARIA risk. This includes knowledge of the risk in the geographical area of travel, length of stay, urban versus rural risk, and sleeping accommodations. Risk may change with seasonal variations and altitude.

- All travelers to areas containing malaria who may be exposed to mosquitoes are advised to take prophylactic medication. Medications should begin before entering malarial areas and continue for one to four weeks after leaving (depending on the medication) to kill any parasites that remain in the liver. Pros and cons of the various meds should be discussed with your healthcare provider including possible side effects and interaction with other medications.

- A very important part of prophylaxis is to avoid mosquito bites. A mosquito net over your bed is highly recommended.

- Bug spray with at least 30 percent concentration of DEET is recommended in endemic areas. Children should use products safer for children.

- Bed nets and clothing impregnated with permethrin has improved malaria prevention.

- Due to rising bacterial resistance to antibiotics, prophylaxis for TRAVELER'S DIARRHEA with antibiotics is no longer recommended.

- Solutions containing bismuth (Peptol-Bismol) have been shown to provide some protection against diarrhea if taken four times a day.

- INFLUENZA (known as flu) is a viral illness causing respiratory and other general symptoms.

- Flu is commonly confused with the common cold caused by other types of viruses.

- Influenza A has several strains with natural hosts in birds. Sometimes Influenza A infects other mammals and humans. These can be very virulent and lead to a pandemic.

- Influenza B is less common and infects humans almost exclusively.

- Influenza C is uncommon and usually only causes mild symptoms.

- Flu shots contain vaccines to Influenza A and B viruses. Because Influenza A mutates rapidly, flu shots change each year in anticipation of the most likely candidates to cause flu. Therefore it is necessary to obtain a shot each year.

- Flu shots increase protection for you and also may prevent you from spreading flu to people in areas where you travel.

- All travelers should consider receiving a flu shot.

Scan for more
resources.

INSECT, SPIDER, SCORPION, & TICK BITES
Venomous Visitors

You have been traveling in a tropical climate and your leg begins to itch in a specific area. There is a small red area that appears to have been getting larger over the past day and you feel more tired than usual. You do not remember any insect bite but there certainly were a lot of bugs and spiders. Should you be concerned?

A wide variety of insects and arachnids (spiders, scorpions, ticks) can inflict bites during travel. Bees, wasps, and stinging ants are the most common culprits worldwide. Bites result in immediate pain or discomfort and range from mild to severe irritation but rarely lead to death. Some caterpillars and large centipedes cause local irritation and, rarely, more systemic symptoms.

KEY POINTS

» Spider bites generally only cause local pain but some species can cause significant tissue destruction. The bite from these certain spiders that run, which include recluse, hobo, wolf, jumping, and certain sac spiders, may not be noticeable initially and there is no effective antivenin.

» Web spiders like the black widow and its Australian relatives can cause severe cramping, sweating, and back and shoulder muscle pain. There are antivenins available usually in the regional area where these spiders are found.

» The very large venomous wandering or banana spiders of Central and South America are now widely recognized for their toxicity and antivenin is available.

125

» Perhaps the most dangerous arachnids are the funnel web spiders of Australia and Indonesia, which are large and aggressive. Antivenin for these spiders is available in Australia.

» Scorpions come in many species throughout the world with the most dangerous in Africa, Asia, and the western hemisphere. Although generally not fatal, bites from scorpions can cause severe pain in the area or extremity. Fatalities usually involve small children or the elderly.

» Scorpions are nocturnal and respond to touch so bites often occur when the traveler puts on shoes left on the ground or steps into the shower without first looking.

» Smaller scorpions tend to be more venomous than larger species.

» Several species of ticks can spread disease from bacteria and other organisms through their bites with common symptoms of fevers, rashes, joint pains, muscle aches, and headaches. Symptoms may present several days to several weeks after the bite. Lyme Disease, caused by bacteria from tick bites in the northeastern and Midwest United States, often has a characteristic bull's eye rash

» An unusual presentation of progressive paralysis in an extremity, most often seen in children, is known as "tick paralysis" and is reversible by removal of the tick. Many diseases spread by ticks require antibiotics so it is important to seek medical care if tick bite is suspected.

» Fleas and chiggers are very annoying, itch, and present with small red dots. Treatment is with local application of lotion and anti-inflammatory medication. Any unexplained fever, fatigue, or skin lesions within a few months of exposure should prompt medical attention because fleas can carry serious diseases.

BASIC PREVENTION AND TREATMENT GUIDELINES

• Most insects or spiders bite defensively so avoid encounters if possible.

• Clean up leftover food and avoid fragrant soaps and cosmetics in areas of high insect concentration.

• Wear light colored clothing.

- Shake your shoes out before you put them on and look in the shower before use.

- People known to be allergic to bees or other insect bites should always carry two epinephrine-loaded syringes (Epi-pen, Auvi-Q, or Adrenaclick) and antihistamines. About one third of victims with a severe allergy will require a second shot

- Remove ticks when discovered. Ticks generally need to be attached for over 24 hours before tick-borne disease occurs. Use a pair of fine tweezers, grasp the tick as close to the skin as possible, and gently pull straight back WITHOUT TWISTING. Do not crush the tick between fingers, dispose by wrapping in tape, dipping in alcohol, or flushing in the toilet. Do NOT use petrolatum jelly or other remedies to coat the tick to await its voluntary release. Wash the bite area.

- Most insect and arachnid bites are best treated by oral antihistamines and non-steroidal anti-inflammatory (NSAIDS) meds like ibuprofen. Anyone who develops more than a local reaction should be taken to a hospital or evacuated from the field.

- Antivenin for spider bites is not likely to be available in rural areas. Pain control and antibiotics are the treatment for suspected recluse spider bites until medical assistance is available.

- Treatment for a scorpion bite includes pain control and use of antivenin if available.

- Use DEET insect repellent, permethrin-impregnated clothing, and tuck pant cuffs into boots to help prevent insect bites and tick infestation. You should inspect for ticks after walking in fields or forests. For children, use insect repellant appropriate to them. Always help children check for ticks.

- Venomous caterpillars and some spiders like tarantulas discharge small spines. If contact has been made and irritation occurs, place a piece of duct tape over the area and remove to extricate irritating bristles. Use of topical anti-inflammatory cream may help.

Scan for more resources.

INSURANCE: MEDICAL & EVACUATION POLICIES
You Better Know What You Don't Know

You are going to hike to Machu Picchu along the rough Inca Trail with heights of nearly 13,000 feet. You have been advised to sign up for travel insurance but there is confusing advice about what coverage you really need. Your physician has little experience with travel medicine. Information about local medical resources is scant and unreliable. What do you need to do to prepare for your travel safety?

No major travel should be undertaken without considering medical and evacuation insurance. Approximately 50 million people travel annually from industrialized countries to the developing world. Access to standard healthcare and medical resources may be quite different than in your familiar surroundings. What you do not know may result in you or your family receiving inadequate medical care while traveling, or in the most severe case, not being evacuated should you need it. Information from the Internet and healthcare providers is readily available but it can be confusing so let's take a look at some things you should know when planning your travel.

KEY POINTS

- » One-fourth to two-thirds of travelers to the developing world report having experienced health problems.

- » Eight percent of travelers (4 million) seek medical care abroad or upon reaching home.

- » Most common illnesses are ones with fever, diarrhea, skin disorders, or respiratory disorders.

» Evacuation for a medical reason occurs in 0.01 percent to 0.1 percent of travelers annually (5000-50,000 travelers).

» 1 in 100,000 people will die while traveling (0.001% or 500 of the 50 million annual travelers).

» Most common causes of death are motor vehicle accidents followed by drowning (much less).

» It is not easy to return the remains of someone who dies on a trip in another country. There are legal issues and possibly public health concerns depending on the cause of death.

BASIC INSURANCE GUIDELINES

• Insurance coverage may be bundled in one policy or require separate policies. There are 3 major components of travel insurance: travel assistance, medical coverage, and evacuation. The most important are coverage for medical costs and evacuation.

- Travel assistance: lost luggage, trip cancellation, visa services, immunization advice.

- Medical coverage: medical expenses with limits and deductible fee.

- Evacuation: necessary medical evacuation of injured person, spouse or significant other, return of mortal remains.

• Check your own medical policy for coverage and exclusions particularly for international travel.

• Even with adequate medical insurance coverage, you may have to pay costs for medical treatment in a foreign country then get reimbursed by your insurance company after you return.

• Common exclusions for medical and evacuation insurance include travel to an area of armed conflict, age greater than 75, adverse events due to alcohol or illicit drug use, withdrawal from chronic alcohol or drug abuse, and exacerbation of known psychosis. Policies often exclude coverage for your planned activities (such as helo skiing, SCUBA, hang gliding). Make sure your policy covers you for adventurous activities.

- Medicare and most health maintenance organizations (HMOs) do not cover medical problems on international travel.

- Tour groups and travel companies do not usually provide medical coverage or evacuation. They will likely assist their traveler but will not cover costs associated with healthcare, transportation, or evacuation.

- Make sure you have evacuation insurance if traveling to a remote area. Most credit cards do not have adequate coverage for evacuation expenses. Evacuation can cost over $100,000. The decision for evacuation and the process is complex and often poorly understood by the traveler and family.

- Find out how an evacuation will occur if needed and how communication will be addressed. Speak to the company holding your policy and ask what happens if you need their services. Find out if you will speak directly to a physician or if communication will occur between the company representatives and the healthcare providers on scene.

Scan for more resources.

INVOLVEMENT WITH POLICE DURING INTERNATIONAL TRAVEL
Basic Guidelines If Police Are Involved

You are in a country where public intoxication is a crime. On the way home after a dinner where you had a few drinks, your driver who also had consumed some alcohol is involved in a motor vehicle accident that is not his fault. However, because your driver and you have consumed alcohol, you are arrested and detained.

Laws vary widely in different countries and what may be legal in one country may be a crime in others. The traveler is subject to the laws of the host country. Arrests occur in countries both friendly and hostile to your home country. About 6000 Americans are arrested annually in foreign countries. Securing release can be quite difficult because of unfamiliarity with a foreign judicial system and may be complicated by international relations between the host country and yours (see Legal Matters).

Criminal offenses are defined differently in each country and what may be acceptable in your country may be a crime in the country you are visiting. Examples of illegal activities that westerners may not appreciate include sharing a hotel room in the Middle East with a member of the opposite sex to whom you are not married or closely related, spitting or littering in Singapore, public alcohol consumption in many Islamic countries, and taking photos of government or military buildings and personnel.

KEY POINTS

»   The criminal process also differs in many countries. Detention rules and bail differ widely, a speedy trial is not guaranteed, burden of proof and trial by jury is not universal. Terms and method of punishment are often different and if incarcerated, jail conditions may be quite inferior.

» An individual detained abroad has the right to notify, be visited, and be represented by your consul. If detained, you should ask to have your consulate notified and to speak to a consulate official. However, this may not be granted depending on current relations between your home country and the one you are detained in.

» The consulate can assist by notifying your family, scheduling visits by family while detained, providing a list of local attorneys, and monitoring your welfare while detained.

» The consulate cannot demand release, act as your legal representative, or pay legal fees

» Try to keep calm and be co-operative.

» Do not be abusive or violent, this will make things worse.

» Your home country laws cannot be used to defend prosecution for a crime.

Scan for more resources.

JET LAG
Sleep Disturbances & Remedies

You are headed to the Far East for important business meetings and want to avoid jet lag which seems to bother you on every trip. You have tried various remedies but none of them seem to work. Is there anything that DOES work for jet lag?

Jet lag is a temporary phenomenon of sleep and alertness disturbance that occurs in travelers who rapidly cross time zones before adjustment of daily circadian rhythms. Circadian rhythm refers to the natural cycles of rising and falling levels of hormones, changes in vital signs, and other metabolic activities influenced by sunlight exposure. Circadian rhythms are slow to adjust with travel to other time zones and may take several days to readjust.

KEY POINTS

» About 15 percent of the United States population has sleep disorders. A sleep disorder may contribute to jet lag. Reported rates of sleep disorders may vary but a significant segment of the population has them in other countries.

» Stress, or the potential of stress, can contribute to jet lag.

» Lack of familiar surroundings, noise level, sleep surface, temperature, climate, and altitude can all affect sleep and contribute to jet lag. Sleep disturbances appear to increase with age.

BASIC PREVENTION AND TREATMENT

• No one method is effective for all people with jet lag and what may be successful to help prevent or decrease jet lag on one trip may not be as effective on the next. What works for one traveler may not work for others. Combinations of methods may improve chances of an diminished effect.

- If possible, select a flight with an early evening arrival and stay up until near your usual bedtime at the local time.

- If you must take a nap on arrival, take a short one in early afternoon and avoid long naps.

- Avoid excesses of caffeine or alcohol, both interrupt sleep.

- Avoid heavy meals or exercise near bedtime.

- Use earplugs and blindfolds to sleep.

- Avoid noise and stress while you adjust, if possible.

- Use of prescription sleep medications will not alter the circadian rhythm imbalance but may help with temporary insomnia. Discuss this with your physician, there are side effects from these medications that may interfere with alertness after medication-induced sleep.

- Use of melatonin is controversial with some claims of improvement but other claims of no effect. Melatonin is a naturally secreted hormone with variable levels throughout the 24 hour day and may have some effect on the sleep cycle. Melatonin is a dietary supplement and not fully evaluated.

Scan for more resources.

KIDNAPPING
How to Avoid Being a Victim

While traveling in a Latin American country on holidays with her husband, a woman decides to stop at a local shopping center in what appears to be a safe part of town. While her husband goes inside, the woman goes back to retrieve personal items from her suitcase in the back seat. Suddenly, she is violently shoved into the back seat and a stranger has jumped into the driver seat and is driving away with her. The woman doesn't know the person, he hasn't said anything, but it is apparent he is armed. She has been kidnapped and her husband isn't even aware of it.

Kidnapping or hostage taking can happen anywhere. It is more prevalent in areas where there is a large inequality of income—the gap between the "haves" and "have nots." Kidnapping can be motivated by a wide variety of issues including political causes, business coercion, monetary ransom, revenge, and religious idealism.

KEY POINTS

> » Kidnap victims can be taken from their house, car, hotel, while walking on the street, or while waiting for a bus or a taxi.

> » Although the chances of you being kidnapped are very small—there are places where a foreigner is significantly more exposed to the risk of being kidnapped than in other places.

> » As with all travel, take the time to "know before you go" and find out if your destination is one of those where the risk of kidnapping should be considered in your travel plans.

BASIC GUIDELINES

- The following recommendations are provided to minimize the likelihood of becoming a kidnap victim.

- If, at any time, you feel someone is following you, make your way towards a place where there are people around—which will reduce the probability of the kidnappers fulfilling their plan.

- As a general rule, where possible walk on the side of the road that faces oncoming traffic. This will make it harder for a vehicle to move up behind you and take you by surprise.

- Make sure someone you know and trust has details of where you are going and when to expect you to return.

- Maintain a low profile and dress modestly and in a manner that is commensurate with your location. Women in particular should wear clothing that would not be considered offensive or provocative in the country destination. Do not wear expensive looking accessories.

- One common mistake many people make is to wear headphones while moving around outdoors. This significantly reduces your awareness of what is going on around you. If you must wear headphones, have the volume set so you can still hear the sound of a spoken voice around you.

- Be extra diligent about the use of ATMs and, if possible, avoid using them altogether if outside at night or in an unfamiliar location. Always check your surroundings when using an ATM to avoid being approached by surprise.

- Avoid sharing an elevator with anyone who makes you feel uncomfortable. Trust your instincts the first time. When you are in an elevator with other people, position yourself close to the control panel and make sure you know where the emergency button is located.

- When using a car, get in the habit of checking in and around your car before getting into it, to make sure it is safe to do so. Similarly, always check your surroundings before getting out of a car. These are vulnerable moments when kidnappers commonly strike.

- Always keep windows and doors locked when driving.

- Be prepared to drive through a red light if you are approached by anyone acting suspiciously or threateningly. It is better to risk being fined than kidnapped or assaulted.

- Do not pick up hitchhikers.

- If you see an accident or a stranded person, report it by telephone if possible, but avoid the inclination to become involved. This is a very common setup for a kidnapping.

- Avoid parking, driving or walking in poorly lit areas—especially when alone or in an unfamiliar location.

Scan for more resources.

LACERATIONS & PUNCTURE WOUNDS
Principles of Wound Care

You are riding a trail bike in the foothills and come upon another trail rider who has fallen and sustained an apparent deep and jagged laceration of the arm, bleeding freely. The victim is dazed and you are not close to rapid medical assistance.

KEY POINTS

A wound is best defined by its geometry and mechanism of injury.

» A laceration is a cut or tear of the skin and can be superficial, involving the skin only, or deep through the skin and involving flesh and significant blood vessels.

» Lacerations can have either a single cut with clean or jagged edge or be caused by impact which splits the skin causing multiple edges.

» A puncture wound is deeper than it is long.

» Both laceration and punctures can be relatively clean or exceedingly dirty.

Each of us has sustained relatively minor lacerations but you may have to deal with a more severe wound when you may not have immediate access to appropriate medical care. An acute traumatic wound in a remote site is a management challenge especially without medical personnel or resources readily available.

BASIC GUIDELINES

• Stabilize the victim. Evaluate for other injuries and prevent movement if spine or neck injuries are suspected. A victim with a laceration may have other serious but less obvious injuries. Make sure the victim is breathing adequately.

- Determine the cause of the injury, this will help determine the extent and management. Get information from the victim about any medications used, particularly anticoagulants and aspirin.

- Put direct pressure on any obvious significant bleeding site while you assess the victim. Use a clean cloth, towel, or similar material. Keep pressure for 10-15 minutes and re-evaluate. Continue with direct pressure Stopping bleeding will also relieve the victim's anxiety.

- Tourniquets should only be a last resort when there is no other way to stop bleeding. They should be used only in life and death situations because loss of the limb is possible.

- Tourniquets should be between 1 and 2 inches wide and stop arterial bleeding. Do not remove a tourniquet without training, removal may lead to more severe bleeding.

- Remove all jewelry on an injured extremity. Swelling may occur and prevent removal later.

- An arterial injury (commonly with pulsatile blood flow) may be accompanied by a nerve injury.

- Stabilize and remain with the victim until medical care can be provided.

- Wound irrigation is key to prevent infection. If medical care is delayed, irrigate the wound with clean water if possible. Remove any obvious foreign material from the wound if possible. Irrigate copiously, multiple times if possible, with pressure from the fluid. A 30 or 60 cc syringe is ideal but you can improvise, for example use a turkey baster or other bulb syringe with enough pressure to simulate a squirt gun. Irrigation is better than antibiotic administration to prevent infection.

- Do NOT use rubbing alcohol, merthiolate, iodine, or other over-the-counter antiseptic. These can prevent wound healing and are often painful.

- Wound closure can be performed using medical glue (not super glue) for relatively smaller lacerations. Do not use for very deep wounds.

- Bandage the wound with a nonadherent dressing and apply a topical antibiotic if it is available.

- Do not splint unless a fracture is suspected.

- Begin oral antibiotics for a severe or dirty wound if an appropriate one is available. If you are unsure about whether an available antibiotic is appropriate for the injury, wait for medical advice. Check with the victim for allergies first if you do decide to provide antibiotics.

- Provide oral or injectable pain medication if available and needed.

- Elevate the extremity or body part with the wound if possible.

Scan for more
resources.

LEGAL MATTERS FOR TRAVEL
What You Need to Know About the Law on Travel

On a trek to Machu Picchu with your college friends you broke your ankle when a piece of equipment malfunctioned and you fell at a campsite. A nurse in your group was able to help somewhat but the travel group company who organized the trip did not have medical supplies sufficient to treat your injury. You had to seek medical care at a local facility and arrange for your own transportation home a couple of days later. Is the company negligent for not having sufficient medical care available? Is the nurse liable because she did not splint the injury correctly? Is the company obligated to pay for your return? Is there product liability?

Adventure and other travel involves risks. Although risks can be minimized, some risks will always remain. Legal issues are a consideration for several aspects of travel. Legal concerns should be part of any trip preparation and not left to only when trouble arises.

Medical care delivered to an injured traveler, whether or not in your group, may have legal consequences. Leaders of a group or expedition have a responsibility to provide an overall safe and healthy environment for the trip and to respond when medical care is needed. An injured traveler in the group should receive the best available care within the reasonable limits of training by those involved in delivery of care.

KEY POINTS

»   Liability varies for those on vacation, business travel, adventure trips, and expeditions. However, the seasoned traveler also understands that unplanned surprises and events may entrap even the most prepared individual. An understanding of basic legal liability and definitions is useful for documents you may be required to sign. The following describes some legal concepts to help guide the casual traveler as well as those on more risky adventures.

» Travelers should seek more detailed discussions of legal aspects from an attorney or legal resources if necessary.

» Laws and legal issues in foreign countries can be very different from the United States. Fines and imprisonment can be severe.

» If you have a legal problem overseas, contact the American Embassy immediately (see several chapters in this book).

FOR TRAVELERS

• Evaluate the risk involved with your trip or activity. Travel to an unfamiliar location likely requires more diligence, ranging from checking on the safety surrounding your transportation and accommodations to full assessment of regional geopolitical unrest.

• If adventurous activities are planned, physical risk, your health status related to the degree of physical exertion and climate, reliability of travel services and transportation providers, medical preparation with vaccines and medication for travel, and travel and medical evacuation insurance are important considerations.

• It is prudent to have your doctor and dentist evaluate you before embarking on remote travel.

• Determining limits of medical coverage and adding to existing coverage may be necessary to protect you in the event of an adverse medical event (see Insurance and Medical Evacuation Policies). Note the exclusions to your coverage in your policies. Ask the company who provides travel insurance about their medical treatment evacuation policies and how they will manage a problem if it arises. You may be required to provide proof of insurance coverage by the event organizer or leader.

• Documents required for travel must be in order and may take longer than anticipated. Passport and visa requirements, special permits for filming and scientific study, country-specific vaccination documentation, permits for special equipment, documentation for carrying controlled substances, and waivers for regulations or requirements must be in order. Copies should be kept with the trip leader and yourself.

FOR LEADERS

- If you are the leader, staff participant, or medical officer on a trip or an expedition, it is very important to determine your legal responsibilities, exposure, risk, and liability. This should be done together with the expedition or event leader and staff.

- For a person who agrees to provide medical coverage, it is imperative to discuss with leaders what and how your response to a medical adverse event will be coordinated, and to understand the limits of the local medical facilities. Also understand medical liability issues.

- All participants must be fully informed of risks. They must also understand that they are voluntarily accepting these risks.

- Travelers should provide proof of appropriate medical and travel insurance coverage including medical evacuation if required.

- In addition to waivers that cover risks, it is valuable to conduct safety briefings before and during the activity, particularly as the potential for various risks changes during the activity.

BASIC LEGAL DEFINITIONS

Travelers should familiarize themselves with basic definitions to read and understand contracts and other legal documents.

- » A contract is a promise between two or more entities that the law will enforce. Travel usually involves a contract whether it is with a travel agency or tour group, an airline or hotel, or a sponsoring organization.

- » Contracts can be written or verbal, and must be clearly understood by both parties. Verbal contracts are often difficult to enforce.

- » You may have legal exposure for the activity in which you will participate. Legal exposure means that you are affected by a situation where you may be exposed to laws that govern the activity.

» Liability may occur when you are legally responsible for something. Areas of traveler responsibility include their behavior and avoidance of illegal activity. People who engage in reckless or intentionally risky behavior in an activity have co-participant liability. In other words, they also bear at least part of the responsibility for a mishap or injury sustained in that behavior. A court will determine the extent of their liability.

» Product liability refers to equipment. Product liability results from faulty equipment design or manufacture that results in injury or harm to a user. Product manufacturers, distributors, retailers, and those who provide equipment can be liable. Operators or equipment providers can be sued for improper fitting, lack of maintenance, or noncompliance with standards or manufacturer instructions. Alteration or use of equipment for other than manufacturer intended purposes can cancel warranties and expose trip organizers or users to liability.

» Causation is the relation of cause to effect and is one basis for legal liability. There must be a plausible connection between actions of the defendant and adverse effect on the plaintiff. In the context of travel medical issues, this usually refers to injury or death.

» Negligence is the failure to use ordinary care, specifically, failure to do what an ordinary person would do under similar circumstances. This occurs when an individual or group providing a service should have recognized an unreasonable risk and did nothing to warn or remove the risk. Negligence is classified as simple, ordinary, or gross and has four areas for consideration:

  - Duty is the responsibility to take reasonable care to protect another person or group. Duty arises when one accepts a position or contract to provide service.

  - Breach of standard of care. Standard of care is what is expected of a reasonable person doing the same activity. Standard of care may be set by law or professional organizations.

- Causation (see earlier definition). The results must be linked by cause to the negligent party.

- Damages (see below). The victim of negligence must warrant compensation for damage.

» Contributory negligence is important to understand. Individuals have a legal duty to take reasonable care to prevent injury to themselves. The individual is responsible for personal unreasonable activities.

» Gross negligence relates to willful or reckless misconduct. Gross negligence is more serious than ordinary or simple negligence and prosecution for this is not prevented by a waiver or release. Gross negligence applies to those who knowingly act or fail to perform a duty or create extreme risk.

» Damages are an award, usually money, to be paid to a person to compensate for loss or injury. Damages are classified as compensatory and punitive. Compensatory damages can be for loss of income, property damage, and medical expenses. Punitive damages are compensation as a penalty for the action beyond compensatory damages such as pain, suffering and emotional distress.

BASIC GUIDELINES

- Trip leaders should complete a risk assessment as part of the basic travel plan, and also develop a plan to minimize or avoid those risks. Individuals should prepare their own plan for a medical or travel logistics problem. Foreign health care providers frequently require payment before services are provided – even emergency room services. Before departure, make certain each travel member has a plan for payment in case of emergency.

- For group leaders, staff, and medical officers of an event or adventure – it is often advisable to provide each participant with a standard form to take to their health care provider for signature to confirm the participant is physically (and mentally if applicable) fit to undertake the activity. This standard form should include a description of the proposed activity and potential risks and also include a statement that the participant has no medical conditions that would affect, or be affected by, such activity. For more vigorous or dangerous expeditions, specific physical requirements may be appropriate.

- For the individual, it is important to make sure you are in good health before you depart. Your physician may be required to provide medical clearance for you to participate in a trip, particularly for adventurous activities. You likely will be required to sign a liability release that you are healthy enough to undergo the exertion but you also assume risk for your own safety provided the event is reasonably safe (see contributory negligence defined earlier).

- It is very important to disclose all medical problems and medication use to the group leader for adventurous activities so they are aware in case of an emergency.

- Do not neglect a dental check-up if going to a remote location.

- Examine your medical and travel insurance policies so you understand their terms and conditions, especiallyregarding medical and other travel emergencies. Insurance is used to mitigate your liability. In the context of travel, insurance is used to protect you or reimburse you when an adverse event occurs. Standard insurance for health and to protect your assets may or may not cover you for travel-related or adventurous activities and it is important to understand the limitations of your coverage. Medicare usually does not cover overseas travel.

- Insurance to cover individual or corporate liability as a group leader, sponsor, or organizer, is beyond the scope of this text and appropriate legal and insurance expert counsel should be sought for those circumstances.

- The more risk involved in the activity, the more broad coverage is desired but this comes at a cost. The right combination for you on your trip might likely entail general coverage for health and travel with medical evacuation (see Insurance and Evacuation Policies).

- A Waiver or Liability Release is a document you may be required to sign before travel, particularly for adventurous activities. These are used by travel organizations to shift legal liability and prevent litigation. These waivers state that the participant agrees to give up the right to sue for an injury or adverse event occurring as a result of participation in an activity or use of a service. This will not apply in cases of gross negligence. Elements of a release should include the inherent risk specific for the activity and address health issues such as ability to perform the activity, authorization to administer emergency first aid and provide medical information to healthcare providers, and authorization for emergency medical transportation. If you have to prepare a waiver as a group leader, this should be constructed with an attorney.

- Medical Release and Permission to Treat is often a separate agreement that relates only to the individual and the medical professionals associated with an activity. A medical release usually states that the signer acknowledges the potential for (a) illness, injuries, and death associated with the activity, (b) possible lack of sophisticated emergency medical resources and evacuation, (c) authorization for necessary emergency treatment and transportation, (d) disclosure of any medical or psychological problems relevant to medical treatment, and (e) permission to release confidential medical information to appropriate parties in case of an emergency.

- It is important for a medical professional to identify and understand local licensure, legal practice requirements, and liability issues. Physicians and other health care providers accept legal responsibility when providing consultation or actual patient care. A physician or licensed healthcare worker who agrees to provide prescriptions for travelers, suggest or administer vaccines, recommend or bring supplies for the group, or provide general medical advice or care is accepting responsibility for those travelers as patients. These activities require medical record documentation. They carry the same legal liability as care for any patient.

- If health care support is provided during travel, medical licensure to practice medicine should be considered. A United States medical license is issued by a state with medical practice only authorized for that specific state. One is not licensed to practice medicine in states where a medical license is not held. Furthermore, international jurisdictions have their own requirements for licensure and medical practice with legal risk for even seemingly simple medical care.

- Medical malpractice insurance is usually specific to the practitioner's office location. Medical advice or "favors", even if informal, constitutes the practice of medicine, with standard medical liability and risk of malpractice. Few medical malpractice insurance companies cover a practitioner for a finite travel time in a location away from their usual office without a hefty and likely unacceptable cost. Fortunately, it has been rare for a lawsuit to arise from appropriate medical assistance without gross negligence in these travel situations.

- Good Samaritan laws are designed to protect bystanders from liability for voluntarily helping a victim of injury or illness. Good Samaritan laws vary among states and countries. In fact, some countries legally require you to render assistance unless it endangers you though this rule may not apply to non-citizens. It is very important for a medical professional to understand that if any medical role has been provided to a group on a trip, the Good Samaritan laws would likely not apply to any care for the members of the group since there is an established relationship. However, emergency assistance provided by the group doctor to someone outside the group would likely be covered by Good Samaritan laws.

- Controlled substance use is governed by law in most countries and requires a prescription.

- Controlled substances for an individual should be accompanied by a record of prescription and instructions for intended use. It is recommended to carry relatively small amounts of such medications so that it is apparent that they are intended for personal use only. It is advisable, however, to bring extra medication on travel because of delays or trip changes may not permit refill of some medications, particularly controlled substances. A letter from the prescribing physician is useful if questioned by authorities.

- Group or expedition leaders, particularly the involved medical professionals, should have jurisdiction over all controlled substance inventory. The U.S. Drug Enforcement Agency or their foreign equivalents may likely require accounts demonstrating amounts and uses of such medications.

- Controlled substances should be kept in locked storage.
- Although it is customary and humanitarian to leave excess or unused supplies behind in underdeveloped regions, the exception to this is controlled substances which must be accounted for to the regulatory agencies.

BASIC GUIDELINES FOR INCIDENT BEHAVIOR AND REPORTING

- The legal responsibility for individuals and particularly for group leaders, staff, and medical personnel extends beyond the resolution of an adverse event. It is very important to document all actions and subsequent responses.

- Some type of medical records should be kept for all medical encounters. Compliance with appropriate confidentiality laws is essential. Part of the initial participant release forms should include release of medical records.

- For general incidents, a case report summary detailing circumstances surrounding an incident, the type of injury sustained, the response that occurred, and recommendations or follow up required is an important document that may have legal, regulatory, or insurance implications. Such a description will be useful to all who analyze the incident to determine liability, if it exists, and to identify and address any behavior or reaction that could be improved. However, unless the participant signs a "release of medical records" some information may be protected by law from release.

BASIC RESOURCES

- Larson K, Knutson T: "Legal considerations during expedition planning." In: *Expedition and Wilderness Medicine.* Bledsoe GH, Manyak MJ, Townes DA (Eds). Cambridge University Press 2009, pp 53-75.

- Barton B: *Safety, Risk, and Adventure in Outdoor Activities.* Paul Chapman Publishing, 2007.

- Heshka J, Jackson J: *Managing Risk: Systems Planning for Outdoor Adventure Programs*
- Kuhne CC: *Adventure and the Law.* American Bar Association, 2014.

Scan for more resources.

LIGHTNING STRIKE
Lightning Can Strike Twice

You are on a sightseeing tour of monuments and a summer squall with thunder rolls in quickly. You are in an open area among tall structures that you think will attract any lightning away from you. Are you safe where you are?

Lightning strikes the earth somewhere about 100 times per second or about 8 million times a day. In the continental United States, it is estimated that an annual average of 20 million flashes occur with the highest concentration in central Florida.

KEY POINTS

» Lightning results when the electrical potential in the atmosphere exceeds the natural resistance of air. This is likely caused by collision of raindrops and particles or by downward convection of negative charges.

» Most lightning accidents occur outdoors, about one-third or more occur indoors, and 10 percent occur during transport in motor vehicles.

» There were 374 deaths by lightning strikes in the United States between 1995 and 2000 with 75 percent occurring in the South and Midwest, and 25 percent were work-related.

» Worldwide, around 24,000 people die each year from lightning strikes with mortality highest in Africa. Lightning injury data is unreliable in most countries and likely underreported.

» Injuries from lightning occur in several ways: direct strikes, contact from touching an object while struck, current jumping from a nearby struck object, current passing through the ground, and blast injuries.

» Fortunately direct strikes (which are usually fatal) occur in only about 5 percent of cases. Persons who are stunned or lose consciousness without cardiopulmonary arrest are unlikely to die.

» The reason that 70 percent of lightning strikes are not fatal is likely because the strikes last milliseconds and have minimal energy transfer to internal organs. However, 75 percent of survivors have some permanent damage such as ringing in the ears, seizures, or blindness. The very short exposure time to extremely high voltage may cause injuries due to high temperatures and blast waves in addition to electrical energy.

» The most common injuries occur to the nervous system with short episodes of paralysis and burning or numbness common.

» Other injuries associated with strikes include: Short-term loss of consciousness, coma, seizures, headache, and intracranial hemorrhage may occur immediately while delayed effects include muscle weakness and subtle cognitive impairment.

» Cardiac problems occur in nearly half of the victims and cardiac arrest occurs without physical damage in about 10 percent due to disruption of automatic heartbeat rhythm.

» Deafness from tympanic membrane rupture by the strike is also common after lightning strike and ear injuries often occur when lightning strikes during telephone use.

» Severe muscular pain and urinary protein excretion secondary to muscle injury sufficient to cause kidney failure if untreated are also often described.

» Superficial burns have a distinctive pattern and severe burns are rare but can be noted at entry and exit points of the current. Burns can be internal and difficult to recognize immediately.

In reality, no place outside is really safe when a thunderstorm hits. Distance and proper shelter are your best protection. Here are some common myths about lightning:

Lightning never strikes the same place twice.
False: Lightning often strikes repeatedly in places prone to lightning (tall isolated objects).

Lightning cannot strike if it is not raining or if there are no clouds.
False: Lightning often strikes 3 miles or more from the storm and can strike 10-15 miles from the storm. A "bolt out of the blue" is exactly that.

Lie flat on the ground if trapped outside and there is risk of lightning strikes.
False: Lying flat decreases your height but increases the chance of being hit by ground current. Best to assume a crouch position if you cannot find shelter.

Inside a house is safe.
Partially true: You must avoid any contact with a conduction path to the outside—phones, appliances, plumbing, water sources, TV cable wires, metal doors or frames.

A car provides safety from strikes.
Partially true, but not because of the rubber tires. The metal roof and sides conduct the current away from you so convertibles and open topped vehicles do not provide protection.

BASIC PREVENTION AND TREATMENT GUIDELINES

- If caught in the open, stay off ridges and away from single trees, remove and stow all metal objects (iPods, carabiners, crampons, ski poles, etc.), and move quickly away from iron ladders and wire ropes.

- Lightning current can follow wet ropes.

- Do not stand near a tall object, you are in danger from current jumping or passing through the ground.

- Assume the crouch position if you note a visible glow or you feel a sensation of your hair standing on end.

- Rescue of lightning victims can be hazardous so wait until the danger of further strikes has passed.

- The victim is not electrified, so begin treatment immediately.

- Treatment of lightning victims is based on the ABCs of resuscitation—

airway, breathing, circulation. Because the heart can frequently restart, begin CPR and continue as long as possible because prognosis is very good if oxygenation is maintained.

- It is important to support the cervical spine because the explosion of the strike may have caused fractures.

- Pain medication and first aid for burns are appropriate if immediate evacuation is unavailable.

Scan for more resources.

LUGGAGE SECURITY
Leave the Louis Vuitton At Home

You are leaving on a two week international trip and need to pack for a variety of occasions. Some of your clothing and accessories are valuable and your female companion is concerned about carrying her jewelry. You will not need your medication until arrival. How do you minimize the chance of lost luggage having a significant impact on your trip?

According to annual worldwide airline baggage reports, approximately 26 million pieces of checked luggage are misplaced by airlines around the world every year. That is the equivalent of one suitcase for every passenger using an airport the size of Washington DC's Dulles International airport in a given year. Even more troubling is that an astonishing one million of these cases are never recovered by their owners – either stolen or simply because the identifying tags had been lost or removed.

KEY POINTS

» The type of luggage you travel with can say a lot about you…and it shouldn't. As a general guide for check-in luggage, it is best to travel with low-key, hard-cased luggage that looks well-used and can be locked. Such luggage provides a modest level of security and at the same time doesn't attract the attention of criminals.

» If possible, lock your luggage and secure it with an external luggage strap with a combination lock. Many cases and luggage straps these days use locks that can be opened by the U.S. Transportation Security Administration (TSA), which can reduce the chances of your luggage lock being cut off when your baggage is opened for inspection.

» In many places, it is possible to have your luggage wrapped in plastic prior to check-in. Where this service is available it should be used, but some destinations will require it to be unwrapped for inspection as part of the customs process.

» When you are given a luggage receipt (also known as bag tags or luggage tickets), make sure you keep your part of it somewhere safe, and ensure the part attached to your bag is properly secured, and that it contains the correct destination code.

» Identify the outside of your luggage with something distinctive, like a ribbon or tape that can be clearly seen from a distance.

» Keep a business card or other label taped to your laptop computer to avoid loss or accidental "exchange" by other travelers.

» Do not put your address on external tags and certainly never use your business card as a luggage tag. External identification tags should be concealed or folded they cannot be casually read by passersby and should only contain your name, phone number (at your destination) and perhaps an email address.

» Put a copy of your passport photo page, and a page with your name and phone number (at your destination) inside a plastic envelope or sleeve, and place this plastic cover on top of your clothing inside your suitcase for positive identification if your case is lost and/or external identification has been removed.

BASIC PACKING GUIDELINES

• Prior to checking in your baggage, always make sure your carry-on luggage meets the airline's size and weight requirements.

• Many countries have adopted the same restrictions for carrying liquids, gels, and aerosols that are common in the United States. Where these restrictions are enforced, all products must be in individual containers that are three (3) ounces or smaller—and be placed inside a quart size, zip top, clear plastic bag.

• Carry only the valuables that are necessary for your trip, and carry them on your person or in carry-on luggage. Never pack any valuables in your checked luggage.

• Critical documents, such as passports and small valuables should be carried in a concealed carrier, such as an under-clothing travelers pouch. Consider carrying cash, traveler's checks, or copies of passports in a concealed money belt.

- If you travel with medications, it is wise to keep them in their original labeled container with a copy of the original prescription folded up inside. If your medications contain narcotics that could be questioned by customs officials, have a letter from your doctor that explains your legitimate possession of these drugs.

- Pack your shoes and other footwear on top of the other contents in your suitcase, this way it is easier for security to check your footwear.

- Wait to wrap your gifts. Be aware that wrapped gifts may need to be opened for inspection. This applies to both carry-on and checked baggage.

Scan for more
resources.

MARINE HAZARDS
Look But Don't Touch

> *You are walking in shallow water in the ocean and suddenly experience sharp, searing pain in your foot. You are not sure what you stepped on but it continues to really hurt so it must be more than just a sharp object. Your friends suggest home remedies. What do you do?*

Anyone who ventures into the sea risks contact with hazardous marine life. Hazards include stings, bites, coral injuries, and poisonous seafood.

KEY POINTS

» Most encounters are accidental and the majority of injuries from marine life are minor if attended to promptly but serious injury requiring first aid and evacuation can occur.

» Higher level of awareness of potential problems is important to recognize and begin on-site treatment to limit symptoms.

» Be careful where you step, what you pick up, and what you eat.

» Wear thick-soled reef shoes and shuffle your feet to avoid entrapping bottom-dwelling venomous fish and rays.

» Aside from large vertebrate predators, many smaller marine creatures can cause severe irritation or even fatality.

» The most likely source of envenomation in shallow water is from jellyfish. The most commonly encountered jellyfish rarely cause serious stings.

» The pelagic Portuguese Man-of-War belongs to the same class as fire coral and though less commonly encountered, still account for over 10,000 annual stings in Australia. Painful stings with welts occur and the pain should subside within an hour or two. Death from an allergic reaction is extremely rare.

» The most dangerous invertebrate is the box jellyfish of Australia and Indo-Pacific areas whose toxin causes excruciating pain and respiratory and cardiac dysfunction.

» Bottom-dwelling creatures can cause problems in shallow water. The gentle stingrays account for over a thousand injuries and about 18 deaths per year. The most famous case occurred when Steve Irwin died after he ignored two of the most important rules regarding stingrays, not to swim directly over or provoke them.

» Envenomation from the dorsal spines of the well-camouflaged scorpionfish and stonefish occurs from stepping or placing a hand on them. Mild to severe pain is experienced, but for stonefish envenomation, the pain is immediate, excruciating, and usually unrelieved by narcotics.

» Coral is not venomous but the calcium framework can lacerate or abrade skin with insertion of organic material leading to itchy lesions that can become secondarily infected.

» Fire coral causes envenomation, even after light contact, though it is not a true coral but related to the stinging hydroids (such as the Portuguese Man-Of-War)

» Sea urchins and crown of thorns starfish contain venom that accounts for the severe pain and swelling seen with puncture wounds. Retained fragments are a further concern.

» Bristleworms, related to leeches and earthworms, are common in tropical and semitropical waters and have very fine spines that easily lodge in skin, causing pain and swelling.

» Sea bather's eruption, also known as sea lice, causes symptoms of burning, itching, and reddish rash caused by the small larvae of jellyfish or, rarely, anemones or crabs.

» Be careful of collecting cone-shaped shells in the water, many live cone snails can inject a lethal paralytic toxin. Look, don't touch!

» The rarely encountered but highly venomous blue-ringed octopus found in the Indo-Pacific is shy and bites only if handled. Its rapidly acting venom causes paralysis requiring ventilatory support. Interestingly, its bite causes no pain.

» The extremely toxic sea snake venom, on the other hand, causes pain with neuromuscular paralysis. Fortunately, these snakes are nonaggressive and usually must be provoked to bite. Their small fangs (less than 4 mm) may not penetrate a wet suit. Sea snake bites are rare but deadly.

BASIC TREATMENT GUIDELINES

- The stinging cells (neumatocysts) of jellyfish are best treated by washing with salt water. Do not use fresh water. Vinegar can neutralize the neumatocysts in some cases but do not apply meat tenderizer or urine. After carefully removing remaining tentacles, wash with hot water for 15 to 20 minutes to denature the toxins. There is no truth to the common tale that urine has any effect on neumatocysts so it is wise to politely decline that option.

- For box jellyfish stings, DO use vinegar to rinse for at least 30 seconds. Vinegar will not relieve pain however. Pressure immobilization, administration of box jellyfish antivenom available in the regional area, and immediate evacuation is advised.

- Treatment for stingray and fish envenomation consists of immersion in hot water until relief. Stonefish antivenin should be administered if available. Xrays are needed to rule out retention of any barbs which can lead to infection if not removed.

- For coral abrasions and lacerations, scrub the wound with a brush and get a tetanus toxoid shot for deep lacerations if you have not had one within ten years.

- Fire coral stings should be treated with vinegar to neutralize the stinging cells.

- Treatment for sea urchins and crown of thorns starfish puncture wounds is by hot water immersion for 30 to 90 minutes. Retained spine fragments can become infected and must be removed.

- Pain and swelling from bristleworm spines may be removed by placing the sticky side of tape and then removing it. Topical pain medication and steroids may be useful.

- Sea bather's eruption (sea lice) may be treated with antihistamines but this is variable in effect. The rash may last 5 to 7 days.

- Cone snail stings cause paralysis and require pressure immobilization and possibly respiratory ventilation support. There is no antivenom. Evacuate the victim immediately.

- Blue-ringed octopus bites cause respiratory failure which requires respiratory ventilator support. Irrigate the wound, immobilize and use a pressure bandage, and evacuate immediately. With ventilator support the victim will survive the incident because the toxin itself is not fatal. The victim may be paralyzed but fully alert during the episode.

- Sea snake bites require immobilization and use of a pressure bandage (snug but not uncomfortable) and immediate evacuation for resuscitation and antivenom use (See Snake Bite).

SEAFOOD POISONING

Marine seafood poisoning is another risk to be considered. It is important to note that NONE of the following toxins are deactivated by heat or refrigeration nor have disagreeable taste, odor, or appearance.

» Ciguatera poisoning usually occurs with ingestion of large carnivorous fish which eat smaller prey which feed on neurotoxin-producing unicellular dinoflagellates. Symptoms are diarrhea, vomiting, abdominal pain, and various peripheral neurological complaints. Treatment is supportive: fluid replacement, pain relief, medication for nausea and vomiting.

» Pufferfish produce a powerful painful neurotoxin which requires cardiopulmonary support for survival. Avoid consuming these species in the field even if prepared by an expert.

» Scombroid poisoning occurs when game fish are not refrigerated allowing histamine to accumulate causing hives, diarrhea, vomiting, and cramps. Treatment is with fluids and antihistamines.

» Shellfish poisoning presents at least four occasionally lethal syndromes with severe gastrointestinal symptoms with or without neurologic symptoms. Some are associated with dinoflagellate overabundance (red tide) and can be airborne. Fortunately, most communities where these occur monitor their occurrence. Treatment is supportive: fluid replacement, pain relief, medication for nausea and vomiting.

Scan for more resources.

MENTAL HEALTH
Behavior That Can Affect Your Trip

Undertaking a long and arduous expedition, you are concerned about how the team members will get along. Behavioral issues add unnecessary challenges particularly under stress. You want to make sure the group is an effective team.

Travelers often join groups during an adventure trip or are placed in groups by the leader. Due to choice of location or predetermined times, members of a group may have little choice in group selection. It is essential for a team leader to be aware of the interpersonal aspects of an expedition. This is something to consider prior to departure but may not always be practical or possible. Components of an effective team or group adventure include both leadership and the personal characteristics of its members. It is often difficult to predict (or control) how people will function in challenging, and sometimes dangerous, situations. If schedules and geography allow, formal or informal pre-departure team building exercises can be helpful and participants are encouraged to attend so both group members and leaders can get an impression of group and individual dynamics. Sometimes persons who are clearly not suited for the adventure will realize this and bow out or be removed from the team roster for other reasons.

KEY POINTS

» Before departure Each team member should be fully informed about all aspects of the expedition—expectations, working hours, and other conditions, risks (physical, mental, emotional), costs, what will and will not be provided, living conditions, and other factors. This discussion will help each potential party member really decide whether this is something they want to do. A positive attitude is a good beginning.

» The leader should determine etermine whether any physical or psychological predeployment "standards" are appropriate. Someone just released from a hospital for major depression may not be an appropriate choice for a lengthy expedition to a remote area. Standards must be fairly and equally applied to all participants. Potential participants should be informed about such standards early in the selection process.

» No medical or mental health history is usually requested for participation in an adventure trip or expedition. Thus, leadership is likely unaware of pre-existing mental health conditions of participants before departure. It is important for you to disclose any mental health issues (such as history of depression, medication use for mental issues, anxiety attacks) to the leader.

» If a trip participant has some history of mental health treatment or is on medication for such conditions, it is advisable for the leader to consult the mental health provider about the readiness for a stressful event. The participant can have the mental health provider sign a simple standard statement provided by the leadership that describes the working environment and likely stresses encountered, stating that the provider concurs that the participant is mentally fit for the trip. This same clearance is often used with the primary care physician of a participant for physical health.

» Some psychiatric medications provide certain challenges in austere environments. Dehydration from heat, nausea or vomiting can pose challenges to persons on lithium carbonate. Monitoring blood levels of drugs such as lithium or phenytoin to avoid serious complications can be difficult on extended travel.

» Travelers with a tendency for mental health issues should understand that the longer they are in a physically or mentally stressful situation, the more they are at risk of developing a problem. This is also true for those travelers who may not have mental health issues prior to travel. Prolonged stress may exacerbate any underlying mental health conditions.

» Travelers should be stable on all their medications before departure. Adjustment of dose or medication change while on travel is difficult.

BASIC GUIDELINES DURING TRAVEL

- For those on trips with defined goals, the leader should set realistic expectations, and arrange work schedules and other activities to reduce stress if possible. Set specific work hours and discourage after hours work. Working 24 hours a day rarely accomplishes more than a normal schedule. Show team members you care about their well-being.

- Leisure and relaxation activities are encouraged for people on a trip with defined goals, and schedule some into the workweek. A midweek day off or an outing to a nearby tourist area is appreciated.

- The team leader should recognize the importance of adequate sleep. If there are significant time zone changes, flexibility added into the work schedule will help accommodate adjustment.

- Congenial and relaxing mealtimes, as well as adequate nutrition, strongly contribute to a an adventure experience or productive work environment.

- Trip members should talk to group leaders about things causing exceptional stress—and work to change them where possible.

- Stresses on the trip can cause new or underlying mental health issues to surface. For example, the team may witness a serious car accident, observe a robbery, or other violence. Look for signs of anxiety and distress, and assist group members to cope.

- A serious new mental health condition or one concealed prior to departure may surface with or without stress. It is a priority for the group leader to seek outside professional assistance if the behavior poses any risk to that person or others, even if it jeopardizes the mission.

- If the trip or expedition was exceptionally stressful, the group leader may want to contact team members if events could lead to post traumatic stress disorder (PTSD). The group leader should educate the team members, and inform them about available community resources.

Scan for more resources.

MISSING PERSONS
What To Do & When To Be Concerned

After finishing college, a young woman joins two other female friends to travel abroad. While they are in France, after an evening of attending different nightclubs, one of the girls fails to return to the hotel where they are staying. Frightened, the remaining two girls wait for the whole next day before reporting their friend missing, in the hope she will just turn up. She does not return.

Unexpectedly losing contact with a travelling partner, family member, business colleague, or friendwhile travelling overseas can be distressing. When travellers venture out into the world, they often leave behind the familiar support systems they have come to rely on, and need to depend on new, untested support mechanisms such as foreign emergency service capabilities, police and medical facilities—and may not be able to receive information or respond as well as they would normally. If you have lost someone overseas, embassies and police will usually assist to the extent they can, but will generally only get involved where there is very well-founded concern for the well-being of a traveller.

KEY POINTS

» If you become concerned about a person overseas, and suspect they may have gone missing; there are some initial steps you can take:

» The first thing you will do is exhaust every means in trying to call the missing person by phone, text message, email, or even post letters to the last places they were known to have been.

» Get in touch with the families and friends of anyone else who was traveling with the missing person to determine if they have heard anything.

» Contact the missing person's employer, if applicable, and seek information about the person's possible movements.

» Do a thorough check of all the social media sites known to be used by the missing person—and get around some of the more common "sharing" security features of popular social networks by contacting the missing person's closest and most intimate friends and getting them to check the missing person's site. They will often see things that you may not be privy to. Post a request to be contacted on every social media site known to be used by the missing person.

» Attempt to determine the missing person's most recent credit/debit card transactions by contacting their financial institution, if you are authorized to do so.

» Attempt to determine if their travel arrangements have been adjusted by contacting the mission person's travel agent or airline, if you can.

» If you are still unable to locate the missing person, and you continue to have serious concerns about their safety and well-being, you should contact your own local police to file a missing persons report. This may seem like a long shot, but this action is necessary for the police to lodge a missing person report with the appropriate government department (Department of State, Department of Foreign Affairs, etc.). You will need to have collated all known details before submitting this report, such as passport number, photographs, travel plans, last contact, and other information.

» You need to be aware that most government departments, such as the Department of State, will only pursue inquiries that are based on a serious concern for the welfare of their citizens overseas and a belief that the person concerned needs consular assistance.

BASIC GUIDELINES

Most people reported missing are just folks who have forgotten to check in while traveling, but unfortunately there are too many cases where people genuinely are missing.

Make sure you take the time to "know before you go" about rules in another country. Being unaware of the local rules and customs can lead to being arrested; for example in some countries you cannot take photographs of military installations or even government buildings. Inappropriate dress, particularly for women can result in detention, or in some places even a pocket knife is considered a weapon.

If the worst happens, there are some important things to remember when you begin trying to locate a person in a foreign country:

- Remain calm. Most missing persons are found safe and well.

- Gather as much information as possible from your inquiries.

- Maintain a record of all the information you gather so you can provide comprehensive details, if required, to others assisting in locating the person.

- Contact INTERPOL which is the world's largest international police organization with 188 member countries. It facilitates cross-border police cooperation. http://www.interpol.int/.

- The International Red Cross/Red Crescent global tracing network may be able to assist. These organizations have a solid reputation for operating in more than 185 countries to re-establish contact between relatives separated as a result of a number of causes including war, internal conflict, or natural disaster. The service is provided free of charge to the public. More details of the work done by ICRC can be found at http://www.icrc.org/eng/.

- The International Social Service (ISS) traces immediate family members who are separated by an international border in conjunction with its social work across 150 countries. It often requests a contribution toward costs for this work. Further information and contact details are available on the International Social Service network (http://www.iss-ssi.org). ISS has websites for different countries too, for example the ISS USA website is http://www.iss-usa.org/.

- There are many private security firms operating around the globe—and some of these firms have very well connected, experienced, and capable security professionals working in their overseas offices, many of whom are former police, government, or military officials. These firms charge for their services, and although most of them are not cheap, in many cases they are able to offer direct access to sources unavailable to you in the country of concern. You will need to do some research to find the firm that is right for your needs, as many of these firms have stronger presences in some countries than others, but their networks of operators are often far-reaching. Major international corporations operating in a city/country are often the best source for information about credible private security firms offering services related to missing persons. By contacting the security director of any international corporation in the location where the person went missing you will generally get the information you need about the firm that has the strongest presence or best capabilities in that country. There are too many private security firms to list here, but, some of the better known international private security firms that should be able to steer you in the right direction include:

USEFUL WEB SITES

Control Risks:
https://www.controlrisks.com/

Pinkerton:
http://www.pinkerton.com/

Olive Group:
http://www.olivegroup.com

Hill & Associates:
http://www.hill-assoc.com/

Academi:
http://academi.com/

Andrews International:
http://www.andrewsinternational.com/

Unity Resources Group:
http://www.unityresourcesgroup.com/

Scan for more resources.

MOTION SICKNESS
Cars, Boats, & Planes

You frequently get motion sickness from the car.
Now your husband wants to go on a cruise, but you're
concerned you'll get seasick. What can you do about it?

With vacation travel, a common concern is motion sickness. Whether it is called sea sickness, car sickness, or results from an airplane or train ride, the problem is really the same. The good news is that most cruise ships are very large, so the rocking motion is minimal, and in good weather very few people become seasick.

KEY POINTS

» The body has several mechanisms to sense motion and position—the eyes, ears, and proprioceptors which send information about position (in muscles, joints, skin).

» Eyes send visual clues to the brain related to a reference point, such as the horizon, to determine motion.

» The inner ear vestibular system also recognizes motion—semi-circular canals detect rotation and the otolith organs recognize vertical movement.

» The skin, joints, and other tissues recognize miniscule changes in pressure, such as the increased pressure on muscles to keep balance when a ship is rocking back and forth.

» Ideally, each of these sensors sends the same signal to the brain. Trouble arises when the messages are different.

» A common cause of motion sickness is reading a book in a car. Sickness results because the ears and proprioceptors detect motion, but the eyes focus on the book and do not sense motion. This conflict of signals sets off the chain reaction of motion sickness symptoms.

» Similarly, on a boat one may feel fine on deck where the body's cues are consistent—the eyes, ears, and proprioceptors sense the same motion. However, if you go below deck where there are no visual cues about motion, but the inner ear and proprioceptors continue to sense motion, sickness can result.

» Motion sickness affects the most experienced sailors in the roughest seas. Astronauts are also affected by it, and the Space Shuttle's zero-gravity toilet has a special setting for "vomit."

» Motion sickness can also result from watching a movie. The eyes sense motion but the ears and proprioceptors do not. This rarely happens if the same movie is on a small screen television because the eyes can also sense that the room around the screen is not moving.

BASIC SYMPTOMS AND MANAGEMENT GUIDELINES

- Motion sickness includes fairly predictable symptoms. First, is slight nausea. This may be accompanied by a cold sweat, flushing, or drop in blood pressure, and general fatigue. Vomiting is the usual last step. The vomiting of motion sickness does not relieve the symptoms, which differs from most other causes of vomiting.

- Behaviors as well as medications can prevent motion sickness. The goal of behavioral approaches is to assure all signals going to the brain about the body's motion and position are sending the same message. In a car, sitting in the front seat so you can see the horizon often helps. Being the driver, so that you can even feel the slight maneuvers in the steering wheel helps even more. In an airplane, the window seats in front of the wings are best—they have the least motion and also allow one to look outside. In a boat or ship, the least motion is generally in the middle of the ship at the water level. The more expensive outer berths with portholes may actually have more motion.

- Just being distracted from the nauseous feelings can help.

- Medications can prevent, but not treat, motion sickness. Use them before you get sick for best effect. Both oral medications and patches are available, with and without prescription. Few medications are safe for children. Talk with your doctor before you leave on your trip to make the best medication choice.

- Take the medication BEFORE you embark. Once motion sickness starts, the medication is less effective.

- General medications to prevent vomiting are usually ineffective for motion sickness.

Scan for more resources.

NOSEBLEED (EPISTAXIS)
Troublesome Hemorrhage

You are traveling overseas in an arid climate and your allergies are acting up, causing you to sneeze repeatedly. Suddenly, you start to have a nosebleed, something you have had before but this time it will not stop. You take a daily aspirin upon advice from your doctor. What should you do?

Nosebleeds (epistaxis) are relatively common but most times can be controlled without seeking further medical attention. Environmental conditions like low humidity, cold, and high altitude can precipitate nosebleeds. Nosebleeds certainly occur with trauma to the nasal area and also can be associated with infections.

KEY POINTS

» Nosebleeds are classified as anterior or posterior depending on the site of bleeding. Anterior nosebleeds originate from the lining of the nostrils and are by far the more common and are more easily managed. Blood typically drains out from the nostrils.

» Posterior nosebleeds are characterized by blood draining back into the throat causing coughing, swallowing of blood, and possibly choking or vomiting. Posterior bleeds are more difficult to control and anyone with a posterior nosebleed usually needs to be evacuated.

» Medications that interfere with blood coagulation can contribute to the occurrence and severity of nosebleeds. The most common of these are aspirin and anticoagulants like warfarin (Coumadin). Chronic use of non-steroidal anti-inflammatory medication (NSAIDS) like ibuprofen or naproxen is also associated with delayed coagulation and increased risk of nosebleed.

» Nosebleeds can be a sign of high blood pressure that has risen out of control. This is a medical emergency.

BASIC TREATMENT GUIDELINES

- Help prevent nosebleeds by lubricating (with Vaseline) the inside of the nose in dry climates or at high altitude. Nasal saline drops are also useful for lubrication. Do not use vaso-constrictive nose drops because vasodilation after stopping the drops can cause bleeding to start again.

- If you have high blood pressure, make sure it is under control before departure.

- For anterior nosebleeds, start by having the victim sit up and firmly press the nostrils together for about 15 minutes; then release to check if bleeding has stopped. If not, pack both nostrils with gauze if available or else use toilet tissue or other clean tissue. Pack tightly and hold the nostrils for another 15 minutes and gently remove. If the nose is still bleeding, repack the nostrils and leave for a couple of hours before attempting gentle removal. Packing can be preceded by application of a nasal spray (Afrin or Neo-Synephrine) that causes vasoconstriction.

- Persons with suspected posterior nosebleeds need to be evacuated. These are very difficult to treat without medical assistance. However, if evacuation is delayed and there is a Foley urinary balloon catheter in the medical kit, the catheter can be inserted into the posterior nasal chamber after lubrication. Inflate the balloon with 10 to 15 ml of saline or water and gently pull forward so that the balloon locks into place. The catheter can be taped in place. The pressure from the balloon will help stop bleeding. Leave it in place until medical assistance is available.

- Reversal of anticoagulant medications is not easy and should only be attempted under guidance of medical personnel. Aspirin and NSAIDS cannot be reversed. However, direct pressure often will work despite anti-coagulation, it will just take longer.

Scan for more resources.

NUTRITION
An Often Unrecognized Need

*You have business travel in Hanoi and several key meetings
are planned in the first few days. You want to be prepared
to eat with you dinner guests but remember your last travel
to Asia was not at all pleasant when it came to food.
While many people complain about having traveler's diarrhea,
you had the opposite problem. Furthermore, it made you
lethargic. You know you need to be alert for these meetings.
You want to ensure you eat right and stay focused.*

Travel is very disruptive to good nutrition. Certainly you have to consider how you avoid picking up food-borne illnesses but your travel diet and nutritional needs are not simply the avoidance of traveler's diarrhea. Keeping in mind a few basic tips can help keep you at your maximum performance even under the stress of jet lag.

KEY POINTS

» When you travel your body is thrown into a circadian clock stress. Your body expects certain kinds of foods (and perhaps caffeine) at certain times of day. When you move into a new time zone your system takes time to adapt. Understanding this is the first step in staying healthy and maintaining a high level of nutritional fitness.

» Another stress that creeps into long distance travel is dehydration. Long flights not only draw water out of you but also cause you to redistribute your water and eventually cause swelling of the hands and feet. Water transits from the gut and therefore constipation is another unpleasant side effect of this type of travel. Maintaining good hydration and avoiding alcohol on long flights is very important to helping prevent this frequent traveler's scourge. Nutritional requirements change for more strenuous activity such as on adventure travel or an expedition. Calculation of caloric requirements are very important to maintain health and morale under stress. The resting energy expenditure for a 100 kg male is approximately 2000 calories and 1400 calories for a 60 kg female. To estimate caloric needs, use the World Health Organization multipliers of 1.8 for moderate activity, 2.2 for vigorous activity, and 3.5 for extremely strenuous activity. So for the man in this example hiking in the mountains (vigorous activity), daily caloric requirements would be about 4400. The requirement would vary each day depending on level of activity. This type of calculation can help you prepare for remote and strenuous trips.

BASIC GUIDELINES

Part of the great joys of travel is being able to partake of the culture including the rich variety of cuisines. Here are a few tips:

- Beware of travel cravings. Particularly on long plane trips. The combination of boredom of air travel along with carbohydrate cravings caused by jet lag can drive even the healthiest of eaters to become junk food junkies. If you have to satisfy those cravings, eating dried fruit and nuts is your most nutritious option. Granola bars are also a good snack option providing energy and much needed fiber.

- Try to eat more frequent, but smaller, meals over the course of the day. That can help prevent the possibility of a travel-related hypoglycemia event (most typically happening around 3 a.m. of your home time). Eating small light meals through the day will help stabilize blood levels of nutrients and ease the absorption in your GI tract suffering the stress of travel. Wheat crackers and peanut butter are a great backup snack combination that is easy to digest and gives balanced energy.

- In many parts of the world, frying or broiling of foods is the best way to reduce the chance of ingesting a food-borne pathogen. You have to be careful, however, about the fat content. This is not just because fried foods are not heart healthy but because foods rich in fats delay GI transit. Eat fried foods in moderation.

- Depending on the region of the world, vegetables can carry disease-causing bacteria. In many developing countries, "night soil" (human feces) is used as fertilizer. If you are traveling to one of these countries beware. Even the most innocuous looking salad can be trouble, even in fancier hotels. Check out the food safety profile on the CDC website (http://www.cdc.gov/foodsafety/).

- Soup is a great meal to have while traveling because the process of boiling reduces the likelihood of transmission of diseases and soups contain much-needed water along with meat, carbohydrates, and vegetables. Soups are also a very social dish across many cultures.

- Jerky is by design a travel food rich in protein. It can also be loaded with sodium. Jerky makes a good backup food to have stashed away when no ready sources of prepared protein nutrition are available. Low sodium varieties of jerky are available.

- Carbonated and caffeinated beverages. The idea that caffeinated and carbonated beverages dehydrate you is a myth. Both the boiling of coffee and the carbonation of water have benefits in making liquids unfavorable to bacteria (boiling far more so than carbonation). It is okay to drink these while traveling. Just be aware that caffeinated drinks can work against your ability to adapt quickly to a new time zone. Be judicious. Also, avoid ice unless you are absolutely certain that it is from a clean water source. If in doubt, then just don't use it.

- Most medical professionals will say that vitamin supplements are probably not needed for those who eat a normal healthy diet. Travel and expeditions, however, are not necessarily periods where balanced nutrition is always guaranteed, it is therefore prudent to consider packing vitamin supplements that balance out your nutrition.

- Food is not simply nutrition, but it is also part of any culture. If invited to share a meal at a person's home, strongly consider this over hotel fare. Fancy hotels in developing countries may have sparkling dining areas but the kitchens in the back are often another story. In general, eating at a private residence poses a much lower risk as fewer hands come in contact with the food and the utensils and at least you will have an opportunity to see the hygiene practices up close to decide if you need to take a prophylactic antibiotic. Remember to eat hot foods hot and cold foods cold.

Scan for more resources.

ORTHOPEDIC INJURIES
Fractures, Sprains, & Dislocations

You are on a hike on a steep wilderness trail and come upon another hiker injured in a fall. What can you do in a remote area without having medical training?

Trauma that involves bones and joints is often dramatic, emotional, and painful. Although some fractures and dislocations are obvious, often the presence and extent of fractures cannot be known without imaging (x-rays, ultrasound). Proper assessment, stabilization, and initial treatment of the victim are very important to limit damage and to salvage limb function. Even with diagnostic limitations, basic first aid and care can be administered if you come across the scene of an accident.

KEY POINTS

A sprain is an injury in a joint where the ligament has been stretched beyond its capacity. If the muscle is torn by the same action, it is termed a strain. A fracture is a break in the bone and is simple or complex (multiple fractures), open or closed depending on skin integrity, non-displaced if still in alignment or displaced if alignment is disrupted.

» The first consideration is to assure your safety and that of other rescuers before approaching the victim. Do not assume the site is safe. It is a natural tendency to rush to the victim but an unstable debris field, electric lines that are down, potential combustion of fuel at a crash site, and other hazards must be recognized.

» As soon as you are with the victim, assess the ABCs—airway, breathing, circulation. If the victim can talk to you relatively normally, it is likely that the airway and breathing are adequate. If not, you must assess those functions and take appropriate action.

» Next, look for any active signs of bleeding or shock. Remember that pelvic and thigh crush injuries can result in a great deal of hidden blood loss.

» Last, evaluate neurologic damage by checking for level of consciousness, movement and sensation in all limbs, and pupil response to light.

» If the victim is stable, evaluation of orthopedic injuries should proceed with particular attention to the skull, spine, and pelvis. Layers of clothing and a harsh environment may make evaluation more difficult.

» Do not move the victim except in a life-threatening situation until it is determined that movement will not worsen the injuries.

» Evaluation for head injury includes determining if the victim lost consciousness, examining the scalp for lacerations and deformities, and determining that the pupils react equally to a light source.

» Without rotating the neck, the cervical (neck) spine should be felt for point tenderness, swelling, or a deformity. Any suspected neck injury requires immobilization before movement.

» Next, while maintaining spinal alignment, the back should be inspected for point tenderness or deformity.

» A pelvic fracture or dislocation can be determined by visual inspection and placing gentle pressure on the hips.

» Extremities are then assessed for circulatory, nerve, bone, and joint function. It is important to note if the injury to the extremity is open or closed.

» Another important aspect is whether a joint is involved. If you can feel pulses beyond the site of injury and the skin color is normal, there is likely adequate circulation.

» Normal movement and sensation beyond the injury site suggests normal nerve function.

» Joint involvement and open injuries are very serious and rapid evacuation is advised. Gentle traction and repositioning of the limb with splinting offers the best chance for recovery in cases of suspected fractures.

BASIC TREATMENT GUIDELINES

Specific treatment for significant orthopedic injuries is beyond the scope of this text and the expertise of the likely reader. Maneuvers to reduce dislocations and fractures require knowledge about diagnosis and practice of technique and should not be undertaken by the inexperienced. However, there are general treatment principles that you can undertake to aid the victim while awaiting more sophisticated assistance and evacuation.

- Orthopedic injuries may cause very severe pain and pain control is an important part of management. Injectable opioid pain medication is probably unavailable, but oral opioids can and should be considered. However, victims with head injuries may not be able to swallow and there is risk of aspiration into the lungs from vomiting. Opioids may also alter consciousness and mask deteriorating mental function that signifies a worsening injury.
- Cleansing an open wound greatly reduces the risk of infection. High-pressure irrigation using a syringe with tap water helps remove bacteria, foreign substances, and contaminants. Washing the wound with soap and water is effective in the field. Avoid using peroxide, betadyne, or chlorhexidine on the wound because these liquids may damage tissues and impair wound healing (see Lacerations).
- Initial treatment of soft tissue injuries of the extremities such as sprains and strains requires the application of RICE—the acronym for Rest, Ice, Compression, and Elevation. Rest and protect the injured area, apply ice or cold to reduce swelling and pain. Gentle compression and elevation reduce swelling. Make sure the compression does not compromise circulation.
- Broad spectrum antibiotics are indicated for any open wound associated with an orthopedic or joint injury.
- Immobilize the fracture or dislocation as well as the joints above and below the injury. Elevate the extremity if possible.
- Rapid evacuation is advised for any significant orthopedic injuries particularly those with open wounds, joint involvement, head or spine trauma.

Scan for more resources.

PEDIATRICS
Travel Health & Safety for Children

We are going on a vacation to a remote beach resort and want to take our two children—ages 6 months and 5 years old. What extra planning should we do?

Healthy infants and children of all ages should be able to travel to all parts of the world—remember children are born and raised everywhere. However, in many areas, the resources are not the same as in a highly developed country. Extra planning is a good idea, especially on a trip to an isolated area or on an extended trip.

KEY POINTS

» First, think about the demands of the trip, any underlying health conditions your child may have, and new health issues that may result from the proposed travel.

» Make a list of your questions and concerns to address with your pediatrician. In general, if your child has certain medical problems at home, they are likely to have these on vacation.

» Changes in food, water, and daily activities also increase the frequency of other problems, such as vomiting and diarrhea.

BASIC GUIDELINES

• Now might be the time to take a pediatric first aid course. This will provide you with basic knowledge to manage various situations that may arise on the trip. Learn to recognize true medical emergencies. Learn how to treat the most common travel illnesses in children, especially diarrhea, vomiting, and respiratory problems.

• As with adults, bring along a basic first aid kit to treat simple scrapes and cuts (see Personal Travel Medical Kits) If traveling to a remote or isolated place where basic supplies may not be available, include:

- Diapers and wipes
- Baby food and formula for flights—check current rules for bringing on airplane
- Baby food and formula for duration of travel (may need to pack in checked baggage)
- For formula—what type of bottle? Disposable?
- Appropriate clothing: Hat for sun protection; sweater or light jacket—infants and young children are more sensitive to cold, including air conditioning; airplanes can be very cold; lightweight long-sleeved shirt and pants for sun protection; two pairs of comfortable shoes that fit—shoes the child has "broken in"; sunglasses.
- Stroller if the child is young; balance size and portability when choosing the stroller and one with an overhead sunshade can be helpful.
- Toys, books, and games to occupy the child during the trip, especially with long air flights.

- Supplies to treat simple scrapes and cuts should be in your routine adult first aid kit. In addition to standard items, include commonly used pediatric medications and supplies, such as an ear thermometer; sunscreen that can be used for infants and young children; insect repellent that can be used in infants and young children; Pedialyte or other electrolyte solution for diarrhea; Tylenol (acetaminophen) in children's doses for fever; pediatric anti-histamine if your child is congested or has earaches. This helps with discomfort while flying.

- Discuss any concerns with your pediatrician.

- Make certain all childhood vaccines are current—measles, mumps, rubella, diphtheria, pertussis, tetanus, hepatitis A, hepatitis B, chicken pox, Haemophilus influenza B (Hib), pneumococcal, rotavirus, and polio. Depending where in the world you travel, these diseases are public health concerns and your child could be infected.

- Older children may require additional vaccinations. Remember, as parents, your adult vaccines need to be current as well. Find out if additional vaccinations are indicated for the geographic location of your travel.

- Discuss malaria prophylaxis if traveling to a malaria area.

- Bring an injectable epinephrine (e.g., Epi-pen) for insect stings and other serious allergic reactions (see Insect Bites).

- Bring prescriptions for any regularly taken medications, for at least 2 weeks longer than the scheduled trip return date in case your trip is unexpectedly extended.

- Find out if your regular medical insurance covers care outside the United States. Consider travel and medical evacuation insurance. See if your physician or health insurance company has a health line you can call with questions during your trip.

- Discuss management if your child has a recurrent illness, such as ear infections, while traveling and whether you should bring additional medication. Understand the signs and symptoms that make it necessary to see a local physician while traveling.

- When you first arrive at your destination, it is a good idea to find out whether the hotel has a physician on call, and what options there are for local medical resources if treatment is needed. Find out if there are local providers who were trained in the United States or who speak English.

- If your child develops health issues while traveling, manage them as you would at home. If a physician visit is needed, work with your hotel or others to identify the most appropriate local provider. If you have travel or medical evacuation insurance, consider calling them for a local referral.

Scan for more resources.

PERSONAL TRAVEL MEDICAL KIT
Don't Leave Home Without It

You are on an extended trip and develop a reddish rash and irritation in the groin area because of the constant humidity. The pharmacy at your location is closed when you arrive in the late afternoon. You sure wish you had something to treat the rash.

It is advisable for all travelers to carry some essential medications for common problems that occur during travel. Do not presume that your trip leader will have extra medication for you or that you can purchase over-the-counter or prescription medications at your destination. Do not depend on a medical officer on the trip or fellow traveler for your needs, they likely have limited supplies. Even if present at your destination, pharmacies have limited hours of operation.

This information is intended as a guideline for advice about what to take with you. You need to decide what is important for your travel needs.

KEY POINTS

» Always carry medications in their original containers, in your carry-on luggage. Remember that all liquids and gels must be less than 3 oz. and be in a ziplock bag to get through airport security.

» If you are traveling with a group, it is likely that other members on the trip who may get sick will ask you for medication. You may consider bringing some extra medication in case that occurs. Do not share prescription medications unless it is determined that they are safe and appropriate for that person.

» Carry personal prescription medications (include the generic names for medications and dose). A note should be carried from the prescribing physician on letterhead stationary for controlled substances and injectable medications. Extra prescription medication is highly recommended in case your trip is delayed or extended.

BASIC MEDICATIONS

- Include necessary prophylactic medications for the specific trip such as for malaria if required.

- Carry antidiarrheal medication, such as loperamide (sold as Imodium) which is available without prescription.

- Ask your physician to prescribe an antibiotic for self-treatment of moderate to severe diarrhea or other infections. A broad-spectrum antibiotic that can be used for diarrhea, skin and respiratory infections is recommended. It is optional to also bring metronidazole which treats non-bacterial diarrhea caused by Giardia and Entamoeba species. Suspect non-bacterial diarrhea if the symptoms are not markedly better within 12 hours. Both of these require a prescription. Make sure you understand the indications, correct dosage, and duration for use of these medications.

- Bring an antihistamine for allergies or nasal congestion.

- Pack a decongestant, alone or in combination with antihistamine.

- Antimotion sickness medication should be included if you are susceptible and will be in a situation where motion could affect you.

- Acetaminophen or aspirin for fever is recommended.

- Ibuprofen for pain and Tylenol with codeine for strong pain (this requires a prescription and is a controlled substance because of codeine content) are both useful for a variety of problems.

- Cough suppressant/expectorant medicines may prove useful, but liquid restrictions on flights may prevent you from bringing more than 90 ml (3 oz.).

- Throat lozenges are often useful.

- Antacids are suggested for people with recurring heartburn or indigestion.

- Hydrocortisone cream should be in your kit to relieve itching.
- Bacitracin ointment or similar antibacterial cream is advised.
- Antifungal cream is important to bring.

Scan for more
resources.

PERSONAL TRAVEL SUPPLIES
Suggested Travel Companions

You are in a rustic cabana in a rainforest lodge and the bathroom is outside down a narrow path. You know snakes and scorpions come out at night. Flashlights are provided but the batteries in yours are weak.

It is advisable to bring supplies that you need with you when you travel. Your personal travel kit should be compact, light, and readily available to you so do not pack it in the bottom of a duffel bag or suitcase. This information is intended as a guideline for advice about what to take with you. You need to decide what is important for your travel needs. The following items are highly recommended.

BASIC GUIDELINES

- Band-Aids, assorted sizes
- Liquid soap
- Lip balm for sunscreen
- Sunscreen that blocks both UVA and UVB radiation
- Sunglasses and sunglass neck strap
- Hat with brim
- Insect repellent containing DEET
- Iodine tablets or ultraviolet light source and portable water filters to purify water if bottled water is not available. Filtration straws are also good.
- Flashlight, small, portable
- Head lamp

- Binoculars
- Camera
- Extra batteries for all devices
- Duct tape. Perhaps the most useful and definitely the most versatile item you can bring. It is great to cover blisters, close lacerations if you cannot get immediate medical care, hold bandages in place, create slings in case of injuries, and patch holes in your bag or tent.

Scan for more resources.

PLANE CRASH SURVIVAL
Surprising Statistics & What To Do

You are going to a remote ecological reserve in a developing country. The only land transportation is a hired taxi with an old car for a six-hour drive. There have been some reports of occasional bandits on this road of questionable condition and you know that the highest cause of injury and death in these types of countries is motor vehicle accident. You have been referred to a small local airline where a bush pilot will get you there more quickly. The weather is good. Should you take this flight?

We have all had at least passing thoughts about being in an airplane crash and chances for survival. Fortunately, statistics for U.S. commercial carriers are highly reassuring according to the U.S. National Transportation Safety Board (NTSB) statistics for U.S. commercial carriers. U.S. air carriers in 2010 logged over 17 million flight hours covering 7.3 billion miles and recorded 26 accidents with no fatalities. This represents over 9 million departures with an accident rate of 0.152 per 100,000 flight hours. Three of the last four years there have been no fatalities with over 700 million passengers on flights per year. Commercial carriers operating large capacity passenger aircraft in other major industrialized countries must follow the strictest safety regulations and their accident rate is also very low. Rare exceptions are the recent Malaysian Airlines crashes precipitated by flying over a war zone in one case and by an undetermined but probable destination change by the pilot in the other.

KEY POINTS

» The most important indicator of overall safety of an airline is how it is regulated by its national civil aviation authority. It is important to note that the fatal accident rate for commercial flight has not changed appreciably in the past 15 years. However, the number of flights performed in the world have more than doubled. Airlines from the United States, Canada, European Union, Australia, and Japan accounted for about 75 percent of all airline traffic, but only 21 percent of the fatal events.

» Smaller aircraft are not certified to the same standards as larger ones and different factors contribute to crashes. U.S. Civil aviation statistics demonstrate that in 2010 there were 1474 accidents in private planes in which 274 had fatalities, totaling 469 people.

» The most important factor contributing to a crash is improper actions or inactions by the pilot. It is estimated that pilot-related errors account for 60 percent of commercial and 70 percent of non-commercial accidents. Mechanical failures have gone way down due to modern, more reliable equipment. However, mechanical contributions must still be considered, such as in aircraft where computers will not let the pilot override the plane. Almost every crash arises from a series of small missteps or factors that add up to catastrophe.

Helicopters have an accident rate about 30 percent higher than the US general aviation accident rate. According to NTSB records, there were 197 helicopter accidents during 2005 in over 2.2 million flight hours. After pilot error, physical structures pose the greatest threat (wires are notoriously guilty) due to flight close to earth or visual flight plans. In a helicopter there is little time to react or fix mechanical problems.

SURVIVAL

Surprisingly, according to NTSB and other statistics, 86 percent of commercial airline passengers and 34 percent of commuter passengers survived crashes over the last 25 years.

• Noted experts differ on the best location to sit in a plane to survive a crash. The most often cited is the exit row but others claim the rear of the plane is best, stating that the only part of a plane you usually see intact after crash is the tail. It does not matter in a helicopter.

• The best position for survival is claimed to be the "brace" position with head pulled down to knees and arms pulled in tight with hands over head. Brace feet against a solid structure in front. Face in the direction of crash to better absorb impact.

- Wear cotton clothes, long pants, shoes, and socks.
- Read the emergency instructions.
- Count the number of seats from your seat to at least two exit rows.
- Know how to open the emergency exit.
- Leave everything behind. Do not delay. You may have minutes to get out.
- Stay low to avoid smoke.
- If the cabin is filled with smoke, you have a very short time to climb over seats and out the exit. The aisles will be filled with people screaming and trying to retrieve overhead baggage.
- Stay low exiting a heliocopter, rotary propellers may still be turning.
- Stay calm, listen to crew instructions.
- Leave the plan rapidly
- The military teaches to rendezvous 100 meters from the plane nose
- In water, put on your life vest but do not inflate until out of the plane.

Scan for more resources.

POISONS:
MEDICATIONS,
MUSHROOMS,
& CHEMICALS
Common Things To Beware Of

You are traveling with a tour group on a day trip from a large city to a rural area to see native handicrafts. The child of your companion starts to have fever and respiratory flu symptoms. Your standard medicine is back in the hotel but another traveler offers aspirin and an Asian lady has some traditional medicine she claims has been used for centuries for fever. Is it safe to give the child something or should you wait until you return to the hotel?

A long list of agents that are potential poisons surround us in our world today. Overdose of nearly every medicine can cause severe problems. Excluding poisoning resulting from recreational drugs, alcohol abuse, and willful overdose, there are common medications and compounds that can be particularly harmful if ingested in amounts above recommended doses. Beware of supplements as well as traditional medicines in other cultures which may contain toxic compounds or ones that interfere with medications taken by the traveler. Be sure you know what you are ingesting. The following are commonly encountered substances that require care.

BASIC GUIDELINES

- Acetometophin, also known as paracetamol, is used for pain relief and fever reduction throughout the world and is found in many cold and flu symptom relief compounds. Commonly used and sold without prescription, this pain medication can be dangerous if not used according to   instructions. Doses of greater than 7 grams in adults and 200 mg in children are considered toxic and can lead to liver failure and death.

- Aspirin is another common medication used for pain relief and fever reduction and should be used within recommended dose ranges. Aspirin will interfere with platelet function so coagulation may be altered if an injury occurs. Aspirin should not be given to children with suspected viral infections because it can cause liver and cerebral damage (Reye's syndrome).

- Caffeine toxicity generally presents as overstimulation of the nervous system with anxiety, increased heart rate, restlessness, insomnia, frequent urination, and rambling thought flow. Acute caffeine toxicity is usually short-lived and resolves within 24 hours. However, severe caffeine toxicity can be life-threatening. Be careful with "energy drinks".

- DEET is the most common insect repellent and because it is applied on the skin, the most commonly reported reactions to DEET are related to accidental inhalation or eye exposure. Serious side effects are very rare. Care should be taken around children to prevent inappropriate exposure, which can cause seizures in rare instances.

- Mushrooms exist throughout the world and about 20 species are considered edible. Many more species contain toxins or mind-altering substances. It is imperative that your mushrooms have been gathered by an experienced collector. Gravies and sauces are classic culprits of widespread mushroom poisoning at family and social gatherings as well as restaurants. Only eat mushrooms that have been collected by reliable hunters who can identify the edible versus toxic species.

- Environmental toxins pose an additional risk. Moderate intake and exposure to the following food groups is recommended, particularly if you do not know where they are grown, raised, or harvested. The most common environmental toxins with the likely sources in parentheses are: PCBs (farm-raised salmon), pesticides (fruits, vegetables, meat), mold and fungal toxins (peanuts), dioxins (animal fat), phthalates (plastic containers and bottles), metals like arsenic, mercury, lead, aluminum, and cadmium (fish, drinking water). However, for most short-term travelers the real risks of most environmental toxins are minimal. Other environmental toxins are in the air, particularly in large heavily polluted cities. Persons with respiratory disease should use care.

Scan for more
resources.

PREGNANCY & TRAVEL
Issues To Consider

You and your partner have scheduled trekking in Colorado. You discover you are pregnant and your trip coincides with the 14th week of pregnancy. Is it okay to be trekking in the mountains at this time or should you cancel your trip?

Women who are healthy and have a normal pregnancy are encouraged to continue a broad range of routine activities including work, travel, and exercise within reason. There are some simple precautions every pregnant woman should take to ensure that she can travel with a relative degree of safety. The advice given in this section is for low risk pregnancies. Discuss your planned trip with your pre-natal healthcare provider.

KEY POINTS

- » As a broad general rule, if you have any doubts about the safety of any activity during pregnancy you should ask your health care provider or avoid the activity.

- » Maintaining physical fitness in pregnancy is important and is protective to both the health of the mother as well as her baby.

- » Higher risk pregnancies have to be treated differently with many more precautions.

BASIC GUIDELINES

There are several changes to a woman's physiology during pregnancy that affect how she should prepare for travel, particularly to rugged or remote locations:

- Fluid management: Dehydration problems for a pregnant woman and her fetus are more acute than for the average traveler. Maintaining a normal level of hydration is important to prevent cramps, contractions, light-headedness, and exhaustion. It is also important because it helps to maintain normal core body temperature. This is particularly important during the first trimester.

- Temperature management: Wearing layers to shed in remote outdoor activities helps in thermal management. This is particularly important for pregnant women, especially in the first trimester, because excessively high core body temperatures can actually harm the growth and development of a fetus. This is why a pregnant woman should NEVER use a sauna or hot tub in the first trimester.

- Center of gravity shifts: As the pregnancy progresses, the center of gravity shifts often leaving a normally nimble individual feeling uncoordinated. This can make a pregnant woman more prone to stumbles and falls. Some women advocate using poles for stability when on uneven trails, particularly later in pregnancy. Falls can lead to miscarriage or pre-term birth.

- Laxity of joints: Hormones released by the placenta soften joints (presumably to allow the pelvic bones to have greater flexibility during childbirth) and as a result pregnant women are at greater risk of soft tissue injury.

- As a general rule, pregnant women should carry less weight if taking packs.

- Snacks: Pregnant women are at greater risk of hypoglycemia. Having readily available health snacks can prevent this. Eating several small meals a day is better than one larger meal.

- Frequent urination: Pregnant women need to take breaks to urinate more often than non-pregnant women. Plan accordingly.

- Altitude: It is all about acclimatization. Pregnant women should check with their physician before planning high altitude activities. There are women who live above 8,000 ft (2,500 M) who have normal healthy pregnancies. Women who live in lowlands should be cautious when trekking at high altitudes and use very conservative ascent profiles providing plenty of opportunity to acclimatize or avoid the high altitude. It is generally advised that pregnant women not take altitude sickness prophylaxis like Acetazolamide but instead go to lower altitudes if any symptoms of altitude illness arise.

- Predisposition to sunburn: Pregnant women sunburn more easily due to hormone related changes in skin sensitivity. Always bring and use sunscreen and protective clothing in sunburn risk activities.

- Foodborne illnesses: There are many travel locations where food safety is not a trivial issue. If you are traveling to a location where food safety is an issue, particularly if parasites or bacterial contamination are known problems in the food supply, then it may be prudent to put off the trip until after safely completing your pregnancy.

- Other infectious diseases. In choosing your travel destinations, and planning your itinerary, consider other infectious disease risks. Some infectious diseases can have significant effects on the unborn baby.

- As you plan your travels, especially extended trips, consider available medical facilities should you have an obstetrical emergency such as sudden profuse bleeding. Know where the most competent medical care is, and how to get access.

Pregnancy is a normal and natural condition and is not a time to suspend many enjoyable physical activities. However, it is a time to be careful and prudent about risk. Many pregnant women can enjoy even remote travel under the right conditions and with the right preparation. Any extended travel, travel requiring any extra exertion, travel to remote areas, travel with other risks, or travel late in pregnancy should be discussed with the pre-natal healthcare provider.

Scan for more resources.

RABIES
Beware of The Dog ...& Other Animals

You have been asked to go on a charitable mission to help those in a low socioeconomic rural area in a developing country following a natural disaster. The nearest medical resource is a clinic fifty miles away. Do you need to worry about rabies?

Rabies is a fatal viral disease transmitted in the saliva of infected animals. Rabies can infect any mammal. In many areas throughout the world, dogs are the most important reservoir. However, both domestic animals (such as cattle and cats) as well as wild animals (such as raccoons, skunks, bats, foxes, and coyotes) can carry rabies.

KEY POINTS

» Rabies is vaccine-preventable.

» Potential exposure to rabies may vary with the location and activity.

» Rabies vaccination is typically reserved for professionals who have a significant risk such as constant exposure to wild animals.

» International travelers with itineraries that include rural areas may also consider vaccination because quality post-exposure vaccination may be difficult to obtain.

» Cave explorers have a significant risk of bat exposure and should consider receiving a rabies vaccination.

» Rabies vaccine may be difficult to obtain and is expensive.

» Vaccination requires three injections over a few weeks.

» Beware of locally produced vaccine if traveling, it may have been derived by different lab processes that make the vaccine less effective with greater risk of side effects.

» Mixing types and brands of vaccine is not recommended except in emergencies.

BASIC GUIDELINES

- Avoid animals in rural villages or unfamiliar locations, particularly in developing countries.

- Remember that everything bites, avoid close contact with stray and wild animals in both rural and urban areas.

- Children are particularly vulnerable. Nearly 40 percent of post-exposure vaccinations are given to children.

- Those planning activities with higher risk of exposure should consider vaccination.

- The incubation period for the rabies virus usually is between 3 and 8 weeks but symptoms may occur months after a bite due to the location of the animal bite.

- Be aware of flu-like symptoms such as fever, headache, and fatigue that progress to gastrointestinal, respiratory, and neurological symptoms.

- These symptoms transition to stages of either hyperactivity and delirium or paralysis and then to coma, and death from respiratory failure.

- Prevention pre-and post-exposure is key to avoid this disease which is fatal if untreated. If potentially exposed, get immediate medical care and the appropriate post-exposure therapy.

- Exposure after vaccination will require two doses of vaccine three days apart. If no pre-exposure vaccine was given, a series of five doses on a strict schedule over four weeks is required along with rabies immune globulin.

- Post exposure vaccine should be given as quickly as possible after the bite.

- Every effort should be maintained, even during a medical evacuation, to obtain the same type of vaccine to assure a complete immune response. Write down the type of vaccine given.

Scan for more resources.

RAPE & SEXUAL ASSAULT
Key Points To Consider

Sally had saved for months to pay for her Caribbean cruise. She was going with 5 of her close friends, 2 guys and 3 girls. They had all gone to school together, then lived and worked close by each other for the subsequent few years.

On the first evening of the cruise, after a day of steady but not crazy drinking, Sally was the first to retire for the night and go to bed. She awoke a few hours later when she heard her two male friends enter her cabin. They were intoxicated, one of them clamped his hand against her mouth while the other held her down. Sally was frozen with fear. These two guys, who she had known all her life, were now on top of her and undressing her. She thought she must be dreaming, but soon realized she was not...it was real...

Rape and sexual assault are among the most heinous and debilitating crimes that a person can experience. Unfortunately the prevalence of these crimes in almost every country far exceeds the number of cases that are reported and prosecuted. Rape and sexual assault can happen any time, at any place, and to anyone—and it is not only females who are victims of these monstrous crimes. Nor are these crimes perpetrated only by anonymous violent criminals; most rapes involve people who know each other.

This brief section is intended to help you minimize the likelihood of becoming a victim and offers some advice if you have become a victim. Although these guidelines are biased toward offering advice to women, they can and should be applied to men and boys equally.

KEY POINTS

» Be observant of your surroundings.

» Take active responsibility for your own safety and avoid situations that put you at risk.

» Be aware and suspicious, and trust your instincts.

» Rape is an act of violence with domination a key factor.

» Rape often occurs between acquaintances or on dates as well.

» Known victims have ranged in age from 6 months to 90 years.

» Most rapists are between 16 and 24 years old.

» Since so few rapists are convicted, they tend to repeat their actions.

» Rapes are often planned but the victim is left to chance.

» Most rapes occur in the victim's home.

» Most rapes occur between 8 p.m. and 2 a.m. and more frequently on weekends.

» Most often a victim caught off-guard is probably less able to fend off the attacker.

» If a victim does not want to identify herself to the police, in the US she can anonymously give a description of the attacker and details of the assault.

» Intoxication with alcohol or drugs puts one at increased risk for rape and sexual assault.

» The victim should have a physical exam as soon as possible, preferably in an emergency room or clinic with expertise and supplies for collecting specimens for both medical and forensic purposes.

» Most rapes are not reported to the police.

BASIC GUIDELINES

- Be situationally aware.

- Avoid establishing routines, particularly those that involve you alone.

- Make noise if you feel threatened, don't be afraid to draw attention to your situation. Some people carry a whistle to make noise if threatened.

- Jog or walk toward oncoming traffic. Don't jog or walk alone in places that you are unfamiliar with.

- Wait for public transport in well-lit, busy areas. Plan your route. Sit near the driver or conductor.

- In bars or at parties, keep your eyes on your drink at all times. Do not allow anyone to add anything to your drink.

- Avoid higher risk environments when possible.

- Consider hotel and transport options carefully.

- Avoid being alone, especially at night—consider use of chaperones.

- Know your environment and be prepared to deal with an emergency.

- Have emergency speed dial numbers on your mobile phone.

- Learn a basic knowledge of release techniques.

- Consider carrying a whistle with keys plus personal alarm/spray (for use only when it is certain sexual assault is the intent—use judgment, as this may cause the attacker to become violent). If used, make certain that you will not be a victim of the spray.

- Avoid excessive use of alcohol and drugs—especially in new, strange environments.

- Ensure someone knows where you are all the time, especially at night.

- Do not wear earphones while walking or jogging—or if you must, keep the volume down so you can hear the sound of a spoken voice.

- Walk with purpose and radiate confidence.

- If you think you are being followed, switch directions or enter a shop/restaurant.

- Be smart about active resistance (shouting, running away, self-defense, use of weapons, any type of physical force). Run away from the situation if possible. Shouting will draw unwanted attention to the attacker. However, using a weapon may anger the attacker even more and intensify the level of violence used against you unless you are successful. Use your judgment.

- Passive resistance (anything that ruins the attacker's desire to have sexual contact) may also abort an attack. Do or say anything to deter attacker from continuing with attack. Vomit? Spit? Swear?

- Non-resistance (submitting) is an option when the victim is in danger of losing his or her life. Compliance is not consent. The objective is to survive.

Scan for more resources.

RESPIRATORY DISORDERS
Asthma, Blood Clots, & Infections

I'm traveling to the far east as an exchange student, and my mother is worried about the various types of dangerous flu there—bird flu, swine flu. I will be going through a Middle-Eastern airport, and now there is MERS (Mid-Eastern Respiratory Syndrome). Is my mother unnecessarily worried or should I be concerned about these?

The risk to the average healthy traveler of getting one of the more dangerous flu strains is extremely low, unless there are current international travel warnings about travel to a particular area (see the U.S. Department of State website). Always heed these travel warnings. Also, follow the usual precautions to reduce transmission of any respiratory disease.

However, seasonal flu is always a risk, especially during the flu seasons which differ in northern and southern hemispheres. If traveling during a flu season, be sure to get a flu shot before you leave. The northern and southern hemispheres usually have different strains of seasonal flu, and thus the flu vaccines vary. If traveling to another hemisphere, getting the flu shots for both hemispheres may be warranted depending upon the length of travel, your activities, and the impact flu may have on your travel objective. Usually only the vaccine for the hemisphere you are in is available, so you may have to get the second vaccination during your travels. However, be very careful to avoid situations with any chance of reuse of needles or syringes, and contaminated multi-dose vials of vaccines. In some cases, the risks of vaccination can exceed the risk of a case of seasonal flu.

KEY POINTS

» A healthy respiratory system is key to adventure travel, no matter what the activity—hiking, climbing, cycling, swimming, skiing, or other activity. A person breathes about 25,000 times a day to take in oxygen and release carbon dioxide—key processes for our metabolism.

» Diseases of the respiratory system can be divided into acute and chronic. Most acute respiratory diseases are caused by infectious agents, usually viruses. Fortunately most resolve within a week or so in healthy people.

» Travelers on long airplane fights and other situations where they are immobile for long periods are at risk for a pulmonary embolism. A blood clot can develop in the legs from the immobility, break off and move to the lungs, and block a blood vessel. The person experiences shortness of breath with low oxygen levels. You can test the blood oxygen levels with a pulseoximeter, which should be in the first aid kit. A pulmonary embolism is a serious and potentially fatal medical emergency requiring immediate medical intervention (see Deep Vein Thrombosis).

» Many chronic respiratory diseases are serious, but the normal traveler is at no increased risk for them, for example, lung cancer, emphysema, and cystic fibroses. However, if you have one of these diseases, travel to areas with highly polluted air can compromise your breathing and lead to a serious exacerbation of symptoms. Persons with a history of asthma should be especially careful, and talk with their health care provider before traveling to determine the best management for an acute asthmatic attack should it occur in an isolated area distant from medical care. Travelers with this condition need to bring their own medication and it is wise to bring an extra amount in case of trip delays or voluntary extension.

» Tuberculosis (TB) is a common disease in many parts of the world, and a traveler in close contact with infected persons is at risk. Travelers to high-risk countries, particularly sub-Saharan Africa and Southeast Asia, are more likely to be exposed to TB. Although TB can present in almost any organ system, respiratory problems are the most likely and well known. Symptoms may take weeks to many months to develop. If you are concerned that you may have been exposed, consider getting a simple skin test, PPD, after you return home. However, if you have ever tested positive for TB, or had a positive PPD, other screening such as a chest x-ray is should be done instead. Consult your physician if you think you have been exposed to TB (see Fever).

» Other unusual infectious respiratory diseases are more common in specific geographical areas though the individual risk for these diseases is usually low. For example, the fungal infection coccidiodomycosis, also known as San Joaquin Valley Fever, is a greater risk to people in parts of the southeast United States than other areas. Reporting your travel history to your medical provider is important if you get sick on your return home.

Scan for more
resources.

ROAD SAFETY FOR DRIVERS & PEDESTRIANS
The Most Dangerous Game

While traveling on holiday in Bali, a tourist was critically injured when the motor scooter he was riding was hit by a pickup truck. His condition required immediate surgery in a local hospital, which was inadequately equipped to deal with the nature of his injures. Because he did not have travel and medical evacuation insurance, his family had to quickly raise more than $100,000 to have him transported home.

Every year, approximately 1.5 million people die on the world's roads and, according to the World Health Organization, between 20 and 50 million sustain non-fatal injuries and permanent disabilities. Pedestrians, cyclists and motorcyclists account for about half of the victims. Injuries from car accidents are the cause of half of the medical evacuations back to the US. Of significance, more than 90 per cent of these deaths and injuries occur in low and middle income countries, with young adults under the age of 25 accounting for almost 1000 of these deaths each day. Furthermore, with more people traveling internationally each year, these numbers can be expected to grow. Use caution when you travel, it is often worth paying a little more for a safe means of transportation. In addition, if you are not covered by travel insurance, recognize that the cost of medical treatment as a result of a traffic accident can result in long-term financial burden for you and your family (see Insurance and Evacuation).

THE RISKS

The risks of driving overseas are substantial. Even if you are a safe driver, unfamiliar roads with different signs and road customs pose additional risks. Risks include dangerous drivers with little or no driver education, poorly maintained vehicles, crowded poor quality roads, ill equipped emergency services, non-compliance with road rules – or no road rules at all, no street lights and wandering animals. However, the most common causes of motor vehicle crashes are speed, fatigue, distractions, and driving while intoxicated; speed is a critical factor in the vast majority of accidents.

THINGS YOU SHOULD DO

Following some general safety guidelines will make you less likely to be involved in an accident and more likely to survive if you are in an accident.

- » Be certain that your insurance covers travel and medical emergencies including medical evacuation or obtain additional insurance (see Insurance and Evacuation).
- » Always wear a seat belt.
- » Avoid traveling at night on roads in countries with poor safety records.
- » Use proper child restraints.
- » Don't drink and drive and don't ride with anyone who does.
- » Take regular breaks while driving.
- » Obey the speed limit. Speed increases the likelihood and severity of motor vehicle accidents. Even small increases above the speed limit significantly increase the probablility of crashing and of injury.
- » Carry a mobile phone and key contact information for emergencies.
- » Learn the local road conditions and traffic culture.
- » Be aware of local laws and security conditions – the penalties for traffic infringements in some countries can be severe.
- » Don't hitchhike.
- » Learn which bus and taxi companies have good safety records.
- » Make sure the vehicle you travel in is equipped with appropriate safety features (including seat belts, air bags, and if required child restraints).
- » Check the tires, headlights, seatbelts and wipers before you drive.
- » Carry a basic break down kit in your car.

» Contact ASIRT for country specific Road Travel Reports with detailed information on over 150 countries (see below).

» The Association for Safe International Road Travel (http://www.asirt. org) offers regularly updated Road Reports for approximately 150 countries. Available via e-mail or download (fees apply), each report covers general road conditions, local driving style and the realities of dealing with the police, public transportation and emergency situations. Other useful features include summaries of especially dangerous roads and phonetic translations for use in unsafe or emergency situations.

» A special note about motorcycles: Motorcycle accidents involving travelers are very common in many parts of the world but more so in many low and middle income countries; and the injuries are often serious or fatal. Regardless of the "flexibility" of many local road laws, motorcycle riders should insist upon wearing helmets, preferably full-face helmets, and other protective clothing to minimize the risk of serious injury. The temptation not to do so can be enticing, but the consequences of not doing so can be ruinous for both the traveler and their families. Use common sense in deciding which routes to take. Select appropriate roads for motorcyclists.

» Make sure you have motor vehicle insurance. It is wise to insure yourself to drive a vehicle when overseas and always carry the insurance papers with you. Make sure your insurance covers breakdown recovery, accidental damage and medical expenses for injuries suffered in an accident. If driving a friend's vehicle overseas, check first that you are appropriately covered by their insurance policy to drive their car. When hiring a car carefully read the insurance document to determine your level of coverage. In some countries, the legal minimum for insurance coverage may be low, leaving you responsible for claims over this limit.

» Consider obtaining an International Driving Permit (IDP). You may contact AAA, or any of its international affiliates. An IDP is a legal identification document that translates driving license information into several different languages including English. To order an IDP, you must be 18 years of age and have a valid driver's license. AAA will ask you to submit two-passport sized photographs as well as a small fee (currently US$15) to obtain an IDP. AAA's website that deals with IDPs is http://www.aaa.com/vacation/idpf.html

PEDESTRIAN SAFETY

- Pedestrians account for a large number of road fatalities.

- Look carefully in all directions before crossing the road. Remember in many countries traffic travels on the opposite side of road from what you are used to.

- Don't assume that drivers will stop at pedestrian crossings or obey other traffic signals or signs.

- Face the oncoming traffic when walking along a roadside so you can see approaching vehicles.

- If walking along a road at night, try to wear reflective clothing or light colors.

Scan for more resources.

SCUBA DIVING PROBLEMS
Safety for Divers

You are on a business trip in Southeast Asia and are invited to go SCUBA diving a few hours outside Manila in the Philippines. You have snorkeled but not been SCUBA certified. Your associates assure you it is fine, they will teach you to SCUBA dive.

SCUBA diving is a spectacular but high-risk sport with 3 to 9 deaths per 100,000 U.S. divers annually. Many accidents are caused by panic; those who exhibit anxiety traits are at higher risk. The Divers Alert Network (DAN) reviewed 947 deaths from 1992 to 2003 and concluded that disabling injuries from asphyxia, arterial gas embolism (AGE), and cardiac incidents were the most common causes of death. Only 15 percent of deaths from asphyxia were caused by equipment failure. Cardiac events were associated with cardiovascular disease and age over 40. An Australian study found that divers were uncertified in 30 percent of deaths, and that triple the number of deaths occurred from shore or private craft dives compared to commercial boats. Bottom line: GET CERTIFIED.

KEY POINTS

» Medical problems encountered in diving usually relate to changes in pressure within a closed body space.

» Ear problems are the most common and the inability to equalize pressure within the middle ear is responsible for many problems.

» Perforation of the eardrum may take a week to heal and is painful, can be associated with infections, hearing loss, and dizziness.

» Inner ear trauma is less common but potentially more serious and must be differentiated from decompression sickness (DCS). Pain on descent is typical of ear trauma but pain upon ascent may be DCS.

» DCS is associated with deeper and longer duration dives.

» Nasal sinuses and the ears are spaces where external pressure equalization occurs through small channels and are subject to pain and infection if not cleared.

» One of the most dramatically painful experiences occurs in teeth with small air pockets from cavities, ill-fitting prostheses, or recent dental work.

BASIC TREATMENT GUIDELINES

• The most serious pressure-related injuries occur with expansion of trapped gases in the lungs during ascent. This is most often precipitated by the rapid ascent of inexperienced or panicked divers while holding their breath.

• Emergency ascent caused 96 percent of cases of arterial gas embolism (AGE). Air may rupture into the lung space or bloodstream causing lung collapse or death from an embolism. Sudden loss of consciousness, confusion, or convulsions within a few minutes of surfacing should be considered an AGE. Treatment for suspected air embolism is immediate surface oxygenation and transport to a recompression chamber. Fortunately, this is the same treatment for DCS that often accompanies this disorder. Because of the difficulty differentiating DCS from AGE, they are now collectively known as decompression illness (DCI).

• Nitrogen narcosis occurs when mental acuity and motor skills are impaired due to an increase in nitrogen pressure that affects neurons in the central nervous system. The effects are first noted around a depth of 100 feet and the possibility of narcosis increases with further depth, making the use of mixed gases highly advisable in these situations. Even highly experienced divers experience narcosis, sometimes unexpectedly, and divers must be alert to changes in mental or physical function that can be subtle. Awareness of the possibility is key to recognition.

• DCS occurs when gas absorbed by tissue during a dive returns to the bloodstream and forms bubbles because of too rapid pressure changes. These bubbles obstruct small arteries and can cause a wide variety of neurological symptoms, pain, respiratory distress, cardiac irregularities, skin rash, nausea, and vomiting. Most symptoms appear within 2 hours of surfacing and may evolve into more serious symptoms over the next 24 hours. The more rapid the onset, the more severe the case. Rapid oxygenation and recompression are required for treatment whether by taking the victim back down in the water for decompression stops or by using a decompression chamber.

A word of caution about the use of closed circuit rebreather equipment by recreational divers to extend dive time. Rebreathers recirculate exhaled air after carbon dioxide is removed by chemical means. Oxygen and carbon dioxide concentration must be maintained within a narrow range and an imbalance in either can be disastrous. Death rates have increased with use of rebreathers related to oxygen levels but suspicion also centers on increased carbon dioxide levels that are not easily monitored. Unfortunately, in some individuals, carbon dioxide toxicity has no warning signs and the first indication is seizures or loss of consciousness—fatal events in the water.

Scan for more
resources.

SEXUALLY TRANSMITTED DISEASES
A Price to Pay For Unsafe Sex

You recently returned from a Caribbean vacation where you had an unprotected intimate sexual encounter. You have some mild irritation when urinating but no visible discharge and have noted what appear to be mild abrasions on your genital organs. Is this a sexually transmitted disease?

Sexually transmitted diseases (STD) are among the top five reasons for adults to seek health care in developing countries. WHO estimates that over 330 million people under age 24 will acquire a curable STD each year. There are more than thirty agents that cause STDs including viruses, bacteria, fungi, and parasites ranging from the relatively harmless to potentially deadly such as human immunodeficiency virus (HIV).

KEY POINTS

» Studies have shown that some travelers may participate in more risky behaviors and are less likely to use condoms with strangers than at home.

» Remember that HIV and other sexually transmitted diseases are endemic in many areas, and risks may be significantly higher than assumed.

» STDs present with varying signs and symptoms. Some of the most common STDs such as non-specific urethritis and gonorrhea inflame the urethra (tube from the bladder to the exterior) and cause burning with urination and a discharge that appear within a few days after exposure.

» Other STDs may present with a growth (venereal warts, herpes) or painless ulcer (syphilis) on the genitalia within weeks to months after exposure. One should not delay seeking medical attention if a genital growth or discharge develops.

» Risk for travelers is directly related to behavior because STDs are transmitted almost exclusively through sexual activity. Not every exposure leads to an STD but there is a 20 to 50 percent chance of acquiring a gonorrhea infection per exposure to someone with the disease.

» STDs are not spread through casual contact or inanimate objects like toilet seats nor by shaking or holding hands.

» Some STDs such as HIV and hepatitis also can be transmitted through body fluids or blood products.

BASIC PREVENTION AND TREATMENT GUIDELINES

• Vaccines are now available for prevention of venereal warts (condyloma) caused by human papilloma virus (HPV).

• Hepatitis A and B vaccine is advised for all travelers.

• Vaccines are not available for most STDs.

• Condom use is highly recommended. Condom use significantly reduces the risk of STDs, but does not eliminate it. Also, other sexual practices can also transmit disease.

• Treatment should be under the care of a competent health care provider. There is a growing problem with resistance of STDs to standard antibiotics and appropriate choice of treatment changes on a regular basis.

Scan for more resources.

SITUATIONAL AWARENESS OF VIOLENCE
The Gift of Fear

You decide to walk back several blocks to your hotel after dinner and sense something is not right. There is a streetlight out halfway up the next block near some bushes and an alley entrance onto this quiet street. You have been told the area is safe and the local people have seemed nice and non-threatening. Do you proceed, cross the street and proceed, select a different route, or hail a cab?

Violence can occur anywhere so it is important to develop your ability to sense when you are in the presence of danger. Gavin de Becker in his highly regarded book *The Gift of Fear* states that everyone has "the gift of a brilliant internal guardian" to warn and guide you through dangerous situations. For more detailed discussion of the principles in this chapter, read his book.

The belief that violence can occur is important to counteract the denial that arises in us when our internal signals of danger become activated. This concept is important for travel group leaders advising their charges about risk, particularly in unfamiliar territory. It is also is important for every individual in daily life.

People in developed countries tend to minimize the need to learn about violence because they feel the police and criminal justice system will handle it. This is not true. Your safety is your responsibility, not that of the government, police, the travel industry, or security guards. We generally assume things are safe without any real assessment. Your personal response to violence will come from a strong inner resource, intuition.

Intuition is the ability to understand or feel something immediately, without the use of conscious reasoning. Intuition results from unconscious rapid processing of multiple subtle signals leaving you with an involuntary impression often called a "gut feeling." In the scenario at the beginning, the traveler noted the subtle signals of danger: unfamiliar surroundings, light out, hidden alley entrance, personal vulnerability while walking. This was subconscious initially but escalated to conscious awareness.

KEY POINTS

» The most serious threat to personal safety while traveling is complacency (it is not going to happen) or fatalism (if it is going to happen, it is going to happen; nothing I can do will stop it).

» Real fear is a survival signal that results from intuition and appears only in the presence of danger. Fear differs from worry, wariness, and anxiety. In a situation with real fear, people react instantly and are not paralyzed.

» Worry and anxiety, often confused with fear, are good evidence that the event you fear is not happening. Worry and anxiety are caused by uncertainty, unlike real fear. Worry and anxiety are used to avoid change. When you worry, you do not act to change the situation.

» When you feel fear, listen to your signal or internal voice.

» Victims of violent crime are most often known in some way by their attackers (see Violent Crime).

BASIC GUIDELINES

• Be prepared.

• Listen to your inner voice.

• Be aware of your surroundings and the people around you.

• Take responsibility for your own safety.

Scan for more resources.

SKIN INFECTION: MRSA
Not Just A Zit

> *Our adventure to Southeast Asia just started, and one of our expedition team members, who is otherwise healthy, physically fit, and frequently works out at a health club, has a skin lesion that seems to be getting worse. He says it began as a small red bump that looked like a pimple or bug bite and now it is becoming a large abscess. It is on the back of his upper leg.*

Bacteria are everywhere in the environment and a wide variety reside within and on the exterior of our bodies in great numbers. This scenario suggests a bacterial infection, likely from a methicillin-resistant Staphyloccus aureus (MRSA) source. Health club gym equipment is one common source to transmit bacteria from one person to another.

KEY POINTS

»   Most bacteria have little or no visible effect on us and may be beneficial. There is increasing evidence that bacteria play a role in insulin regulation and possibly other hormonal systems.

»   Most non-native bacterial incursions into our bodies are kept at bay by our immune systems. However, if a bacterial infection evolves, most can be treated with antibiotics. Bacteria can develop resistance to antibiotics because they mutate to adapt to antibiotic effects. Therefore, it is important to use antibiotics for appropriate indications, at proper doses, and for correct lengths of time.

»   *Staphylococcus aureus* is a common bacterium frequently present on skin surfaces, in the nose, and in other body structures. Occasionally it causes infection. For years, such an infection was easily treated with a penicillin-related drug. Resistance to the penicillin family of antibiotics first was reported in the late 1960s and these infections with resistant organisms are now termed methicillin-resistant Staphylococcus aureus (MRSA). Fortunately, these difficult infections can be treated with other classes of antibiotics.

» MRSA infections now are fairly common community-acquired infections and are spread by personal contact with an infected individual or surface in the environment. They are usually limited to the skin—the victim has a red, swollen, often pus-filled sore that may look like an insect bite which can be painful. The victim may have a fever. The infective site is often in an area that had a small cut or abrasion, or in areas with hair follicles (such as groin, buttock, armpit).

» Occasionally, MRSA infections can become more severe. This is very rare in otherwise healthy people, and is usually limited to people with other diseases and generally fragile health. Pneumonia, septicemia (infection spread in the blood), bone infections, and other problems can occur.

BASIC GUIDELINES

• If a MRSA infection is suspected, that person needs to see a health care provider. Treatment often includes a controlled disruption of the lesion to drain the exudate (pus), coupled with antibiotics.

• It is critical to keep the wound covered with a dry, light dressing to prevent spread to others. Impeccable personal hygiene is essential—not only for the victim but for everyone—to prevent infection. Hand washing is a must to prevent developing an infection or spread of an existing one. —Frequent handwashing should be done after touching the wound or dressing, but also after using the toilet, before eating, and before and after communal activities. Don't share towels, clothing, or toiletry items.

• Good hygienic practices should become a routine part of everyone's life to prevent MRSA and other infections, and to maintain good health.

Scan for more resources.

SKIN RASHES
Annoying But With Few Emergencies

Our team is in Egypt, excavating ancient ruins. We are in the heat all day. Several of us are developing a rash that looks like little bumps on our back and abdomen. The men found it goes away if they don't wear shirts in the heat.

Prickly heat, or heat rash, occurs when someone perspires heavily in the heat. Sweat gland ducts become clogged, and the perspiration gets trapped and irritates the surrounding tissue causing a rash that usually goes away when the area is cleansed and cooled. No specific treatment is needed.

KEY POINTS

» Fortunately for travelers, few skin disorders are true emergencies, though they can be very uncomfortable and annoying. Symptomatic treatment is generally adequate.

» Many skin disorders are chronic conditions that do not require urgent treatment while on travel unless severe or complicated by secondary bacterial infection.

» Other rashes may have an infectious origin—fungal, bacterial, or viral. Athlete's foot is an example of a fungal skin infection. Rashes from viral sources are usually systemic infections including measles, rubella, and chicken pox. Others, such as warts, are more localized lesions (see Fungal Skin Infections).

» Most bacterial infections of the skin like MRSA begin localized though they can become systemic in people with decreased immunity. Bacterial skin infections require treatment if extensive, not improving, or visibly worsening (see Skin Infections MRSA).

» The most serious skin diseases, such as various skin cancers, often have no symptoms except the lesion itself—they do not usually itch or hurt.

» Other rash-like skin disorders are related to allergies. Contact dermatitis is a skin reaction in the area of contact with something causing an allergic reaction—chemicals in tanning leather and plant resins like urushiol in poison ivy are examples of compounds that cause rashes.

» Some skin reactions, such as hives, are reflections of systemic allergies to foods, medications, and other substances. Hives can be a warning sign of future life-threatening severe allergic reaction known as anaphylaxis (see Allergic Reactions). Skin photosensitivity to certain medications (such as some classes of antibiotics and diuretics) can cause rashes in people when exposed to UV rays found in sunlight.

» Some apparent skin rashes are actually a result of insect bites. Venom injected by the insect causes a reaction with itching.

» Bed bug bites cause discrete welts on most people.

» Scabies bite in patches corresponding to areas of itching and oozing.

BASIC GUIDELINES

- The topical treatment for skin diseases includes antifungal cream and hydrocortisone cream which should be located in the first aid kit. Oral anti-histamines can help with itching.

- An antibiotic cream is useful for cuts and small lacerations to help prevent infection but it is rarely effective for an established bacterial infection.

- Simple cotton dressings are also useful to protect skin lesions and keep ointments in place.

- Wound care should be instituted for any infection or rash that appears to be becoming infected if you cannot get medical attention (see Lacerations). Appropriate oral antibiotics should be started after asking about allergies to medications.

Scan for more resources.

SNAKE BITE
What You Really Need To Do

You are on a nature hike in Central America and veer off the trail to look at a beautiful butterfly. Not watching where you are walking, you step over a log and feel a sharp prick in your lower calf. You did not see a snake but have two relatively small puncture wounds.

Fear of venomous snakebite is disproportionate to the actual risk for the usual traveler not involved in high-risk behavior in venomous snake territory.

KEY POINTS

» Only about a quarter of the 2700 snake species are venomous, though about 40,000 annual deaths result worldwide from snakebite, many occurring in rural areas in undeveloped countries.

» Reports of venomous snakebite vary from 5000 to 8000 each year in the United States with about 3 percent from captive exotic species.

» Snakes responsible for bites are unidentified about 25 percent of the time, making treatment with specific antivenin difficult.

» The incidence of envenomation increases in areas freshly disturbed by tropical violent storms. But snake envenomation presents a small risk unless deliberately handling local reptiles.

» Vipers which include copperheads, cottonmouths, and rattlesnakes account for 99 percent of the native venomous snake bites in the United States and are responsible for 9 to 15 deaths per year, mostly among the young and elderly. The cottonmouth (or water moccasin) is the most frequently misidentified snake due to confusion with more common harmless water snakes. Cottonmouths are not usually aggressive unless grabbed or restrained. Copperheads, on the other hand, often strike when provoked and account for a large portion of snake envenomations.

» Snakes produce toxins in two general categories, one that disrupts blood functions (hemotoxin) and one that affects neurological activity (neurotoxin).

» Hemotoxins tend to work more slowly than the rapid effects of neurotoxins.

» Bites from pit vipers interrupt coagulation and cause hemorrhage, severe pain, swelling, and death of muscle tissue.

» In addition to a hemotoxin, certain rattlesnakes have now evolved to produce a neurotoxin that can lead to visual disturbances and respiratory paralysis.

» Coral snakes are brightly colored smaller relatives of cobras, mambas, and sea snakes which are secretive and seldom seen. Despite their highly neurotoxic venom, these snakes account for only 1 percent of United States' venomous snake bites and almost always result from intentional handling. Contrary to popular myth, coral snakes do not need to "chew" for an extended time to envenomate. The country adage "red on yellow, kill a fellow" to distinguish coral snakes from similar appearing non-poisonous snakes applies only to North American coral snakes and not to their southern relatives.

» Medically important snakes in other parts of the world also include the family of cobras (Africa, tropical and subtropical Asia), mambas (tropical Africa), kraits (south and SE Asia), coral snakes (southern United States to central Argentina), and sea snakes (tropical western Pacific, eastern Pacific tropical coast, and Indian Oceans).

» Australia harbors many highly venomous snakes, including the taipan and common brown snakes, considered to have the most toxic venom in the world. The 50 or more sea snakes species evolved from Australian venomous land snakes. These usually non-aggressive but extremely venomous snakes live an entirely marine existence. However, they are found in two landlocked fresh water lakes, one in the Philippines and one in the Solomon Islands.

» Pit vipers constitute about 120 species of venomous snakes in the Americas and much of Asia and 40 species of Old World vipers in Africa, Europe, and Asia. Many of these are the sources of bites but with low death rates.

» Russell's viper found from Pakistan to Taiwan is highly lethal because it is well adapted to agricultural areas.

» Saw-scaled vipers found in arid and semiarid regions of India, the Middle East, and Africa likely cause more fatalities than any other snakes in the world.

» The stout-bodied, wide-headed African vipers have some members with spectacular appearance (Gaboon viper, rhinoceros viper) but rarely bite humans.

» Puff adders, however, prefer grassland and are a major cause of snakebite in Africa.

» About 3000 people a year are bitten by vipers in Japan with about 10 deaths.

» In the tropical Western Hemisphere, about 30 species of moderate to heavy pit vipers, often lumped together under the name fer-de-lance, account for most of the serious snakebites in Latin America. The bushmaster is the largest neotropical pit viper whose bites are rare but usually fatal.

» Although not venomous, constrictors can deliver nasty bites. These ambush predators rarely attack humans but large adult specimens can kill people and at least 9 cases of suspected death from pet constrictors have occurred in North America over the past two decades. Large constrictors have now become established in the United States with breeding colonies in the Everglades spreading to other southeastern states. Reports of attacks on human beings, once more common in South and Southeast Asia, are now very rare. No deaths have been attributed to South American anacondas, the largest constrictor species.

BASIC PREVENTION AND TREATMENT GUIDELINES

• Familiarize yourself with indigenous venomous species and their habits if you will be in rural areas.

• Wear loose-fitting bloused trousers, boots.

• Avoid placing hands and feet in places that cannot be visually inspected.

- Avoid blind contact with brush or tree limbs in flood water areas.

- Move out of the strike range of an identified snake (1 body length).

- Do not provoke or handle a snake. Keep the victim of a snake bite calm, warm, and rested.

- Identify the snake and photograph if possible (cell phone).

- Remove all jewelry from the injured extremity to prevent compromise of circulation.

- Immobilize injured area with a loose-fitting dressing.

- Elevate injured body part to the level of the heart.

- Evacuate the victim as soon as possible to the nearest medical facility.

- Closely monitor progression of swelling during transport. Marking the advancing edge of swelling can provide valuable information to the physician.

- Encourage fluid intake

- DO NOT CUT AND SUCK BITES, APPLY VENOM EXTRACTION KITS OR TOURNIQUETS, OR PLACE COLD PACKS. These have all been shown to potentially worsen the bite outcome and are strongly discouraged.

- If a suspected neurotoxic species (coral snake, mamba, cobra, krait, sea snake) caused the bite, a pressure bandage wrapped over the entire extremity with immobilization helps impede toxin spread.

Scan for more resources.

SPACE TRAVEL
So You Want to Fly in Space

You have always been intrigued by space travel and you are fortunate enough to afford the Virgin Galactic space flight. You want to reserve a seat but have some health and safety concerns. What should you worry about?

The progress for the potential of civilian space flight has created great interest resulting in a considerable number of people on a waiting list for commercial space flights. Flight costs are expected to drop as space tourism continues development. As this sci-fi fantasy nears reality, major concerns about safety persist.

There are unique medical problems associated with space travel. Microgravity, space radiation, and isolation and confinement all can produce changes in physiology and behavioral health. Changes that occur in your physiology in space can increase the risk of pathologic conditions on Earth. These may be transient and return to normal function upon return to Earth or more extended, possibly permanent. Some examples of this are adaptations of the neurologic and vestibular (balance) systems, bone mineral density loss in microgravity, loss of muscle strength in microgravity, possible immune compromise, and development of cataracts years earlier than expected for a comparable age group. Other problems, possibly unique to space travel, will likely emerge as our knowledge and experience grows. Space crews experience G forces 3 to 8 times those on Earth.

KEY POINTS

> » Human space fight experience so far shows that travelers can probably experience the space environment for short durations (such as suborbital flight profiles) with medical conditions comparable to those acceptable for travel to remote and extreme terrestrial environments. The longer the duration of stay, the higher the risk of an underlying

medical disorder causing untoward consequences, just as in travel to remote and extreme terrestrial environments.

» Ionizing radiation is more intense in outer space and is different from most terrestrial sources of ionizing radiation. Space radiation consists of particles (protons, electrons, neutrons, and the nuclei of elements) traveling at light and near light speed. These particles cause damage at the cellular level as they pass through tissues. Biological effects of this unique radiation are not well known. Spacecraft afford some protection from space radiation, and most contain areas where the crew can take shelter in the event of a space radiation event (such as a solar particle event). Research needs to continue to search for more effective shielding materials and methods.

» Isolation and stress could create psychological problems and travelers should be screened for psychological stability for participation in space flight.

» The known long term effects of microgravity relate mainly to loss of bone mineral density, cardiovascular deconditioning, and loss of muscle strength. These are addressed and minimized by aggressive aerobic and resistive exercises on orbit, and aggressive rehabilitation on return to Earth.

» A syndrome of vision change, optic nerve swelling, change in the shape of the eyeball and retinal change has been described in crewmembers participating in space flight missions of several months duration. Intracranial pressure also be increased. These changes tend to return to normal post flight. The long term implications of this syndrome for very long term missions in low earth orbit and beyond are unknown at this point.

» Nutrition is a great challenge on space flight. Space crews report that food tastes more bland than on Earth. An interesting and varied diet that fulfills nutritional requirements is an important goal.

» Technologies to monitor traveler health continue to develop. The International Space Station can monitor vital signs and EKG, perform diagnostic ultrasound, send photos and use video telemedicine, and perform limited diagnostic laboratory tests. Spacecraft designed for transportation to orbit currently have much less capability.

» Communication in case of an adverse medical event is limited. Communication delays in low Earth orbit (LEO) are minimal but many periodic black outs may be experienced depending on specific orbits. Communication delays range from seconds to 20 minutes beyond LEO.

Scan for more
resources.

SUBSTANCE ABUSE
Recognition & Management on Travel

I will be a leader for a one-month expedition to an isolated area. What should I do to prevent alcohol or drug use from interfering with our mission? I am concerned about health and safety issues, as well as legal problems.

Managing others misusing alcohol and/or drugs (legal or illegal) is very challenging. People with substance use disorders often deny having them, and can become aggressive if confronted about them, especially when intoxicated.

KEY POINTS

» Alcohol intoxication impedes judgment, and when intoxicated, people tend to take risks they otherwise would not take in both their job and social activities. Their actions can endanger others as well as themselves.

» Prescription drugs, especially opioids, sedatives, and stimulants can be abused. Misuse of prescription drugs causes essentially the same health and behavioral problems as chemically related illegal drugs.

» Drugs can be used through various routes of administration—oral, inhaled, snorted, injected, or absorbed through the skin and mucous membranes.

» Everyday substances can be abused. Glue and other volatile chemicals are sniffed to get "high." Deaths have even been reported from excessive caffeine use and abuse.

» Drug-seeking behavior can lead to theft and other disruptive and illegal activities.

» Illegal drugs can become a problem when traveling, particularly when readily available in some parts of the world. Further, the actual chemical content of the drug you are buying may not be accurately represented. Concentrations are unknown (heroin may be stronger resulting in a deadly overdose.) Known drugs can be laced with even more dangerous compounds to increase the "high" or contaminated with toxic substances.

» Many illegal drugs such as PCP and LSD cause unpredictable behavior that can be dangerous for everyone.

» Drugs easily obtainable in a foreign country does not mean they are legal to use there. Legal issues regarding drug use by foreigners differ in many countries. Risks of arrest and imprisonment are real (see Legal section).

BASIC GUIDELINES

Many alcohol and substance use problems can be prevented before travel. If traveling with a group, it is the leader's responsibility is to establish a culture of appropriate behaviors regarding substance use. If you are that leader, you may want to consider the following:

- Select participants or fellow travelers who don't abuse alcohol or other drugs. If participants are not well known to you, a background check (for DUIs, drug convictions, and other charges) and a urine drug screen (for current drug use) can be helpful, but not definitive.

- Have a written policy regarding transport of drugs—prescription drugs, over-the-counter drugs, herbal preparations and illegal drugs—on the expedition. Many prescription drugs are the source of abuse. Will persons on prescription narcotics and other related drugs be allowed to participate on the expedition? If so, under what parameters?

- Have a written "no tolerance" policy that clearly outlines the consequences of inappropriate substance use, which usually means immediate return home. Have each participant sign the policy and make certain they understand it.

- Understand and be able to recognize the signs and symptoms of abuse and the life-threatening medical emergencies that accompany substance use disorders.

- As a group leader, understand the legal aspects of inappropriate substance use in the areas where you will travel. Educate all travelers in your group about these.

- Know that many drugs (prescription and illegal) and the regular heavy use of alcohol cause physical dependence. If the drug or alcohol is abruptly stopped, withdrawal effects result. Suspect substance dependence if a fellow traveler has unusual behavior in a remote area without access to alcohol. Denial of excessive alcohol or drug use is common.

- Sudden withdrawal of heroin and opioid pain medications causes a very unpleasant withdrawal characterized by nausea, vomiting, abdominal cramps, and other symptoms, but these are not life-threatening.

- Withdrawal from benzodiazepines as well as alcohol can cause fatal seizures.

- In a remote situation, the best emergency treatment for withdrawal may be to give the person just enough of the substance being withdrawn to control symptoms until more definitive care is available.

- Many medical evacuation companies will not evacuate someone in withdrawal. Many of them have clauses that exclude their service in those circumstances.

Scan for more resources.

SUBTERRANEAN ENVIRONMENTAL HAZARDS
Going Into the Bat Cave

You are on a business trip in Central America and your host suggests a visit to a cave previously inhabited by pre-Columbian natives. A local guide will lead the adventure. What are the risks?

Whether visiting an abandoned silver mine, an underground archaeological site, or caving for recreation, travelers face safety and medical challenges. Some of the most diverse subterranean adventure destinations pose problems for the novice as well as for the highly experienced cave explorer. Development of modern protective equipment and improved technology have combined to make this adventure more popular. The subterranean environment is unique because of its combination of lack of natural lighting, dampness, constant exposure to mud, cold temperatures, frequent partial submersion, and possibly long periods of isolation.

KEY POINTS

» There are medical concerns beyond those associated with dark, damp, cold places and anyone heading into a cave, even if well known as safe for cavers, is advised to pay attention to these issues.

» Aside from superficial occurrences, fungal infections are uncommon infections from common environmental fungi and usually associated with an unusual exposure or compromised immunity. Visitors to caves risk exposure to fungal infections by disturbing soil contaminated with bat guano. Inhalation of the spores or contact with fresh guano can lead to systemic infection. The most common agent is *Histoplasma capsulatum* but other fungal species also cause infection. Over 90 percent of cases either have mild or no respiratory symptoms after an incubation period lasting up to 2 weeks. Most cases resolve without treatment but some victims present with high fever, chest pain, and non-productive cough and require treatment with antifungal medications. Loose masks do not prevent the infections and sealed masks have never been studied for prevention of disease transmission in the caving population.

» Rabies is a fatal viral disease transmitted in the saliva of infected animals. Rabies can infect any mammal. In many areas throughout the world, dogs are the most important reservoir. However, other domestic animals such as cattle and cats can carry rabies. In subterranean areas, bats are the source of rabies and one should avoid bat contact. Anyone bitten, scratched, or exposed to bat saliva must receive immediate postexposure prophylaxis to prevent this nearly universally fatal disease if it is left untreated. (see Rabies)

» Long exposure to a cold and wet environment creates a risk of developing hypothermia. Cave visitors should layer clothing with an outer waterproof garment. Learn to recognize the signs of hypothermia, which include prolonged shivering, confusion, loss of muscular control manifested by staggering, clumsy movements, and inability to perform simple physical tasks (see Hypothermia and Frostbite). Anyone with suspected hypothermia needs to be escorted out of the cave for evaluation and rewarming. Bat droppings can also spread disease.

» Caves are normally well ventilated but air low in oxygen or containing noxious gases can be encountered. Air pockets within a cave may concentrate carbon dioxide or gases and care must be taken. Certain types of limestone can create carbon dioxide that also collects in low areas because it is heavier than oxygen. These are potentially fatal circumstances which can cause asphyxiation.

» Falls resulting in trauma are a constant concern in caves. Management of trauma is discussed elsewhere (see Trauma to the Abdomen, Trauma to the Chest, and Orthopedic Injuries). Circumstances encountered during more complex caving expeditions such as prolonged entanglement, management of waste, and water purification are beyond the scope of this text.

Scan for more resources.

SUICIDE
Recognizing Risk Factors

A casual acquaintance on an adventure cruise has withdrawn from the group and made some strange comments about death and appears depressed about a personal event. Is this person suicidal? What should you do?

Suicide is a difficult subject, and is more easily ignored that addressed. However, learning about suicide and knowing what to do if someone shows signs of hurting oneself, is important to preventing it. You can save someone's life.

KEY POINTS

» There is one suicide in the United States about every 15 minutes; more than 33,000 people kill themselves each year.

» About 400,000 people are seen in emergency rooms annually due to self-inflicted injuries.

» In young adults, there are more than 100 attempts for each completed suicide.

» In older adults, about one in four attempts result in death.

» Never assume a suicide attempt is just "acting out;" acting out can lead to death, too. Every suicide gesture should be taken seriously.

» About four times as many men kill themselves as women. For men, firearms are the most common method; for women, it is poisoning (including drug overdose). In men, the suicide rate is highest over age 75; in women, the rate is highest in the 45-54 age range.

BASIC GUIDELINES

• Some general risk factors for suicide include a previous attempt and a family history of suicide or other violence; depression, schizophrenia and other mental health diagnoses; and serious physical illness.

- Alcohol or substance abuse is frequently associated with suicide attempts.

- Suicide is a reaction to extreme emotional pain and is a desperate act often in response to what the person perceives as a desperate situation. There may be a specific loss or "trigger" such as disruption in a relationship, death of a loved one, severe financial strain, legal problems, or diagnosis of a serious disease.

- A person often gives some type of warning before suicide such as talking or (or even "joking") about suicide, death, or no reason to live. The person may be experiencing extremes of emotion such as anger or rage, or seem very anxious, confused or disorganized.

- Look for isolation, withdrawal from usual interests and activities, and signs of depression.

- Sudden sleep problems may be signal of depression and suicide potential—nightmares or sleeping too much or too little.

- There may be an increase in alcohol or substance use.

- The person may give away treasured possessions.

- Behavior may be impulsive, or very risky.

- The person may look for firearms, drugs (prescription, over-the-counter, illegal), rope, or other objects that can be used.

- If you have concerns about someone, talk with him or her. Provide a nonjudgmental environment where the person feels comfortable talking about sensitive subjects.

- If they talk about hurting themselves or someone else, take this seriously. Never let someone who may be dangerous to themselves or others be alone. At least one or two people should be with them at all times until professional help is able to manage the situation. If you are in a remote area, recognize that it can take hours to days to access professional help.

- If you suspect someone is suicidal, don't ignore it, take action. First, don't leave the person alone—at least one responsible adult should stay with the person while others get help immediately.

- Help can come from immediate consultation with a health/mental health provider or a clergy member. If geographically practical, and if the person is willing, a trip to the emergency room may be indicated. If you suspect the person has taken an overdose of drugs, call an ambulance immediately and try to determine what was taken, how much, and when. At least in the United States, the local police and emergency response personnel are another resource—don't be afraid to call 911.

- In the United States, the National Suicide Prevention Hotline is available at 1-800-273-8255. There is always someone to help.

Scan for more resources.

TAXI SAFETY & SECURITY
Tips for Urban Travel

A business traveler staying at an upmarket international hotel, had been invited to join some expatriate acquaintances for a happy hour at another hotel. Walking out onto the busy road outside his hotel, he flagged down a local taxi. Ten minutes later, the driver, who had been on his cell phone, pulled into a side road and stopped to allow two men to jump in the backseat on either side of the passenger. He was robbed at gunpoint and thrown out of the car.

For many travelers, the use of taxis can be an intimidating experience. When you get in a taxi, you are putting yourself in the hands of someone you do not know and entrusting yourself to them. Taxi drivers can be an excellent source of local information, in particular about places foreigners should avoid. If you sense your driver is someone that could be trusted, feel free to engage him or her on such matters. However, being aware of a few practical measures before getting into a taxi can reduce the chances of your trip becoming an experience you would rather not have.

BASIC GUIDELINES

- Before traveling, ask a knowledgeable source what the typical fare would be for the trip you plan to take. Then, before getting into the taxi, ask the driver to give you an approximate cost for the trip, and make sure it is close to the amount you have been told.

- Write the name of your current address and your destination—as well as phone numbers for contacts at both locations—in the local language, so you can show it to the driver as necessary.

- If you are traveling with luggage, make sure you stay outside the cab to see your luggage loaded and the trunk locked before you get into the cab. Similarly, at your destination, do not pay the driver until your luggage has been removed from the trunk and is in your control.

- Know the tipping policies in your location—and apply them. Do not be over generous or too stingy.

- Know the local currency well enough to know the bills and coins you need to use, and to be able to know that your change is correct. Also have denominations that will be as close as possible to the anticipated bill. Some taxi drivers will claim they have no change. Do not display large amounts of cash.

- Ask a trusted source such as a hotel concierge or local friend to provide the name of a preferred, reliable taxi service to use.

- Taxis should, if possible, be booked via telephone rather than hailed in the street. Watch carefully at the manner in which a hotel doorman obtains your taxi, and do not use the taxi if there was anything suspicious about the manner in which it was hailed.

- Before using a taxi to any destination, ask what you need to know about the return journey (such as availability of taxis) to ensure you will be able to get back safely.

- Be extra cautious at taxi stands in foreign places, as these are common sites chosen by criminals for their operations.

- In countries where taxi drivers are required to be licensed, ensure you see the license and the driver's photo matches the driver.

- Always lock taxi doors and put windows up.

- Do not allow the driver to add extra passengers, and do not get in a cab that already has a passenger in it.

- If you feel uncomfortable about anything after getting into a taxi, have the driver return you to your point of origin. Make an excuse if necessary such as that you forgot an item.

Scan for more resources.

TERRORISM
Traveling to High Risk Locations

> *A traveler sitting in the Java coffee shop at Nairobi's Westgate mall, was abruptly interrupted by loud bursts of machine gun fire. In this real life scenario, gunmen from the Islamist group al-Shabaab commenced an attack on the upmarket Westgate shopping mall - firing and throwing grenades at passers-by and slaughtering people en masse. The attack lasted more than 80 hours, and resulted in the violent deaths of 67 people with 175 wounded.*

While acts of terror can occur almost anywhere these days, certain places throughout the world are more prone to terrorist activities than others. Terror tactics involve the use of violence intended to create fear and achieve some political, religious, or ideological goal, and almost always avoid or disregard any concern for the safety of innocent bystanders. The United Nations has struggled to agree on a definition of terrorism due mainly to the differences of opinion that underpin global security issues. Essentially one man's terrorist is another man's freedom fighter. Terrorism has been used in almost every country in the world to achieve either some domestic, regional, or international goal. Acts of terrorism range from small scale incidents such as local violence to state terrorism in support of national purposes.

KEY POINTS

Prior to traveling, it is always wise to do some research about the place you are visiting. If there is a history of terrorist violence in your destination, there are some preliminary actions you might like to consider:

> » Make sure your travel partners and someone who is not traveling with you, such as family or a friend, has a detailed copy of your itinerary— and if it changes, make sure to let them know.

> » Do some research, and prepare a contact list of the appropriate diplomatic missions and any other known contacts that can assist in

an emergency, in a place where it will be easily located when needed. Register your proposed trip with your diplomatic mission ahead of your departure.

» Keep a copy of critical travel documents and contact details on a public domain email service (such as Yahoo or Gmail) that can be easily accessed from hotel business centers, or Internet kiosks and similar Internet access portals.

» Have a plan. You and your traveling partners should know what action to take if you (or any of them) are caught up in any act of terrorism. Make your family and work colleagues aware of the plan.

» As morbid as it may seem, prior to any travel you are advised to revise and update your will, and other important documents such as powers of attorney.

» In places where your planned mode of transport could be unreliable, research alternative transportation options and have contact details available.

» Pre-arrange hotel stays, airport pickups and transfers, and arrange for transportation providers to use an easy-to-remember signal to confirm their identity upon arrival if appropriate.

» Do not travel wearing any clothing that identifies you as a foreigner. In particular avoid wearing anything that could identify you as belonging to any country, or organization that might be considered confrontational at your destination.

» Use non-descript luggage when traveling—and especially avoid using luggage and even luggage tags that make it clear you are a foreigner.

» Dress and behave in a manner that is low profile and consistent with the dress and behavior of your host city/country. Minimize your time in the common areas of an airport, which are less protected.

» Leave the airport as quickly as possible after getting your luggage. Always move confidently and don't do or say anything that demonstrates you are a newcomer to the location. This requires you to have done your planning and preparation prior to departure.

BASIC GUIDELINES

- Keep your personal details and business details confidential. There is nothing wrong with being friendly, but exercise caution when talking about personal matters in public, or with strangers.

- It might sound like a cliché, but minimize time spent in the normal tourist venues where foreigners would usually congregate—this is particularly important in places which might be a focal point for cultural and/or ethnic animosity. Hotel concierges will normally be able to identify such places for you.

- Constantly look for places you might use to get assistance or to take shelter, such as police stations, hotels and shops, hospitals as you travel around.

- Be conscious of people who may be following you and people who you observe watching you.

- If you have to meet someone in a high risk location for the first time, select the time and place for the meeting yourself if possible—and make it somewhere public, not too remote.

- Don't open your hotel door to anyone whose identity you are uncertain of.

- Don't hand out your business card casually---think carefully about who you give your card to.

- If using a taxi, use only taxis that are recommended by hotels or other trusted sources. Do not enter a vehicle you believe to be a taxi unless it is clearly identified as such, and before getting into a taxi, check to see if there is a license displayed and, if so, quickly match the fact of the driver to the photo on the license.

- If you have your own car, always make a visual inspection as you approach the vehicle, looking for any signs of interference or tampering.

- If possible, use inconspicuous vehicles instead of luxury showy cars.

- It is important to avoid a set travel or transport routine. Vary your routes and timings each day if possible.

- Make sure you are certain of the route to be taken before you depart. Avoid taking unplanned detours if there is doubt about where it will take you, especially if it takes you into restrictive or remote areas.

- Get into the habit of always putting windows up and locking doors when traveling in crowed areas. This will protect against doors or windows being easily opened and objects being thrown inside.

- If the unthinkable happens, and you are caught up in the vicinity of a terrorist type attack, the first thing you must do is try to remove yourself from any imminent further danger.

- If the attack is just somewhere in the vicinity of your location (eg., if you hear an explosion nearby), take yourself into the nearest safe looking place such as a hotel or office building and take cover.

- If you are in your hotel when you hear an explosion, do not look outside the window as secondary blasts are very common following a bombing. Close the curtains, and extinguish the room lights and take shelter in a bathroom or interior stairwell. Try to get anyone else who is traveling with you to come together in one place. Remain sheltered until you are certain the danger has passed.

- If gunfire erupts, drop to the floor, or get down as low as possible, and try to shield yourself behind or under a solid object such as a heavy piece of furniture.

- As soon as possible, contact your nearest diplomatic mission, and ask for guidance.

- Never argue or attempt to fight with terrorists unless you are certain it is a life or death decision. Otherwise follow all instructions and orders from terrorists or responders.

- When responders arrive on the scene, adopt a position that makes it very clear you are a victim, not a combatant. Do not pick up anything or jump up to run toward the responders. Wait until the responders give you instructions and follow those instructions.

Scan for more resources.

THEFT & LOST DOCUMENTS
Prevention & Replacement

You are in a foreign country shopping in a popular crowded local market when you realize your passport and credit cards have been stolen. You have no idea who took them and doubt that you will get them back.

There are plenty of valuable items to worry about when you are travelling, including the security of your money, jewelry, cameras, computers, phones, credit cards, and travel documents. These days, you can also add your identity to the list of valuable items you need to protect.

Replacing valuables is arguably easier than dealing with a stolen identity, and the consequences of the latter can be significantly more devastating. If you do become a victim of theft despite all the precautions you have taken, act quickly to minimize damage.

If your credit cards are stolen, immediately contact your credit card companies to cancel the card(s) and notify the credit reporting agencies. Know how to report and deal with suspected identity theft.

KEY POINTS

» As obvious as this may seem, get travel insurance before you travel, and know exactly what the policy covers and how to report a claim. Check the small print on your credit card website before you go, some cards include various insurance capabilities as part of their service if the card is used to pay for your travel.

» Do some research, and ask a trusted local about safe places to go and places where you might need to be extra cautious.

» Whenever you venture out, know what you have on you...and think carefully about what you carry and leave behind. Think about separating your sources of cash. Consider leaving some cash and a credit card in a safe place, and only venturing out with what you think you will need for that day/night.

» Consider buying a cheap mobile phone with a local SIM card in it, or even putting the SIM card from your expensive smartphone into it when you go out. This allows you to leave your valuable phone and all its data back in a safe location.

» Consider carrying a "throw down wallet" in places where you suspect the risk of robbery or theft might be high. This is an older wallet containing an expired driving license, expired credit card, some other "filler" cards and a small amount of cash, which can be given up if a wallet is demanded. Of course if your life is threatened, just give the assailant what he wants.

» Money belts are very effective for concealing an emergency stash of cash. Some money belts made today are very inconspicuous and the hidden zipper pocket can hold thousands of dollars in cash or travellers checks.

» Photocopy or scan your passport (including important visas and entry stamps) and credit cards in a safe site, perhaps in an online email account or dropbox, which you can access from an Internet cafe if necessary. Keep a file with all contact phone numbers to report lost credit cards and other valuables. You should also keep a copy of your travel insurance policy in a place that can be accessed while travelling.

» Try not to be an obvious tourist or traveller. The less attention you bring to yourself, the lower the chance of being singled out by criminals.

» Don't underestimate the skill of pickpockets. Check your pockets after any contact with a stranger no matter how inconsequential it might appear at the time.

» Modify your behavior to match the degree of familiarity with your surroundings. For example, do not put yourself in the situation of being intoxicated in a place unfamiliar to you.

» When checking into a hotel, ask for a room near the elevator. This location is likely to have more passing pedestrian traffic and be less attractive a target for a criminal intent on breaking into a room.

» Place cash, passport and other valuables in the room safe or contact the reception for safe-deposit facilities every time you leave your room—there are a number of tools thieves use to get a hotel door open including electronic breaching devices, but getting into a room safe is significantly more difficult.

» Do not leave handbags, laptop computers, wallets, bags, documents, and other valuables unattended in hotel conference rooms, restaurants, or other public areas.

» Leave your room key and other valuables with reception or a trusted friend/colleague if using hotel facilities such as a swimming pool or sauna. Do not leave them unattended in clothing or bags nearby.

» Do not leave "Please Clean" or "Make Up My Room" signs outside your door. This announces the room is probably unoccupied. Just ask the reception to have your room made up.

BASIC GUIDELINES

• Call your credit card issuers to notify them of your travel plans before you leave on a trip.

• Have your home mail deliveries stopped or picked up by a trusted neighbor for the duration of your travel. There is a lot an identity thief can learn from your mail.

• Ensure that all your financial business transactions are taken care of face-to-face, and never give your credit card details to a stranger or an unknown caller.

• Use cash whenever possible, but if you must use a credit card, watch the transaction completely. Be sure no one is writing down your number or skimming your card.

• Avoid using your credit card number on public computers or at least ensure you are on a secure website, such as an HTML address that starts with https://. If you have to do this, make sure your information is removed prior to leaving the computer.

- Try to use only secure (closed) wireless networks. The free Wi-Fi networks at cafes, in hotel lobbies, and in other public places are notoriously not secure because they often lack data-encryption protections that closed networks have.

- Put a password lock on your smartphone. The amount of data most of us keep on our phones these days is astonishing. Not just emails and text messages, but bank details, addresses and contact details of friends, account passwords, photos of home, and travel details. Leaving this information unprotected makes it way to easy for hackers and identity thieves. Be smart and protect your phone with a home-screen-locking password or, if available, a fingerprint scan.

- Use ATMs very cautiously and whenever possible use only ATMs that are in bank branches during normal banking hours. Another good option if available is to use cash-back options at convenience stores, pharmacies, and shops. If possible, use a colleague to stand behind you to watch your back and block others from viewing your screen. Always tear up ATM receipts immediately.

- Check your credit card statements regularly while traveling. In these days of smartphones, many credit card providers offer an app that alerts you to any expenses on the card. Regularly checking your credit card account will quickly alert you to any unusual or unauthorized expenses.

- Do not use your passport as your default form of ID. Use a drivers license or other form of ID if possible.

- If you are the victim of theft while traveling, you must report it to local police as quickly as possible. You should also ask for a copy of the report as you will need it to replace your passport or make a claim on your travel insurance.

- Replacing lost travelers checks is easy. Just phone the emergency contact number shown on the check receipts or stubs and report the ones missing. Some companies will even offer a free collect call from abroad to report lost checks. Your check-issuing company will give you instructions for replacing the checks, generally within 24 hours in most locations.

- Make sure to advise your travel insurance provider at the earliest possible time after a theft. Many insurance policies have strict time limits on reporting thefts, so check your policy to understand what is expected of you in case of theft or loss. Your insurance provider will almost certainly need to see a copy of the police report.

- If your passport is lost or stolen while traveling, report it to the local police immediately. You will need a police report to get a new passport in most cases. Also immediately notify your nearest embassy, consulate or high commission, so that your passport can be cancelled—to avoid anyone using it illegally. The embassy will let you know exactly what to do. If you find your passport after reporting it lost or stolen you won't be able to use it and you should return it to your embassy, consulate or high commission, who will issue you with replacement travel documents for your return home. You may be charged a fee for this service which you should be able to claim on your travel insurance

- If you are on a package holiday, talk to your organizer's representative who will advise you on what to do if you lose your travel documents. If you are an independent traveler, contact your travel company or ticketing company immediately. Many organizations will charge a modest fee for replacement tickets, but with the proper identification, replacements are relatively easily obtained. The ticketing company may ask you to pay for a replacement ticket and then claim a refund from the company upon your return home.

- If you want to learn more about how to deal with and report identity theft, visit the U.S. Department of Justice's Identity Theft site at the site below: even if you are not a U.S. citizen, you will learn much about how to deal with this crime. http://www.justice.gov/criminal/fraud/websites/idtheft.html

Scan for more resources.

TORNADO
What To Do If Caught In the
Path of Destruction

A cell of severe thunderstorms with heavy winds is headed your way. The weather has been hot and humid but a cool front is forecasted to arrive soon. What should you do?

A tornado is a violent rotating column of air extending from a cloud and in contact with the ground. Tornadoes have been reported on every continent except Antarctica but the high concentration of these storms occurs in North America primarily in the U.S. midwest and south. The United States has four times as many tornadoes as all of Europe. Frequent tornadoes also occur in South Africa, Argentina, Paraguay, Brazil, the Netherlands, the UK, Bangladesh, eastern Asia, Australia, and New Zealand. They are also called cyclones and twisters, though cyclone is also used to describe large circulating hurricane-like storms of South Asia.

KEY POINTS

» Tornado severity is graded by different scales based on width and velocity and damage caused. These highly destructive storms have wind speeds ranging from 40 mph (64 kmh) to greater than 300 mph (480 kmh) and have widths from a few meters to over 2 miles (3.2 km). Less than 1 percent of tornadoes are extremely violent.

» Tornadoes usually occur in late afternoon after solar heating.

» Tornadoes stay on the ground for very short distances to many miles in extreme cases.

» A tornado can be a variety of colors depending on the debris in the funnel but is not always visible and may be obscured by rain, dust, or darkness.

» Other types of weaker and less destructive tornadoes include waterspouts and dust devils. Waterspouts vary in intensity and can be very powerful and dangerous if they develop from severe thunderstorms. Dust devils are not connected to a cloud.

BASIC GUIDELINES

- If you are in the path of a tornado you have little time to prepare.

- There is no geographical area safe from tornadoes. Tornadoes climb hills, go into valleys, and have been noted in all locations.

- Go to a basement or an interior first-floor room of a strong building or a storm shelter if available. Get under a table, staircase, or sturdy furniture. The side or corner away from the direction of approach is safest.

- If in the open, park your car at the side of the road and seek shelter in a sturdy building or basement. If not available, get into a ditch.

- If no ditch is available, stay in the car with the seat belt on. Put your head down below the windows. Cover your head with your hands and a blanket or coat if possible.

- Do not hide under a highway overpass or bridge. This is one of the most dangerous places to be during a tornado because of increased air flow and flying debris.

- Do not waste time opening windows in the house or building where you seek shelter. It makes no difference and actually may increase damage.

- Do not try to outrun a tornado in your car. Winds may exceed 200 mph, there is driving rain, and power lines may be down.

- If you are far enough away, drive at right angles to the storm.

Scan for more
resources.

TRAUMA TO THE ABDOMEN

You are on a rural bike trail and come upon another rider who has fallen and is clutching his abdomen and writhing on the ground. He has significant pain and is not very communicative. What is the best course of action?

Traumatic injury can be due to a direct blow (motor vehicle accident, fall, strike from hard object) or penetrating in nature (knife, gunshot, sharp object). Obviously, in severe trauma both can occur. All victims with significant abdominal injury should be evacuated rapidly.

Life-threatening hemorrhage can occur within the abdomen but diagnostic capability is limited and treatment is very difficult in areas without access to advanced medical care.

BASIC GUIDELINES

- The degree and angle of force and mechanism of injury will raise suspicion for abdominal injuries. Falling on a bicycle handlebar can cause injuries as severe as motor vehicle accidents.

- Examine the victim's abdomen while he or she is lying down. If there is significant tenderness or muscular rigidity, an internal injury should be suspected and rapid evacuation is advised.

- All penetrating wounds of the abdomen are surgical emergencies.

- Severe abdominal trauma often causes injuries to multiple organs.

- A strong blow to the upper right abdomen should raise concern about liver damage. Although the victim is likely to have significant tenderness and muscular rigidity in the face of liver injury, rather extensive injuries may have disproportionately less pain and rigidity. Be alert for liver injuries if there are multiple anterior or lateral lower right rib injuries.

- A strong blow to the upper left abdomen should raise concern for injury to the spleen. Again, pain and muscular rigidity may be disproportionate to the extent of injury. Multiple anterior or lateral lower left rib injuries should alert one to the possibility of spleen injury.

- Liver and spleen injuries can be accompanied with serious internal bleeding, a medical emergency.

- Lower abdominal trauma may also have associated pelvic fractures and other injuries where significant and potentially life-threatening hemorrhage can occur.

- Do not give oral fluids, pain medication, or other medications until evaluation in a medical facility has occurred.

**Scan for more
resources.**

TRAUMA TO THE CHEST

Walking in a forest, your companion stumbles and falls onto a tree stump hitting his chest and now has difficulty breathing and significant pain on that side. What should you do?

Traumatic injury can be from a direct force (motor vehicle accident, fall, strike from hard object) or from penetration (knife, gunshot, sharp object). Severe trauma can have both types of injury. Injury to the chest is one of the leading causes of death after trauma. All victims with significant chest injury should be evacuated rapidly. All penetrating wounds of the chest are surgical emergencies.

KEY POINTS

» Blunt injury can break ribs and/or the collarbone and can make breathing very painful.

» A broken rib, if it is a solitary injury, can be managed conservatively in a remote area until medical care can be sought.

» Multiple broken ribs suggest significant force and greater trauma necessitating evacuation for evaluation and treatment.

» Broken lower ribs may also indicate liver injuries on the right and possible spleen injuries on the left.

» Broken ribs in the back should raise concern about kidney damage as well as vertebral and spinal cord injuries. Kidney injuries can bleed significantly and is suspected if blood is in the urine. Any suspicion of spinal cord injury requires immobilization before moving the victim.

» Multiple fractures in a row may affect lung expansion and contraction in a condition known as flail chest. This causes severe respiratory dysfunction.

» Pneumothorax is a collapsed lung due to an air leak into the chest wall that prevents expansion of the lung. Pain, shortness of breath, difficulty breathing, and loss of breath sounds from the affected side are characteristic of pneumothorax.

» Any open wound should be rapidly covered with an impermeable bandage: vaseline gauze, tape, or cloth.

» Hemothorax is hemorrhage into the chest cavity. This often accompanies a pneumothorax in severe trauma. Hemothorax can be extensive and cause lung compression. The lung fails to expand on breathing and the patient struggles to breath.

» Pulmonary contusion is a bruised lung that can cause difficulty breathing and possible coughing up of blood.

» Cardiac contusions should be considered with motor vehicle accidents due to steering wheel blunt trauma.

» Serious injuries like pneumothorax, lung contusions, cardiac contusions, and rupture of internal organs such as the bronchi and esophagus may not present initially with significant distress but are potentially life threatening.

BASIC TREATMENT GUIDELINES

• Cushion the patient in a comfortable position and evaluate frequently for breathing difficulties.

• Do not tape or tightly wrap the chest to prevent compromise of lung expansion.

• Provide pain medication.

• Encourage at least one deep breath or cough each hour to keep lung expansion and help prevent pneumonia from developing. The victim will resist this because it is painful.

• Transport the victim to receive medical care at the earliest opportunity.

Scan for more resources.

TRAUMATIC BRAIN INJURY
Concussions to Coma

You and a friend decide to explore old French Foreign Legion forts in Morocco. The guide leads you up a steep set of steps to a parapet when your friend slips and falls hitting his head against a stone pillar. He suffers a brief loss of consciousness, makes a few jerking movements, and then regains consciousness. He appears confused and has a small cut that is not bleeding significantly near his right temple. You try to help him up but he refuses your help and says "I'm okay."

Traumatic Brain Injury (TBI) is a broad category of injury that includes any type of injury to the brain ranging from concussion or mild TBI to penetrating injuries of the brain.

Only milder injuries will be considered in this chapter because a traveling companion can have an impact to improve the outcome or even save a life.

KEY POINTS

» The brain is a 3-pound soft organ encased in a hard box. The job of that box is to protect that soft organ from injury. For much of our lives the box or braincase (skull) protects the brain from bumps or bruises. It can also be part of the problem in a brain injury so sorting out a possible brain injury early is key.

» If the victim has profuse bleeding, objects protruding from the skull, visible pieces of skull fragments protruding from the scalp, visible brain protruding from the scalp, is unconscious, is actively seizing, or is pulseless, then this is a dire emergency for which immediate evacuation and supportive care is the only option. Maintaining the airway, attempting to stopbleeding, and positioning the victim to prevent choking on blood, vomit, or biting their tongue are about the only measures to do while arranging for a rapid evacuation either by EMS in urban environments or an emergency evacuation plan in a remote area.

» Remember that any significant injury to the brain is also a potential injury to the spine. Neck stabilization is necessary to evacuate a person with a significant TBI.

» Even if apparently not immediately life threatening, be careful not to ignore ominous warning signs, Loss of consciousness, vomiting, unequal pupils, bizarre behavior, severe headache, or excessive sleepiness are all signs of a serious emergency.

BASIC GUIDELINES

- For less serious injuries, take the person to a safe and quiet place in order to start the evaluation process.

- Determine if there are there any visible signs of injury including cuts, bruises, or deformity. Determine if the victim is lucid or confused and how quickly they respond to questions or physical stimuli.

- If the victim appears to have a minimal injury, is lucid, and responds to questions reasonably, you can administer a simple concussion examination. There are several concussion assessment tools available for purchase, or that can be downloaded as mobile apps. Included is a link to the MACE or Military Acute Concussion Evaluation as an example. Others include IMPACT, SCAT2, and the King-Devick tests. An objective measure is helpful to determine a baseline status to monitor any change in mental state. This is also helpful in communicating with remote health care providers to determine evacuation.

- Regardless of how minor a brain injury might be (a concussion is still a brain injury) anyone who sustains a TBI should be seen by a healthcare provider. A small percentage of even mild TBI sufferers will ultimately develop chronic post-concussion syndrome. It is important that the organ of decision making, the brain, be cleared by someone trained to do so.

Scan for more resources.

TRAVEL IN ARID CLIMATES

You are on summer vacation in New Mexico and plan to hike 5 miles to an abandoned silver mine up in the hills. The elevation is 5000 feet and your plan is to start early but you will have to hike back in the afternoon. What special precautions should you take?

Travel in the heat can be quite taxing and requires attention to safety. Lower humidity in an arid climate can be deceptive because the heat index is less despite high temperatures and may lead to less concern for safety. An arid climate is not just found in the desert: paradoxically, marine vessels on the open water can create an arid environment on a sailing or commercial voyage.

BASIC GUIDELINES

- Plan ahead and pay attention to weather forecasts.
- Try to avoid times of the most intense sun (generally 10 am to 4 pm).
- Hike earlier in the day and do not be overly ambitious.
- Take frequent breaks.
- Wear lightweight, light-colored, and loose clothing.
- Hats with a brim, sunglasses, and sunscreen to block UVA and UVB radiation are very important.
- Higher elevation is generally cooler but sun intensity and fluid loss increase.
- Hydration is essential.
- Start hydration early, before your activity. There is a tendency to wait too long to begin hydrating.
- Drink frequently in smaller amounts to optimize hydration.

- Eat snacks with salt and drink sports drinks with electrolytes if possible to help replenish minerals lost in sweat. Large volumes of water consumed without mineral and electrolyte replacement is also dangerous.

- Do not drink alcohol when on activities in these climates because alcohol increases fluid excretion and overrides the body's mechanism for water conservation.

- A good rule is to monitor your urine output and quality. If you have not urinated every few hours you are likely becoming dehydrated. Dark urine likely means you need more hydration.

- Children and the elderly are more susceptible to dehydration.

- Be aware of the signs and symptoms of heat exhaustion and heat stroke (see Heat Exhaustion and Heat Stroke). Heat exhaustion presents with a rapid weak pulse, dizziness, nausea, headache, diarrhea, and mild temperature elevation. Some confusion or irrational behavior may occur. Sweating may be either present or absent and skin of the patient may feel cool to the touch.

Scan for more resources.

TRAVEL IN COLD CLIMATES

You are headed to Yellowstone for a multi-day snowmobiling adventure. There is good snow cover with more snow forecast and a cold snap is headed down from Canada. What special precautions should you take?

Travel in cold climates requires planning for safety and awareness of the environment. Being unprepared for sudden decreases in temperature and changing climatic conditions can be disastrous.

BASIC GUIDELINES

- Listen to the weather forecast. Pay special attention to the possibility of precipitation and wind chill warnings.

- Adjust your plan for outdoor exposure according to changing conditions. Outdoor time should be decreased with dropping temperatures and increasing wind chill. Have a safety plan if conditions deteriorate beyond the expected and seek shelter.

- Pay attention to any warnings of avalanche and avoid potential danger (see Avalanche Survival).

- Dress in layers and cover as much exposed skin as possible. Wear a hat because significant heat can be lost from a bare head. Extremities lose heat the fastest so wear gloves, mittens, and cover your nose and ears with a scarf or balaclava.

- Waterproof and warm footwear is very important. Wear non-constricting warm socks to promote circulation.

- An outer wind resistant layer is advisable.

- Sunglasses are very important in bright sun with snow to prevent corneal injuries and snowblindness (see Eye Injuries).

- Stay dry. Wet clothing increases heat loss and chance for frostbite.

- Keep active.
- Check on children and older members of the group frequently, they may not adapt adequately to the cold.
- Limit use of alcohol which increases circulation to the skin and heat loss.
- Know and look for the signs of hypothermia: prolonged shivering, confusion, loss of muscular control manifested by staggering, clumsy movements, inability to perform simple physical tasks (see Hypothermia and Frostbite).

Scan for more resources.

TRAVEL IN TROPICAL CLIMATES

You have signed up to go to a nature reserve for eco-tourism in a tropical country for ten days. What special preparations will you need?

Unless you live in a tropical climate, you will not be acclimated to the heat and humidity nor will you be familiar with local flora and fauna. Both physical and mental stability begin to deteriorate after two weeks on an extended stay in remote tropical environments if under stress.

KEY POINTS

» When planning for a tropical adventure, nutrition is an important consideration because of increased energy requirements. Safaris likely have sufficient food but if you are trekking, hiking for long in the jungle, on a dive expedition, or similar activity dependent on your own food sources, the right mix of food and nutrients must be calculated because physically demanding activity increases caloric needs. High heat and humidity will add to those caloric needs. Food is very important for good morale (see Nutrition).

» Potable water is as necessary as food and you should plan to drink 4 to 6 liters per day if physically active. Natural water flows should be considered contaminated until treated or disinfected. People often need to be encouraged to drink more water in tropical climates so make sure you have enough bottled water.

BASIC GUIDELINES

• Plan your trip to avoid undesirable local climate conditions. Travel and climate are likely more favorable between rainy seasons when some areas of desired travel may be inaccessible.

• Pay attention to the political situation at your destination. Check with your embassy or national consular department to determine safety of the intended location for travel.

- Learn about the flora and fauna of the destination to familiarize yourself with potential risks of exposure to noxious plants and dangerous animals, large and small.

- Make sure you have up-to-date vaccinations.

- Light, loose clothing with long sleeves and pants are surprisingly cool and help protect you from insects, scratches from brush, and unnecessary sun exposure.

- Sunglasses, a hat with a brim, and appropriate sunscreen should be used with direct sun exposure (see Burns). Sun exposure increases in intensity the closer you get to the equator.

- Proper footwear is essential. Break in any new boots before your trip to avoid blisters. Knee-high rubber boots are very practical and protective in rainforests.

- Assemble a personal travel kit and personal medical kit (see Personal Travel Medical Kit, Personal Travel Supplies).

- Bring extra medication if taken daily. This will avoid having to refill prescriptions if your trip is delayed or extended. Your medicine may be unavailable at your destination.

- Ziplock bags of different sizes are very useful for protecting medication, phones, cameras, and other materials sensitive to moisture.

- Shake out boots and shoes before putting them on in the morning to detect any spiders, scorpions, or other undesired visitors that may have crawled in at night.

- Do not wander off the trail or planned route.

- Do not swim in fresh water bodies because of parasites.

- Do not attempt to touch any wild animals or insects. Remember everything bites!

Scan for more resources.

TRAVEL PREPARATION
Be Prepared: More Than Just a Motto

You have been invited to go on a fishing excursion in the boundary waters and your trip organizer tells you the team will be two weeks in austere environments with little contact with the outside world. There will be an expedition medical kit and each team member is asked to put together their own personal kit. What are the key items to consider and assemble for a trip like this?

Preparing for remote travel entails significant preparation to ensure that you have the essential clothing, equipment, and personal supplies to enjoy and survive your adventure. Attention to detail is very important to avoid not only minor inconveniences but also potentially very troublesome problems. The time and trouble expended for trip preparation will be well spent.

BASIC GUIDELINES

- Allow enough time to prepare properly. Try to avoid scurrying around at the last minute to get supplies, equipment, necessary vaccinations, and medications. While there are often a few items to collect as departure nears, basic supplies and clothing can be stockpiled ahead of time.

- Make sure that you are physically fit to undergo the adventure. It is recommended for you to have had a recent physical exam by your physician, particularly if the trip will be physically demanding. You may be required to have medical clearance to participate. It is important to uncover a medical condition which can be corrected in time to go or to find out that you are not able to participate before a lot of money is spent on travel reservations and gear. It is advisable to have a copy of your medical record, emergency contacts, and other vital health details on a flash drive with you in case of emergency. Provide a copy to the group or expedition leader or let them know about the flash drive.

- Do not neglect dental care. A dental abscess in a remote area is excruciatingly painful and can be avoided by a recent dental exam.

- Determine with your healthcare provider that all regular vaccinations are up to date prior to departure. Also determine if you need any vaccinations or medications for prevention of diseases specific for the area of travel (see Immunizations and Prophylaxis). Some vaccinations may be difficult to get or require a series of injections to complete.

- Find out your need for insurance coverage. Examine existing policies for exclusions, limits of coverage, and determine if you need evacuation insurance. Travelers to remote areas should have medical evacuation insurance (see Insurance and Evacuation). Speak to the provider to determine how an evacuation will occur if needed.

- Research the area of travel to learn about climate, geopolitical considerations, culture, currency, illegal or forbidden practices, necessary permits for your activities (fishing and hunting licenses, photography and video permits, travel to restricted areas), transportation to remote areas, and overall safety and security.

- Prepare a personal travel medicine kit to include your prescription medications and those used for common ailments (see Personal Travel Medical Kits). Be efficient with packing, bring extra critical medications in case of travel delay or change in plans.

- Prepare details of your itinerary and leave with relatives or a close friend. Contact your embassy or consulate if you are going to a developing country to let them know once you are in country. This is particularly important if you are going to a remote area.

- Determine well in advance your need for a visa. Visa requirements change and you may need several weeks to obtain a visa. Visas for travel to Brazil and India are classic examples of this issue for Americans.

- Be sure to bring notebooks and pens to record your experiences and thoughts. Photographs are usually considered by travelers but they may forget to bring writing items.

- Learn about cell phone options – especially if you plan to use your current cell phone overseas. Costs and services vary widely. Some people choose to purchase a local phone with paid minutes in the foreign destination or rely on public pay phone options.

- Last, be flexible. Very few extensive or complicated trips have no glitches or delays. Keep a good attitude and you will maximize your experience.

Scan for more resources.

TSUNAMI
When the Unthinkable Occurs

Your business trip to SE Asia has provided an uexpected gap that allows you to go to a beach resort a few hours from the major city where you are staying. As you are leaving on the trip, the news reports an earthquake of 5.9 in the southern Philippines. Should you be concerned?

A tsunami is the series of waves produced by underground or underwater disturbances such as earthquakes, explosions, landslides, and glacier activity. Tsunamis are different than normal sea waves because of their very long wavelength. Rather than a breaking wave, tsunami waves resemble a rising tide, and consequently have also been called tidal waves.

KEY POINTS

» Ocean waves from wind average about 100 meters between crests and 2 meters in height while tsunami wavelengths can be as long as 200 km with a height of only 1 meter. Such large waves can travel at 500 mph (800 kph) in the ocean but slow to 50 mph (80 kph) near the coast as the shallow water decreases the wavelength but increases the height enormously.

» The time between waves can range from minutes to hours and, depending on the magnitude and distance from the underground event, can result in huge waves with heights of many meters. Damage and loss of life is generally confined to the coastal areas but can be tremendous and extend to countries along an entire ocean basin.

» About 80 percent of tsunamis occur in the Pacific Ocean.

» Damage from tsunami waves occurs with both the smashing ridge and the trough withdrawal. Sometimes the trough arrives first on land and the curious phenomenon of a retreating sea and exposed seabed is noted followed a few minutes later by the arrival of the wave peak. This sequence is repeated several times.

» If the tsunami strikes a heavily populated coastal area, loss of life can be catastrophic. The 2004 tsunami killed over 230,000 people in countries surrounding the Indian Ocean, some of them quite far from the epicenter.

BASIC SAFETY GUIDELINES

- It has not been determined why all earthquakes do not cause tsunamis but many of them do so if an earthquake has occurred, be on alert for a tsunami emergency.

- Do not stay in low coastal areas after a strong earthquake in your area.

- There are multiple waves in a tsunami so stay on high ground until cleared by authorities.

- Immediately evacuate if you note an unusual fall in the coastal water. The same holds true if you see a noticeable significant rise in coastal water.

- No false alarms are issued by the Pacific Tsunami Warning Center.

- Never go to watch a tsunami. If you can see the wave, you likely will not escape unless on significantly high ground.

- Cooperate with local authorities and follow their advice.

Scan for more resources.

TYPHOON & HURRICANE
Beware of Big Winds

You are in a coastal town in an area where typhoons or hurricanes are known to occur. A tropical depression is forming and is predicted to hit land fifty miles away. Speculation is that it will get worse though it is unknown whether and to what degree it will intensify. What should you do?

Typhoons and hurricanes are different names for the same type of violent, circular storm. These storms are called typhoons in the Pacific NW basin and can occur year round while similar storms in the Atlantic and eastern Pacific are called hurricanes and are more seasonal, occurring between June and November with a peak from mid-August to late October.

KEY POINTS

» A tropical circular storm is called a tropical depression if wind speed is less than 40 mph, a tropical storm with winds speeds between 40 and 75 mph, and a typhoon or hurricane if wind speed exceeds 75 mph. In some areas like the Philippines, tropical storms are called Category 1 typhoons, storms with winds between 75 and 100 mph are Category 2, and those in excess of 100 mph are Category 3.

» The Philippines, closely followed by China and Japan, have the highest incidence of typhoons.

» No matter the classification, these storms are all dangerous and capable of causing significant destruction and loss of life. Typhoons and hurricanes can bring heavy, damaging rain, cause storm surges and extensive flooding, and spawn strong thunderstorms and tornadoes. Landslides can occur from the heavy rains.

» Generally, there is a warning of a few days, allowing time for evacuation or stockpiling of food and supplies but remote areas may have less notice.

» Circular (cyclonic) storms are characterized by a central zone of low storm activity called an eye with resumption of turbulence after it passes.

BASIC SAFETY GUIDELINES

Surviving a violent storm of this type may depend on your preparation, protection during the storm, and observation of safety rules in the aftermath.

- Large violent storms may occur over a few days and restoration of electricity and resumption of public services may take several days to weeks.

- In the days before a storm arrives, pay attention to updates of developing weather from radio, television, or Internet sources.

- Board up the windows or place storm shutters if available.

- Collect enough drinking water in large containers to last several days.

- Stockpile food sufficient to last several days. You may be without refrigeration.

- Have enough medication for chronic disorders to last for a couple of weeks.

- Have batteries, flashlights, battery-operated radio, first aid kit, and basic tools (such as manual can opener) available.

- Have some books or other entertainment.

- Prepare a secure room in the interior of the building away from all windows if possible.

- During the storm, stay away from windows.

- Stay under a table or stairwell in your secure room during the brunt of the storm if possible.

- Avoid phone use if lightning is occurring.

- Monitor weather reports.

- Be prepared to evacuate if near a large body of water that could flood from storm surges or massive rain.

- Resist going outdoors when the eye of the storm passes over. Power lines may be down and flying debris is dangerous. The storm will resume shortly.

- Make sure the storm has completely passed before going out.

- Beware of and stay away from downed power lines

- Make sure drinking water sources are not contaminated.

- Be patient, resumption of normal utilities and services may be delayed.

Scan for more resources.

UROLOGIC PROBLEMS
From Stones to STDs

You are on an extended business trip overseas and have noticed some discoloration in your urine that may be blood. You also experience some discomfort when urinating. You do not have a history of urinary problems but you know the possibility increases as you get older. You notice you are urinating more frequently. Should you be concerned?

Urinary tract problems can occur in the kidney, ureter (tube between the kidney and bladder), bladder, urethra (tube from the bladder to the outside), and in the male genitalia.

KEY POINTS

» Visible blood in the urine (hematuria) is disturbing but rarely life threatening unless massive or if significant trauma has occurred in which case more than one organ system is usually involved. Many conditions can cause hematuria and a little bit of blood looks like a lot.

» Painless hematuria needs to be evaluated in a timely fashion but is rarely a cause for evacuation.

» Hematuria with pain can be caused by common conditions like urinary calculi (stones) and bladder infections.

» Passage of urinary calculi is very painful, associated with flank pain that may radiate to the lower abdomen or groin, waxes and wanes, and may be associated with nausea and vomiting. Small stones may pass but larger ones can cause complete obstruction. Obstruction is a medical emergency because the trapped urine can damage the kidney or lead to an infection which is potentially life threatening. Any fever other than low grade in this situation is an emergency because of the potential for overwhelming infection. Treatment consists of pain control, hydration, and use of an alpha adrenergic blocker (tamsulosin, alfuzosin), which relaxes smooth muscle to aid passage. The victim may need to be evacuated for fever or pain control.

» Bladder infection is characterized by frequent urination accompanied by burning and there may be a foul smell and blood in the urine. Recent sexual activity may be related to the infection. Treatment consists of appropriate antibiotics, hydration, pain medication in severe cases, and medical attention if accompanied by a high fever. Drinking cranberry juice does help prevent urinary tract infections in women.

» Acute urinary retention is the inability to pass urine and is accompanied by severe lower abdominal discomfort. This is most often seen in males and commonly related to urethral scar tissue in younger males and prostatic obstruction in older males. This is a medical emergency that is often preceded by difficulty with urination. Antihistamine use can be a cause of urinary retention in men. Alpha adrenergic blocker medication (tamsulosin, alfuzosin) may help with this problem but urologic consultation is required to address acute urinary retention.

» Testicular torsion is the twisting of the testicle that causes obstruction to its blood supply. This surgical emergency is accompanied by acute pain and most commonly occurs in adolescents and younger men. The testicle will not survive if the strangulation of the blood supply is not relieved within 6 to 10 hours. Any severe pain in the testicle should be evaluated for torsion, which may be mistaken for an infection.

» Epididymitis is a painful swelling of the back of the testes caused by an infection. Urinary tract symptoms of burning and frequency of urination may be present. Treatment consists of pain medication and appropriate antibiotics under the guidance of a health care professional. It is very important to rule out a testicular torsion.

» Sexually transmitted diseases (STD) can cause burning during urination and a discharge. Both gonorrhea and non-specific urethritis from other organisms are prevalent throughout the world and occur within a few days of exposure. Broad spectrum antibiotics are required. Other sexually transmitted diseases include HIV/AIDS, syphilis, and other painful or ulcerating disorders that usually manifest from weeks to months after exposure. Do not treat sexually transmitted diseases with just any antibiotic – seek medical attention to assure prescription of the proper antibiotic in an adequate dose.

Scan for more
resources.

VICTIM OF VIOLENT CRIME
Avoiding & Reacting To Violent Crime

You are out for dinner in a foreign city and on the way home from the restaurant you are accosted and robbed of your wallet and jewelry. Your companion is assaulted when he resists, sustaining injuries that require medical care.

Violent crime targeting foreigners and/or travelers is becoming increasingly prevalent in many countries. Although we need to acknowledge that there is no such thing as a risk-free environment, it is important to minimize both the likelihood and the impact of such crimes. Violent crimes can happen—and do happen—in almost every city of the world, in particular those places that have been hardest hit by economic downturns. What is not generally known is that the victims of violent crime are most often known in some way by their attackers—even if only marginally, such as having been identified as a traveler. Travelers are generally more likely to submit to the demands of criminals without the use of force, and therefore are among the most common victims of crime. Naivety and complacency are among the most common reasons people become a victim of violent crime.

KEY POINTS

»   Familiarize yourself with the laws and customs of the countries you are visiting. Laws can be quite different than what you are used to in your home country and often differ because of variances in definitions of crime based on culture. Language can be a barrier to understanding legal circumstances or interpreting laws. Legal rights may be quite different from what you are used to.

»   Travel advisories should be checked. The U.S. State Department advisories are a good resource for Americans. Other countries also have travel advisories.

» Consider registering with the U.S. State Department Smart Traveler Program.

» If you are the victim of crime, get help to make sure you are safe

» Contact the U.S. embassy or consulate to report a crime and seek assistance. There is an emergency duty officer even when the embassy or consulate is closed.

» The U.S. Embassy can provide immediate assistance in person or on the telephone, information about the role and services of local law enforcement, coordination of services with local governments and resources, emotional support, and assistance for victims of crime who must return to a country to testify. Citizens of other countries should contact their consulate for assistance, similar services are often provided.

» Consular representatives can provide valuable assistance in cases of robbery, sexual assault, missing persons, parental child abduction, and death of a citizen.

» Some countries like the United States and the United Kingdom have an office for terrorism victim assistance. These provide assistance with injuries, evacuation needs, companion family members, payment of immediate medical expenses, compensation for material loss, and repatriation of remains.

BASIC GUIDELINES

The following advice is intended to serve as a practical checklist to reduce the risk of becoming a victim:

• Criminals prefer single targets. Keep this in mind when venturing out.

• Criminals will generally select the most vulnerable, weakest looking individual to target. Don't allow yourself to look vulnerable or weak.

• Understand that most violent crimes occur after dark or in the very early hours of the morning and in the more squalid parts of a city, such as outside bars, ports, bus stations, empty parks, alleys, and unlit side streets.

- Always appear to be confident and focused about what you are doing even if it is just walking down the street.

- Do not refer to maps in public, or create the appearance of being lost by asking for directions in public. If necessary, do these things inside a shop, away from the street.

- Understand that many criminals feel they have nothing to lose. Don't respond in any manner that forces the criminal to respond with violence, and look for ways to give the criminal an easy opportunity to escape.

- Stay aware of your surroundings, glance around occasionally and if possible use window reflections to check to see if you are being followed.

- It's good idea to carry a "throw down" wallet when traveling. Keep a small amount of cash and some expired credit cards in it to make it look authentic.

- If confronted by an armed criminal, cooperate fully, give the attacker only what he asks for, and do so without hesitation.

- Once you have given the criminal what he wants, back away slowly and leave the area calmly, and go to the nearest safe place to report the incident (police station, hotel, public building).

- If you are traveling out of the country, report the incident to your embassy.

- Do not try to respond with violence or by using any form of offensive weapons such as pepper spray. Such weapons are generally not effective and only serve to make the criminal angrier.

- Try to remember details of the attacker's appearance without making it obvious you are doing so. This way you will be able to provide a description to the police.

- Request a copy of the police report for insurance purposes.

Scan for more resources.

WATER SAFETY
Pay Attention to Basic Principles

On our family vacation this year, a lot of time will be spent in the pool and also in lakes and rivers. What safety measures should I take?

Many types of travel have an involvement with water, whether it is recreational swimming, boating, or similarly related activities. Whatever the activity, certain safety precautions are essential.

KEY POINTS

»   Drowning is probably the best recognized risk of water activities. Drowning is the second leading cause of unintentional injury deaths in children, and ranks fifth for all ages. Children can drown in just a few inches of water, even in a shallow bathtub. Over two-thirds of children under four years of age who drown do so in swimming pools. Make certain pools have locked fences, teach children (including toddlers) to swim and to respect the water, young children should wear life jackets in pools. Children should always be supervised around any water (see Drowning).

»   Adults should never swim alone, and know your swimming limits. Preferably, swim where there are lifeguards. Follow warnings for no swimming when there are rough tides and currents, or sharks or jellyfish. Stay out of the water if there is any threat of lightning.

»   When boating or water skiing, always wear appropriate personal protective gear—almost 90 percent of boaters who drown were not wearing life jackets.

»   Infectious diseases are becoming an increasing problem in the water. Respect your fellow swimmers, and shower with soap before entering a pool. Though chlorine can kill many organisms in swimming pools, Cryptosporidium often survives. This organism causes diarrhea and is transmitted by the oral-fecal route. Pools become contaminated from microscopic amounts of fecal matter. If diapered children are allowed in pools, diapers should be changed often. Children and adults with diarrhea should not be allowed to swim in pools or other areas. Never drink the water when swimming.

» Organisms, such as Pseudomonas, can grow in hot tubs. This organism can result in an itchy red skin irritation called "hot tub rash." The bumps can become infected around hair follicles. Prevention includes showering before entering a hot tub, and removing swimsuits and showering with soap when leaving the hot tub. (Also wash your suit after each wearing.)

BASIC GUIDELINES

- Make certain that the chlorine (or other disinfectant) and pH levels are monitored and properly maintained in pools and hot tubs.

- When traveling, especially outside of the United States, use caution when swimming. Many hotel swimming pools are not chlorinated to U.S. standards, and can spread disease. Outside swimming locations—beaches, rivers, and lakes—may be contaminated by unprocessed residential sewage. Just because others are swimming there does not make it safe. If you choose to swim in these areas, be very careful not to drink any of the water. Shower completely after swimming, and wash your swimsuit.

- Use extreme caution when swimming in lakes, rivers, and ocean beaches; swim only in areas marked for swimming, and preferably where there is a lifeguard. Natural water areas can have dangerous eddies, undertows, and other deadly water features that threaten even the strongest of swimmers.

- If you are prone to swimmer's ear infections wear earplugs and keep your ears as dry as possible.

- Some pool disinfectants can irritate eyes, especially if the air around the pool is not well circulated.

- If you snorkel or SCUBA dive, follow accepted safety precautions. Rent gear from reliable sources, especially if outside the United States.

- Remember to wear sunscreen when exposed to the sun, and refresh often when in the water (see Burns).

- If you boat often, consider taking a boating safety course.

- Alcohol and water sports, whether boating or swimming, don't mix. Never drink any amount of alcohol if you will have any boating responsibilities including as the mate.

Scan for more resources.

WOMEN: PROBLEMS UNIQUE TO

You are going on a six-week trek to an intermittently inaccessible area. Are there special safety and health issues women travelers should consider?

Women travelers, especially if traveling alone, face certain specific challenges. From a safety aspect, women alone are often seen as potential targets for crime. Pay special attention to other sections of this book regarding lost persons, assault, rape, and violent crime. From a medical perspective, the sections on travel and pregnancy, and sexually transmitted diseases are especially relevant to female travelers.

From a general gynecological health perspective, women should pay special attention to several areas, especially planning before they depart.

KEY POINTS

The goal is to prevent illness, especially emergency situations or serious illness, during travel. Women should consider the following:

» Make certain your general preventive gynecologic and other exams are current and that any issues have been addressed. If your next checkup is due during the travel period, complete it before you leave. Be up-to-date on:

- Mammogram (and remember to continue breast self-exams during your travel)

- Pregnancy test—if the travel would be a risk to the pregnancy, such as mountain climbing

- Other routine preventive services, including dental (this holds true for men).

» If you have any gynecologic symptoms, however minor, seek definitive treatment. Don't assume they will get better—get treatment instead.

A minor vaginal infection can develop into a major concern in the heat and moisture of a jungle, isolated from medical care. A simple urinary tract infection can become debilitating. Pelvic inflammatory disease (PID) can advance to a tubo-ovarian abscess becoming a true medical emergency requiring immediate treatment. Bleeding fibroids can become a life-threatening medical emergency in a remote area.

» If you have a history of vaginal infections, determine what treatment medications you may need during your travels, learn when to use them, and bring them with you.

» Consider whether any prescription contraception medication or related over-the-counter supplies (such as condoms) will likely be needed, and, if so, bring an adequate supply with you. Remember only barrier contraceptives like condoms help to prevent sexually transmitted diseases and HIV/AIDS.

» Bring adequate tampons or sanitary pads; they may not be obtainable where you are traveling. Also, remember to change tampons at least every six to eight hours to prevent toxic shock syndrome.

» Various unavoidable gynecologic health issues can occur while traveling. Though some can be very uncomfortable, most are not dangerous, and can be managed.

BASIC GUIDELINES

• Severe abdominal pain that may be accompanied by nausea and vomiting can be a sign of a ruptured ectopic pregnancy, ruptured ovarian cyst, or adnexal torsion. All three are true emergencies—the first two result in excessive internal bleeding that rapidly leads to shock, and even death. Adnexal torsion (twisting of the ovary and possibly the fallopian tube) can cut off the blood supply and result in necrosis and life-threatening abdominal infection.

• Severe gynecologic trauma or hemorrhage requires immediate medical care.

• Do not ignore warning signs such as severe, sudden abdominal pain. That can be a sign of significant internal bleeding which can kill quickly. Sudden severe vaginal bleeding can be a sign of miscarriage or other acute event that can be dangerous if not treated immediately. When there is a sudden change with severe symptoms (pain, bleeding, etc.), pay attention and seek medical consultation immediately.

Scan for more resources.

INDEX

AUTHOR BIOGRAPHIES

MICHAEL J. MANYAK, MD, FACS

Dr. Michael J. Manyak is a urologist, explorer, and corporate medical executive with significant expertise in expedition medicine. He is the former Chief Medical Officer for Triple Canopy, Inc., a large international high threat security firm. Dr. Manyak received the Distinguished Eagle Scout Award from the Boy Scouts of America, awarded to one in a thousand Eagle Scouts. He serves as Vice President of the National Eagle Scout Association and heads the NESA World Explorer Program, sending nationally-selected Eagles on expeditions.

Dr. Manyak maintains an avid interest in field exploration and expedition medicine and edited the highly regarded resource *Expedition and Wilderness Medicine*. He is a consultant to the medical office of the National Geographic Society and consulted for NPR Radio Expeditions and *USA Today* for travel medical issues. He was the urologic consultant to the Peace Corps. Dr. Manyak has served on the NASA Aerospace Medicine and Occupational Health Advisory Committee. He served on The Explorers Club Board of Directors for 10 years and is an Associate Editor of *The Explorers Journal* where his column on Expedition Medicine appears. Dr. Manyak has led a scientific expedition to the Ndoki rain forest in the Congo Basin in a collaborative effort with the World Wildlife

Fund, has dived the Spanish galleon Nuestra Senora de Atocha in search of artifacts, was the ship physician on the icebreaker *MV Polar Star* for an Antarctic expedition, and was the medical director for the *RMS Titanic* salvage expedition and dove to the *Titanic* wreck site in the Russian MIR submersible. In recent years, Dr. Manyak was the medical officer on an expedition to the deepest canyon in the world in Peru, on the first scientific dive in Mongolia in Asia's second largest lake, on an expedition to evaluate a new spectacular finding of early human footprints in Tanzania, rode camels in the Gobi Desert observing the very highly endangered wild camel, and explored the Amazon rain forest in the Yasuni National Park of eastern Ecuador.

Dr. Manyak has received several awards for educational and editorial activities, is a frequent national and international speaker, has numerous appearances on national networks, and was profiled by *Washingtonian Magazine* as one of 50 people selected as The Best and Brightest of Washington. He has published over 200 professional abstracts, book chapters, and refereed journal articles and has been granted 11 patents. He maintains his academic appointments as Adjunct Professor of Urology, Engineering, Microbiology, Immunology, and Tropical Medicine at The George Washington University.

Scan for more resources.

Colca Canyon, Peru, 2006

REAR ADMIRAL JOYCE M. JOHNSON, DO, USPHS (RET)

Rear Admiral Joyce M. Johnson, DO, USPHS (Ret) is a physician with a breadth of global public health experience. She serves on various for-profit and non-profit boards and advisory committees.

Dr. Johnson has worked on all seven continents. She has particular interests in systems development, third world health care delivery, emergency preparedness and disaster relief. She has been an "on site" responder following a number of floods and hurricanes, and most recently was in the Philippines following Typhoon Haiyan, one of the most ferocious typhoons ever recorded. For over a decade she has been a consultant to the National Science Foundation on development of the health care system for Antarctica, and has been to the South Pole twice.

RADM Johnson served in the US Public Health Service (Rear Admiral, Upper Half). Her last active duty assignment was with the US Coast Guard as director, health and safety ("surgeon general"). She managed the Coast Guard's health care system, including 150 sickbays and clinics worldwide. She also had responsibility for the Coast Guard's safety, security, and work-life programs.

Other government assignments included senior scientific and management positions with the Food and Drug Administration. At the Centers for

Disease Control and Prevention, she was an Epidemiologic Intelligence Service (EIS) Officer and staff epidemiologist in the Center for Infectious Disease, and was one of the first HIV/AIDS researchers, with a focus on the disease among Haitians.

Dr. Johnson is active with numerous organizations, including The Explorers Club and the Society of Women Geographers. She has been a medical director with Project HOPE in Asia and Africa. She has been a volunteer with DoCare to Central and South America.

Dr. Johnson is board certified in three specialties - Public Health and Preventive Medicine, Clinical Pharmacology, and Psychiatry. She is also a Certified Addiction Specialist and Certified Food Services Executive. She is a Governance Fellow, National Association of Corporate Directors. In addition to her medical degree, she earned a master's degree in Hospital and Health Administration. She has been conferred five honorary doctoral degrees.

Dr. Johnson writes the monthly "Ask the Doctor" and "Nutrition" columns for the *Military Officer Magazine* (readership about 500,000), the regular *Health Today: Q&A* for *Uniformed Services Journal*, and writes on a range of health topics for lay and professional audiences. She is a frequent speaker at professional meetings. She is active with many professional associations and has served on expert committees including the National Academy of Science, Institute of Medicine.

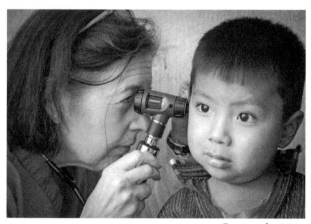

Guatemala, 2009

WARREN J. YOUNG, MBA

Warren J. Young is the Director of Security Services and Business Continuity for the International Monetary Fund (IMF), based in Washington DC. In this capacity he is accountable for designing and implementing the safety and security program responsible for employees who travel to, and work in all 188 IMF member countries. To assist the IMF in achieving its objective of fostering global growth and economic stability worldwide, Mr. Young is responsible for the travel safety and security preparedness of up to 600 traveling personnel per day, who conduct an average of 8,500 overseas missions per year – many of which take place in some of the most challenging security environments on the planet. He is a former Head of Security for the Asian Development Bank, based in Manila Philippines and a former Regional Director of Operations (Asia Pacific) for the global risk and strategic consulting firm, Control Risks. He is a former Australian Army officer who served his country for 22 years in both conventional and Special Forces, participating in several overseas deployments including an operational tour of duty as a commander of a multi-national military force in Afghanistan, for which he was awarded the United Nations Special Service medal. Among other military awards, Mr. Young is also the recipient of the Australian Defense Force's Conspicuous Service Cross. As a security professional with more than 15 years of post-military international security experience, Mr. Young has traveled extensively throughout the world and has worked in many of the world's most dangerous countries to fulfill his responsibilities to these international organizations, often during periods of significant unrest or open conflict.

Mr. Young is a member of the United Nations Inter-Agency Security Management Network (IASMN) – an organization that brings security leaders from every UN agency together regularly to cooperate in designing and sharing security policies and best practices for worldwide security operations. He is a member of the prestigious International Security Managers Association (ISMA) whose membership is restricted to only the highest levels of security leadership among the major multi-national corporations and Fortune 1000 companies. He is also an active member of the American Society for Industrial Security (ASIS). He has participated in several speaking engagements on the subject of international security, especially on the subject of staff evacuations from foreign countries and emergency response planning, and has been a guest speaker on International Security Planning at Harvard University's Weatherhead Center for International Affairs in Cambridge Massachusetts.

Mr. Young is a graduate of the Australian Army Command and Staff College, where he later served as an instructor in leadership and military history and he has a master's degree in Business Administration.

Afghanistan, 1991

Dallas, Texas

ABOUT WINDRUSH PUBLISHERS

Founded in Dallas, Texas, WindRush Publishers excels at bringing books of exceptional quality and content to the minds of discriminating readers everywhere. With an eye for excellence we are always on the search for new inspirational and motivational topics by expert authors in a variety of subjects. With more great books to follow, WindRush remains devoted to producing exciting works designed for audiences of all ages and interests.

Stay Informed and Inspired at www.WindRushPub.com

Scan for more resources.

NOTES

NOTES

NOTES

NOTES